KU-186-297

Management an
Organisational
Behaviour

A STUDENT WORKBOOK

Management and Organisational Behaviour

A STUDENT WORKBOOK

Karen Meudell and Tony Callen

For all our students, past and present, whose healthy cynicism keeps us not only on our toes but sometimes on the back foot as well.

PITMAN PUBLISHING
128 Long Acre, London WC2E 9AN

A Division of Longman Group Limited

First published in Great Britain in 1995

© Karen Meudell and Tony Callen 1995

ISBN 0 273 61253 0

British Library Cataloguing in Publication Data
A CIP catalogue record for this book can be obtained from the
British Library.

10 9 8 7 6 5 4 3 2 1

Typeset by PanTek Arts, Maidstone, Kent.
Printed and bound in Great Britain by Clays Ltd, St Ives plc.

The Publishers' policy is to use paper from sustainable forests.

Contents

Preface

This workbook has been written to complement our colleague, Laurie Mullins's book, *Management and Organisational Behaviour*. It incorporates many of the assignments and activities in that book and also provides numerous new and additional exercises.

Aims and objectives

In putting this book together we had in mind both lecturers and students. Our experience over many years of teaching organisational behaviour to both undergraduate and postgraduate students has indicated that there are two main obstacles which have to be overcome: first, the very name of the topic itself is offputting to students (whether it is called 'OB', 'behavioural science' or a variation thereof such as 'social and organisational behaviour'); and, secondly, the fact that each topic area can get lost in a quagmire of theories and research studies which students have difficulty relating to a 'real world' context. By the very nature of these two identified difficulties, it takes time for lecturers to invent interesting and stimulating activities which will address these issues.

The aims of this book, therefore, are fivefold:

1 To provide lecturers with a planned and flexible scheme of work to complement a formal lecture programme for one or two semesters.

2 To give students some topical debates and real-life examples of how the various theories can actually work in practice.

3 To allow students the opportunity to research the various subject areas and to relate them to 'real world' situations.

4 To encourage the development of student skills in the areas of research, critical analysis, and oral and written presentation.

5 To allow opportunities for group working wherever possible.

Distinctive features

- The workbook is extremely flexible in approach. It can be used by both lecturers and students, in part or in entirety, to complement both lecture and seminar programmes.

- It can be used on both undergraduate and postgraduate/post-experience courses.

- In these days of ever-increasing class sizes, its contents and layout present the lecturer with ready-thought-out exercises, assignments and examples.

- It is 'real world' related, with contributions not only from educationalists engaged on current research but also from industrialists and trainers.
- It is topical and up to date, drawing on recent research and using case studies based on current issues and well-known public figures both from Britain and also from abroad.
- It encourages students to research topics for themselves, facilitating the development of critical analysis by asking them to analyse their findings against the various theoretical models and frameworks.
- It deliberately provides a mix of activities, assignments and debates some of which are more demanding of the student than others.

Plan of the book

The book has been designed to complement a one- or two-semester lecture programme and follows the traditional 'micro to macro' approach. It can be used in several ways:

- As an addition to formal lecture input by using parts of each chapter as considered appropriate.
- As a complete seminar programme: each chapter provides a variety of seminar-type topics and these can be either lecturer- or student-driven.
- As a combination of the above whereby, for example, a 'pause for thought' could be taken as the lecture topic and the remainder of the chapter used in a subsequent seminar.
- As an additional text to aid student learning and understanding and as a revision aid.

Chapter outline

Figure P.1 indicates the link between the chapters in this book and the various chapters in Mullins. Each chapter takes the same format, as follows.

Case studies

These are all 'real world' related and wherever possible the actual companies have been named. However, there are occasions when, for the purposes of maintaining confidentiality, the name of the organisation has been changed.

Activities and assignments

These can be completed individually or in groups and are based on a 'learning by doing' approach. We have generally specified a word length for assignments and activities of approximately 2,000 words. However, this is by no means prescriptive and lecturers can substitute whatever requirement they consider appropriate.

Fig. P.1 The link between this workbook and L. J. Mullins, *Management and Organisational Behaviour*

Chapter	Title	Related chapter in Mullins*
1	An introduction to organisational behaviour	1
2	Learning	4
3	Personality	4
4	Perception	5
5	Attitudes	4
6	Motivation	14,15
7	Leadership	6, 7, 8, 13
8	Groups	6, 7
9	The context of the organisation	3, 9, 11
10	Organisation structure	10, 11
11	Organisational culture	20, 21
12	The nature of management	2, 12, 13

* L. J. Mullins (1993), *Management and Organisational Behaviour*, 3rd edn, Pitman.

Debates

These can either be used for discussion or as a formal debate with the audience voting at the end. For each topic we have included a couple of starting points both for and against the proposition together with some further reading that we strongly recommend students use.

Pause for thought

This can be used as a basis for discussion, as a lecture focus or simply as a means of encouraging students to stop and think about something.

'Look, it really works!' and 'Still not convinced?'

Both these sections take the various theories and research studies and relate them to situations with which students of all levels can identify.

Note: Where we have directed the reader to the Mullins publication, we are referring to the third edition (1993).

Acknowledgements

We would like to thank all our colleagues and friends whose ideas, encouragement and advice during the writing of this book have been invaluable. Specifically, we would like to thank the following people:

- Penelope Woolf, our Publisher at Pitman, who twisted our arms in the first place and really *did* demonstrate that 'there's no such thing as a free lunch . . .' (You can stop feeling guilty, now, Penelope, we enjoyed it, honestly!).
- Eric Baldwin who kept up the supply of ideas, suggestions and support.
- All our contributors who had *their* arms twisted (without the benefit of a free lunch) and who delivered, as promised, and on time.
- And finally Laurie Mullins without whom there probably wouldn't have been a book in the first place.

We have tried to reference all our sources of work by other writers but apologise to anyone whose acknowledgement has been inadvertently omitted.

An introduction to organisational behaviour

HIV/AIDS policy decisions at Beaver Industries

Background to the case

Beaver Industries is a large manufacturing company which makes components for boats and yachts and employs approximately a thousand people. The company was launched in the early 1970s by the current managing directors, brothers John and Sam Beaver. Originally the company was housed in a large wooden shed beside the harbour where John and Sam employed five men to help them make the components. As the business expanded, the company moved into larger premises located on the outskirts of the large south coast town in which Sam and John lived with their respective families.

Today there are two operating units on the site which run along formal top-down lines of communication, with Sam and John making policy decisions and cascading them down through the levels. (Policy decisions at Beaver Industries tend to be based upon existing legislation which all companies must adhere to. John and Sam duly comply with this legislation and strictly follow guidance regarding policy implementation.)

Janet Foster has been the personnel manager at Beaver Industries for the past five years. Until recently she has been satisfied with the way decisions are made concerning policy design and implementation, but to her increasing concern, no policy exists within Beaver Industries which deals with HIV/AIDS, and the implications that this disease has for workplace practice. She voiced her concerns to Sam and John at their last meeting and they said that they believed the needs of employees living with HIV/AIDS could be adequately addressed within the framework of the existing Health and Safety policy.

Although Janet accepts that it is feasible that this policy could be manipulated in order to deal with these issues, she is concerned by the fact that a Health and Safety policy is not geared to deal specifically with issues relating to HIV/AIDS. In the journals the company subscribes to she has noticed a number of articles which confirm her misgivings. They illustrate the benefits of implementing a specific HIV/AIDS policy or of at least including a section which refers to the issue in an existing policy. One American journal in particular has made increasing reference to problems personnel managers have faced when dealing with HIV/AIDS in the workplace (see, for example, Banas 1992). With such a potentially serious and sensitive issue for employees and the company, Janet is convinced that what Beaver Industries needs is a proactive scheme which will prepare both manage-ment and employees alike for the possible and increasingly likely impact of HIV/AIDS on the company. She is convinced that this approach would be far better than Sam and John's present philosophy: 'We'll face it when it happens'. Janet has observed that the journals have reported ungrounded fears and preju-dices arising as a result of HIV/AIDS which can affect morale and productivity. She therefore maintains that the issue is one which must be directly addressed. To rely on existing strategies and approaches would be inappropriate and potentially harmful for the company.

To safeguard the company from this eventuality, Janet first had to convince senior management that a different approach was required. She thought long and hard about which would be the most cost effective and efficient means of distributing the information and finally decided that the best method available to her was via leaflets inserted into employees' wage packets. Choosing this approach meant that all employees would receive the factual information. By following this path of action, Janet has begun to follow the guidelines suggested by the Society for Occupational Medicine as a way of implementing HIV and AIDS awareness training. (A description of the guidelines is given at the end of this case.)

In an ideal world, Janet would have liked to have run seminars and workshops to tackle employees' attitudes and fears directly. This would have allowed her to convey factual information in a manner which had meaning for employees and which related the information to their work environment. Pragmatically, however, she realised that such methods are costly in terms of both time and money and were something which senior management felt was unnecessary. Distribution of leaflets would at least reach all employees with the minimum of expense and was something that Sam and John were prepared to accept.

A case of AIDS?

Until recently there had been no known cases of HIV or AIDS within the company. However, last month June Bolton, a clerical worker in her early thirties and who had been with the company for four years, had began to take a series of absences from work. She was losing a lot of weight and her work, which had always been of a high standard was beginning to decline. This meant that the workload on her colleagues was increasing as they tried to cover for her. June's department was one which was central to the company as a whole; its reputation was going downhill and staff were becoming thoroughly demoralised.

Although June's absences were all covered by medical certificates from her GP, they referred to a 'viral infection'. The 'rumour mill' was already beginning to grind into action and speculation about her symptoms and decline in work was rife. Since the HIV/AIDS leaflets had recently been distributed in wage packets, many of June's colleagues were beginning to wonder if she was actually the cause of the recent initiative. Some of her colleagues took the step of seeking confirmation of their suspicions that she was in fact living with HIV or AIDS, while others became wary of working alongside her. This cautiousness was illustrated by some colleagues writing their names on coffee mugs and not sitting too close to June while working. The rumours did not take long to reach June who was horrified to discover what her colleagues were saying about her. She decided to go and speak to Sue Brown (her departmental manager) about the issue immediately. Sue had been concerned about June's health, as well as the change in the atmosphere of the department, and had been intending to have a word with June anyway about her general health and wellbeing.

During the course of the meeting it transpired that June was not, in fact, living with HIV, but was coping with glandular fever. June was so upset and angry by this incident that she was seriously considering resigning and claiming constructive dismissal. Sue was relieved to find out that June was not, in fact, living with HIV or AIDS because this meant that the situation would be defused fairly easily providing that June was willing to allow other employees to know the nature of her illness. She was also very disappointed with the way June's colleagues had reacted, although she understood that they had done so through a lack of understanding of HIV and AIDS.

Having spoken to both June Bolton and Janet Foster, Sue suggested that a meeting of all managers was required to determine what could be done to sort out the present crisis and avoid a repeat of the episode in the future.

The meeting

This incident was extremely distressing to the senior management. Despite the lack of a formal policy concerning HIV/AIDS, they had believed that because of the widespread distribution of the leaflets, the company was well prepared for the possibility of an employee becoming HIV positive. The reaction of their employees towards June (someone who had worked for the company for a number of years and who was well respected) both surprised and dismayed the management team. If there was such strong feeling over a case of glandular fever, what would happen when the first case of HIV/AIDS required action? At the end of the meeting it was decided that the company's whole approach to this difficult and sensitive issue required re-evaluation. Rather than maintaining the existing *laissez-faire* philosophy, it was suggested that Janet Foster's proactive approach was in fact more appropriate for this type of situation. What was needed was a full scale audit which would ascertain where they as a company had made mistakes in their approach to the HIV and AIDS issue and how a more proactive approach could best be initiated.

Activity brief

Your brief is to design a research study which explores the relationship between employee attitudes towards HIV and AIDS and the nature and effectiveness of employer responses in terms of workplace education and training. As a member of the audit team, you are required to prepare and submit a report (of approximately 1,500–2,000 words) indicating clearly:

1 How you will collect a comprehensive set of data relating to attitudes, values and definitions of AIDS as a workplace issue (i.e. questionnaire, survey, case study, interview?).

2 How you will use this data to identify areas of workplace behaviour relating to AIDS which are of priority interest in terms of education, welfare provision and support.

3 What sorts of employees you will need to contact. How you will do so. How many you will need to contact.

4 Whether your research project will be qualitative or quantitative in emphasis, and why.

It is important to remember that the research strategy or strategies, and the methods or techniques you employ must be appropriate for the questions you want to answer. One simple approach which is widely used distinguishes between three main strategies: experiments (measuring the effects of manipulating one variable on another variable); surveys (the collection of information in standardised form from groups or people) and case studies (the development of detailed intensive knowledge about a single 'case' or a small number of related 'cases'). However, it may well be that some combination of strategies may be appropriate for the research with which you are involved.

Occupational health guidelines

● Secure the support of the company's board and chief executive.

● Consider carefully the company's culture, needs, risks and preferences.

● Prepare the ground by training managers and supervisors to be confident and competent in managing, constructively and sensitively, any employee who may be HIV positive or who develops an AIDS-related illness. This should include training sessions and the provision of briefing packs.

● Consider introducing, where possible and appropriate, flexible working hours, part-time working and special leave arrangements.

● Distribute and display information on access to counselling services provided within the company and outside in the community.

● Display information about HIV organisations offering help and support.

*Case provided by Karen Gadd, University of Portsmouth.

Further reading

Hakim, C. (1992), 'Nothing prepared me to manage AIDS', *Harvard Business Review* July–August, 26–33.

Huczynski, A. and Buchanan, D. (1991), *Organisational Behaviour: An Introductory Text*, Prentice Hall.
Robson, C. (1993), *Real World Research: A Resource for Social Scientists and Practitioner Researchers*, Blackwell.

 # Bucken Marine

This case investigates the use of cognitive mapping to examine how individuals view their world.

In times of high uncertainty, traditional industry and market analysis models are often inappropriate and managers (and researchers) are forced to rely on subjective interpretations of 'what is happening'. This subjective view is the enacted environment of individuals, people's perceptions based on knowledge, experience and their own psychological make-up.

The case raises issues relating to psychological, social and cultural systems.

Background

This study forms part of a much larger research project concerning the competitiveness of a particular UK industry in comparison to other similar industries in other countries. The industry in question is the inland waterways boat-hiring industry, which includes boating holidays on rivers; the Norfolk Broads, and narrow-boat holidays on the canals. The industry is highly fragmented and is made up predominantly of small, owner-manager businesses, frequently husband and wife teams, supported by one or two employees. The industry is notorious for its inadequate and unreliable data and, with the onset of the recession, it experienced serious environmental turbulence with dwindling holiday bookings from both at home and overseas.

The industry study undertaken by the researcher indicated that the holidays were seen to be expensive in comparison with overseas package tours and self-catering cottage holidays in the UK. All the managers of the boat-hiring firms explained the relatively high price of their holidays as being due to the capital cost of the boats which have a useful life of only eight to ten years and that these assets depreciated whereas cottages (in the long term) appreciated. Holiday-makers do not want to hire the same boat they had ten years ago and, if available, they would prefer to have the latest one in the fleet – at no extra cost. Holiday-makers have also grown accustomed to having *en suite* bathrooms and colour television sets when staying in hotels. And, when on self-catering holidays, they want freezers, microwave ovens and all the other modern gadgets. One owner of a narrow-boat fleet told the researcher that women customers insist on having a hairdrier on board – from the customer's point of view, an apparently simple and inexpensive item to supply, but to the owner one £9.00 hairdrier needs £900 worth of 240 volt installation with a generator for each boat as well as several power points down the length of the canal.

The industry reached its peak turnover figures in the early 1980s, but there has been a steady decline in holiday sales ever since, with a corresponding decline in the number of boats available for hire. This reduction in the size of the hire fleet has been attributed by some commentators to the withdrawal by the British government in 1980 of the 100 per cent tax relief on investment in new boats. This tax incentive led to many 'outsiders' commissioning boats and hiring them out, resulting in many new craft flooding the market. Yet, despite the sudden increase in the number of boats, both the newcomers and the established hire businesses were enjoying, at that time, a period of unprecedented boom. The UK then led the world in providing inland waterway holidays and this international standing remains true to this day. The explanation is that British waterways are relatively narrow and therefore free of commercial traffic while the waterways in other parts of the world are broad and crowded with heavy shipping and barges.

Why the demand for boating holidays in the UK has waned is not clear and forms part of a larger research study. What is irrefutable is the despondency felt by those who are still in the industry and their pessimistic view of their environment. This case study is an example of one owner-manager who is particularly downcast about the future of his firm, although it is necessary to point out that not all the respondents in the study were so downhearted.

The organisation

(For reasons of confidentiality the name and location of the organisation have been changed. Any similarities to existing or former organisations are purely coincidental)

Bucken Marine is situated on the River Severn several miles inland from the estuary, amid green rolling hills and tree-lined banks. The firm has been a family-run boat-yard for three generations and is currently owned by two brothers. Originally, the firm made wooden boats but branched out into boat hire in the 1920s when this leisure activity became more popular. It maintained its boat-building side of the business until the early 1970s when the new material, glass-reinforced plastic (GRP), began to dominate the boat-building industry. Coincidentally, the demand for holidays afloat began to increase dramatically and the present owners decided that they would switch their resources from building to hiring. At first, things went well and the two brothers expanded their fleet to forty boats, ranging in size from four berths to ten berths. The boats were smart, up to date and, in keeping with the times, simply fitted out. In those days, customers saw the holidays as 'camping on the water' and therefore did not expect the luxuries they had in their own homes.

With the onset of the 1991 recession, bookings for the boats dried up to a trickle and Bucken Marine withdrew more than half their fleet. The few customers that remained no longer booked their holidays in advance, thereby denying Bucken Marine the deposits to improve their cash flow during the winter months. The hiring season for the firm shrank from twenty-eight weeks to as little as twenty-two weeks and, with the uncertainty over bookings, the firm is existing literally from one day to the next.

The study

Although the researcher knew the UK and international leisure marine industry for seagoing boats very well, he was not familiar with inland waterways. His first priority then was to understand the industry and how it operated. Not wanting to impose his own interpretation on the industry but rather to let the practitioners 'tell their own story', he chose to adopt inquiry research methods that he has used in the past. Using unstructured interview techniques, the researcher asked respondents just one question: 'How do you see your business today?' This question usually led to a conversation that lasted between one-and-a-quarter to two hours. In most cases the respondents automatically described the future for their firms but, if they did not, a second question was asked: 'How do you see your business in three to five years' time?'

The interviews were recorded and the tapes transcribed. Observational notes were also taken and written down immediately after the interview, often while in the car. These notes helped to add 'flesh' to the interview; for instance, in the case of Bucken Marine, the researcher noted the state of the boat-yard, the buildings and the boats themselves.

From the transcription the researcher highlighted key issues and recorded them as concepts on a cognitive map using the computer software 'Graphics COPE'. Cognitive maps are visual representations of an individual's or group's enacted environment. In other words, how people interpret their world.

In previous studies the researcher validated the map he constructed (i.e. his interpretation of the data) with the respondent by asking if the map tallied with what the respondent had said. In this study, such validation was not possible. The maps from all the respondents were combined and analysed for similarities, differences and exceptions, building up a picture for the researcher of the issues confronting the managers of these firms. However, the researcher felt uneasy about the validity of each individual map and felt that the assistance of another researcher in linking the concepts would identify his own bias and possible errors, giving greater credibility to the analysis.

Linking the concepts

Graphics COPE allows the researcher to link concepts in three different ways:

1 Causal links imply that one concept leads to, or affects, another concept in some way.

2 Connotive links are bi-directional links which associate concepts in some way but not causally.

3 Temporal links represent a relationship in time from one concept to another.

The list of concepts from which the map (Figure 1.2) was constructed is given in Figure 1.1.

Fig. 1.1 Key issues underlying the management and organisational behaviour of Bucken Marine

No.	No.
1 Worked with schools on work experience	45 Other countries do not go along with them
2 Very positive response	46 Holidays to foreigners are about 25% of the total now
3 But shortage of money prohibits training	47 People are booking later now
4 Since 1980 it has not been possible to take on more people	48 The socioeconomic group is B down to E
5 Cannot afford to train someone full time	49 So the big problem is shortage of capital in the industry
6 Possibility that people will not stay with us	50 Most of the inland waterways fleets are over 20 years old
7 Cannot afford to do it at present	51 Revamping the interior is not the answer
8 But . . . developing a new service	52 People do not want the same boat they had ten years ago
9 The problem with the hire fleet industry in this country is the product is not good enough	53 The boats must be like floating hotel rooms
10 We must compete with all the other types of holidays	54 The equipment inside them must be modern
11 I have been on industry management courses	55 These last two years have been *very, very* difficult
12 But courses cost money	56 There is a future in boat hiring
13 Courses cost time	57 But we need to be able to invest in the industry
14 This is a 7-day-a-week job	58 But we do not have the investment
15 We cannot afford to improve the products	59 The standard of living in Europe is on the increase
16 There has been an increase in the number of foreigners taking holidays	60 What people want now is quality
17 Especially Germans, Canadians and Americans	61 If we had quality boats we could charge higher prices
18 We want to get more Europeans to come over	62 We could then reinvest in the industry
19 We have the sort of holiday they want but not the product	63 If we want to attract overseas customers the boats must be improved
20 A third of the current bookings are from previous customers	64 The service must be improved
21 But we need to provide a better product to keep bringing them back	65 We need to cut down on 'red tape'
22 Our fleet is old	66 My brother spends all his time on the books and VAT
23 Everyone's fleet is old	67 We would like to pay our two employees more
24 We do not have the money to invest back into the business	68 Our main mechanic has been here 28 years
25 We do not make profits on hire fleets	69 We pay him £15,000 a year
26 The business *just* provides an income for the four who work here	70 He has a wife who earns more
27 We cannot justify others investing in this business	71 This releases the pressure on me
28 We used to get 100% tax relief on new boats	72 The young lad gets £14,000 a year
29 The tax relief was both good and bad for us	73 My brother and I take about the same
30 Good: more new boats for us	74 We have been fighting the bank for eight years now
31 Bad: encouraged city slickers to swamp the markets with boats	75 We have managed to reduce our overdraft
32 Since the boom 15 years ago, it's been downhill	76 Any money coming in is used to pay the overdraft
33 Flights to this country are too expensive	77 A customer bought one of our assets, which we lease back
34 Ferries are too expensive	78 This saved us three months ago
35 The Channel Tunnel will be too expensive	79 We do not spend money willy-nilly
36 We should get right out of the centralised European system	80 We do not have a computer, word-processor or fax
37 We could run our business properly in the 1970s	81 Banks are very domineering over small companies
38 We only had the laws of this country to worry about	82 The BTA is not doing a good job overseas
39 We have stupid EC directives	83 The key to this business is getting overseas trade
40 They are time-consuming	84 Any way of keeping British holiday-makers at home
41 They are ruining a lot of businesses in this country	85 I don't see what the future will be
42 It is difficult to give examples	86 I do not have £50,000 to invest in a new boat
43 OK, probably many do not affect me personally	87 The government could help by reducing the VAT rate on holidays
44 We seem to be the only country in Europe that goes along with EC directives	88 The government could give grants to revitalise the industry
	89 Our asset is 'liquid history'
	90 We must stop the British going abroad

Issues raised by the case study

If individuals within organisations are influenced by and, in turn, influence their environment, what evidence is there of psychological, social and cultural environmental issues in the map?

1 *Psychological factors* Is the respondent's attitude to his circumstances reflected in what he says? The respondent expressed some very strong views about his situation as he saw it. Does he explain how he came to be in this position and, if so, what are the causal links?

2 *Social factors* Is there any evidence of societal changes? If there is, are they real or imagined by the respondent?

3 *Cultural factors* Given that cultural factors are notoriously difficult to define, could this category of environmental influences be useful to the researcher in understanding what is going on within the industry and this organisation?

 ## Activity brief

1 Examine the map (Figure 1.2) and decide what types of links the researcher has allocated to the concepts. Critically evaluate these links.

2 Review the list of concepts and relate them to psychological, social and cultural categories. With this information, group the concepts into sets.

3 Redraw the map incorporating your understanding of the psychological, social and cultural factors.

Further reading

Eden, C. (1983), *Messing about in Problems*, Pergamon Press.

Moriarty, K. and Jones, M. (1992), *Graphics COPE Reference Manual*, Strathclyde University.

Mullins, L. J. (1993), *Management and Organisational Behaviour*, 3rd edn, Pitman, chs 1, 5–8.

*Case study provided by K. Alan Rutter, University of Portsmouth.

 # Eric and Kipsey

See Mullins, pp. 23–9.

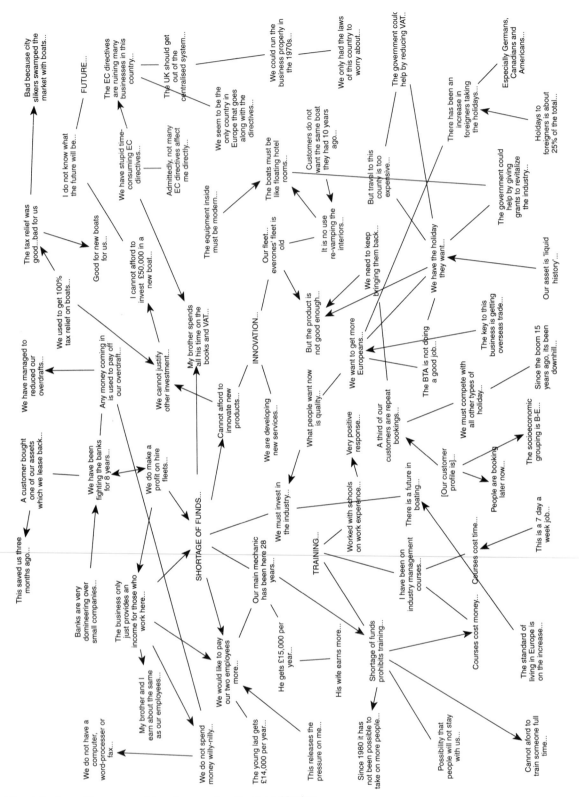

Fig. 1.2 Cognitive map of key issues for Bucken Marine

Activity one

In small groups of not more than five people, design an activity which illustrates one of the topics considered in chapter 1 of Mullins. For example, this could be a group exercise, a card game, a quiz or a 'Question Time' type group discussion.

Play out the activity with the rest of the group and then prepare a verbal presentation based on the following points:

● How successful was the activity? Why or why not?

● What modifications, if any, would you make to your activity?

● How does the success (or otherwise) of your activity link with issues concerning the study of OB?

 ## Activity two

Using the text in Mullins (pp. 19–21) and information from the reading list below, prepare a students' guide to undertaking case studies from *one* of the following two perspectives:

1 A first year undergraduate with little or no work experience.

2 A mature part-time management student with considerable work experience.

Further reading

Cameron, S. (1994), *The MBA Handbook*, 2nd edn, Pitman, ch. 10.

Easton, G. (1992), *Learning from Case Studies*, 2nd edn, Prentice Hall.

Mullins, L. J. (1984), 'Tackling Case Studies', *Student Administrator*, 1 (5).

 ## Debate one

'The study of organisational behaviour is really an art which pretends that it is a science and produces some spurious research findings to try and prove the point.'

Starting points

For

● OB deals largely with intangibles. Not only is it difficult to observe and measure, it is also difficult to establish links between cause and effect.

● Science aims to be able to control. There are moral and ethical considerations in OB which militate against this.

Against

- The problems of considering OB as a science occur only if we try to apply rigid scientific practices to the subject.

- OB is a science in that it follows similar principles (i.e. to describe, explain, predict and control) but it is a *different* type of science – a social science and thus cannot be compared directly.

Further reading

Mohr, L. (1982), *Explaining Organizational Behavior*, Jossey-Bass.

Ryan, A. (1970), *The Philosophy of the Social Sciences*, Macmillan.

Shipman, M. (1981), *The Limitations of Social Research*, Longman.

 Debate two

'Anyone who teaches management and anyone of even moderate intellect and experience who is subjected to such teaching, soon becomes aware that the theories used are often of limited scientific validity in terms of the explanations or predictions which they offer. At best they are partial; applied in the wrong way, without understanding of the necessary complementary caveats and provisos, they may even be misleading' (Lee and Lawrence 1985).

Starting points

For

- The research studies are not only inconsistent but also contradictory – nothing can be gained from 'meddling' in this way.

- Social behaviour is, for the most part, genetically determined. We would do better to study sociobiology rather than psychology and sociology.

Against

- Research by psychologists, sociologists and anthropologists has enabled considerable progress to be made in being able to explain and predict people's behaviour.

- Admittedly, understanding human behaviour is not as simple as understanding the behaviour of a chemical, but any attempt to do so should be welcomed.

Further reading

Lorsch, J. W. (ed.) (1987), Handbook of Organizational Behavior, Prentice Hall.

Mullins, L. J. (1987), 'The Organisation and the Individual', Administrator, 7 (4), April, 11–14.

Whyte, W. F. (1987), 'From Human Relations to Organizational Behavior : Reflections on the Changing Scene', Industrial and Labor Relations Review, July, 487–500.

✓ Look, it really works!

1 One of our students on our part-time MBA course came to the Stage 1 OB unit with a degree of trepidation and cynicism. A systems engineer by training, she expressed grave reservations about successfully completing a unit in 'such a fuzzy, unquantifiable subject'. The introductory lecture, 'The Nature of Organisational Behaviour', did very little to change her opinion. In fact, if anything, it reinforced it – this was definitely a subject that Lyndsey felt uncomfortable with. A quick straw poll of the class showed that she was not the only one to feel this way – over 50 per cent of the students thought the same (we'd like to think that it was because they were all engineers and scientists rather than because we were lousy lecturers . . .).

Anyway, we ploughed on and about two-thirds of the way through the course Lyndsey came up to one of us after the lecture and said, 'You know, it actually works!' 'What does, Lyndsey?' (you get a bit gobsmacked after three hours of 'Great Leadership Theories I Have Known' . . .). 'This whole thing,' she replied. 'I had to do a presentation on performance-related pay to the main board last week and to back up my point that we didn't need it, I used all the research findings on motivation and money. The board ended up agreeing with me and said afterwards that it was largely because I could prove my points with research data – I'd never have done that prior to the course.'

Hopefully this not only provides an example of how OB *can* work in practice but it might also be useful to look at the model of attitude change here (see Chapter 5 and Mullins, pp. 114–15).

2 Steve White is the head chef in a large London hotel. He's been in the industry for twenty-five years, starting off as a 'button boy' (a kind of junior hall porter-cum-gopher) before moving into the kitchen and gradually working his way up. He's been a head chef in various hotels for the last ten years and in his last three jobs he's been recruited prior to the opening of the hotel so he's been required to help design the kitchen, recruit his brigade, sort out menus and generally get the show on the road. There is a limit to how many times anyone can do this and, frankly, Steve is bored. He joined his current company because they seemed to offer wider opportunities than just kitchen work and, having opened the hotel, he is now looking to change.

Before we go any further and for those not intimately connected with the hotel industry, perhaps we ought to establish a few facts:

- Tradition says that 'once a chef, always a chef' – they're experts in their own field but can't (or don't want to) move into any other.

- Rule 1 says that 'the chef is always right'.

- Rule 2 says that if the chef is wrong, Rule 1 applies.

- Chefs are not, generally, known for their democratic approach to managing people. This can range from a slight raising of the voice when contradicted to hurling whatever is in the hand at the time (if you've ever been on the receiving end of a red-hot wok, as one of the authors has, you'll know what we mean).

- Having said all that (and to avoid having one's kneecaps filleted at the table and served with a vinegar and mustard *timbale*), chefs are known for their undying devotion to their craft. They are synonymous with training, development and maintaining their networks – all chefs know each other and can point to who they have trained and to who they have encouraged to leave for a promotion which they've organised.

Back to our bored Steve . . . he's now been at the hotel for two years (and is breathing a sigh of relief because he now can't be sacked without a good reason). He's seen two food and beverage managers (his immediate boss) come and go and he is looking for something else. The hotel manager approaches him one day and asks him if he would like the job of food and beverage manager. He jumps at the chance because he knows that he can promote his existing sous chef and still keep control in the kitchen whilst furthering his own career.

A few weeks later a former colleague of his rang him up to congratulate him on his promotion and to ask how things were going. He replied: 'I hate it. I have to wear a suit all day, carry a bleep, I'm at the beck and call of everybody, the bar and restaurant staff don't understand where I'm coming from and I've had two waitresses and one barman in tears – I'm thinking of jacking it in.'

Can you see where the psychological contract might fit in here? When he joined the company Steve clearly had his *own* psychological contract, as did the company. Where did it go wrong?

 ## Assignment one

Using the metaphors suggested by Gareth Morgan (Mullins, pp. 5–7), apply one or more to your own organisation. If you are not currently working, take any organisation that you know – this could be a sports club, the Students Union, or somewhere where you've worked during your vacation.

Prepare either a verbal or written (maximum 1,500 words) report of your findings.

 ## Assignment two

In small groups, using the first 'Pause for thought' in this chapter (see below), the text in Mullins (pp. 13–19), and the reading list below:

- Explain why certain business activities have become increasingly harmonised across the world.
- In what ways would you expect work organisations to vary in different societies? Will these differences always exist?

Present your findings to the other groups in whatever format you consider appropriate to the topic.

Further reading

Torrington, D. (1994), *International Human Resource Management*, Prentice Hall.

Trompenaar, F. (1993), *Riding The Waves of Culture*, Economist Publications.

Welford, R. and Prescott, K. (1994), *European Business*, 2nd edn, Pitman.

Assignment provided by Dr Ray French, University of Portsmouth.

❗ Pause for thought

1 The world is getting smaller. No, not an example of catastrophe theory in physics or the message of a religious sect predicting the demise of the planet; rather this statement reflects for many the opening up or demystifying of the rest of the world.

Few significant businesses do not think of themselves as other than international and the concept of a global business environment is accepted by more and more commentators.

There is a paradox. Increasingly products, services and the means of providing them are becoming more homogenous. Japanese-owned car producers such as Nissan and Toyota have not only set up manufacturing plants in Britain but have also 'imported' their own organisational practices. McDonalds have opened outlets in the former Eastern bloc, to great initial demand from the local clientele. In the summer of 1994, that archetypal French event, the Tour de France, came to the south coast of England. An estimated three million spectators witnessed the event over two days – and they said it would never catch on! (A cricket competition was also arranged in Corfu to coincide with the European Summit in June 1994 but the English weren't allowed to participate because they were thought to be too good!).

But if many aspects of life which were once culturally distant are now similar, most of us recognise that culturally derived attitudes and patterns of behaviour remain significant across the world. We continue to believe, with justification, that Italians, Australians and Swedes display distinctive cultural identities which will impinge upon the business world. Few would expect these to disappear even in a truly global environment. Torrington's advice in a recently published textbook (1994) to 'think globally and act locally' perhaps comes closest to explaining this paradox.

2 It is well known that the United Kingdom joined the European Economic Community, as it was then called, in 1973 along with Denmark and the Republic of Ireland, thus increasing the size of the Community from the original six members to nine. However, the UK had made several previous attempts to join, the first being in the early 1960s.

The original application was vetoed by the then president of France, General Charles de Gaulle, in 1963. In his New Year's message that year he pondered whether Britain was really 'European' enough to join the community. After vetoing the British application he stated that 'in her daily life, her habits and traditions are very special and very eccentric'. He further suggested that Britain would always act as a 'Trojan horse' for the American domination of Europe.

Is there such a thing as an Anglo-American type of culture? Several writers on the subject, including Hofstede (see Mullins, p. 17), certainly think so. What are the crucial elements of this Anglo-American culture? How do these manifest themselves in terms of organisational behaviour? How might these features change, and can Britain ever become a 'good European'?

Pauses provided by Dr Ray French, University of Portsmouth

❓ Still not convinced?

1 It's 9.10 on a rainy Monday morning in February. The lecture theatre is filling to capacity with wet first-year students who will, judging by the already gently rising steam cloud, dry themselves off during the next hour.

Into the lecture theatre walks a middle-aged man who goes to the lectern and begins to speak: 'Good morning, ladies and gentlemen, my name is Michael Morris and I'd like to welcome you to this introductory lecture in Behavioural Science. Indeed, that is as good a starting point as any – is it a science at all? Pedagogically speaking the critics would argue . . .'. The voice droned on, the steam rose, heads began to droop and eyelids began to close.

At the end of a seemingly endless hour the lecture was over and groups of students filed out: the keen ones to the library, the majority to the refectory. Over coffee, Julian said to his friends: 'Well, if that's what we've got for the rest of this semester, then it confirms everything I ever thought about the subject – boring, dry, lifeless and uninspired. I suggest we get a rota going, take it in turns to attend and copy each other's notes. What do you reckon – one lot turn up and the rest have a lie-in and watch The Big Breakfast?'

Not convinced about OB? Well, given this scenario, you'd probably be very justified. However, give the subject a chance. OK, not all lecturers (for whatever reason) are going to make it into an earth-moving experience (the thought of students at 9.15 on a Monday morning is frequently no more attractive than the thought of you having to face us !). Not everyone sees OB as the exciting and dynamic subject that we do, but try and look for examples of how it might relate to the 'real world'. We've tried to provide them in sections like this throughout the book – any more you come up with, please send to us, we'll be pathetically grateful!

2 Sit cross-legged on the floor, circle your thumb and forefinger together and repeat after us: 'OB is dynamic, OB is exciting, OB is real-world related. . .' Not working? OK, follow one set of the following instructions:

1 Tune in and follow regularly any soap opera, drama or other series. Each week, take one concept of OB and apply it to whatever you're watching. Some suggestions to get you going might be:

   (a) *Prisoner, Cell Block H* (leadership, informal groups, organisational bureaucracies, organisation culture).
   (b) *Neighbours* (attitudes, motivation, perception).
   (c) *MASH*[1] (organic and mechanistic organisations, groups, informal leadership, motivation, attitudes).
   (d) *The Original Star Trek*[1] (leadership, groups, cultural differences, perception, personality).
   (e) *Blind Date* (perception, personality, attitudes).
   (f) *Coronation Street/Brookside* (all of the above and then some).
   (g) *Question Time* (attitude change, communication).

2 Take any novel or play and analyse it in OB terms. As an example, let's take *Hamlet*:

   (a) **Hamlet** thinks the rest are out to get him (perception, personality).
   (b) **Ophelia** (the female love interest) is infatuated with Hamlet (attitude and motivation, gender stereotyping) but doesn't know if he feels the same (perception).
   (c) **Gertrude** has recently remarried and so remains Queen (organisation theory, motivation).
   (d) **Polonius** wants everyone to like him (attitude, perception).
   (e) **Horatio** tries to pour oil on troubled waters and protect his friend (perception, attitude, motivation).
   (f) **The Grave Diggers** have a lousy job to do but manage to make the best of it (job satisfaction, motivation, attitudes).
   (g) **Rosencrantz and Guildenstern** are trying to cope in a turbulent and changing environment and to stay together without having to do the Elizabethan MBA (motivation, attitudes, perception, groups, organisational culture).
   (h) **Fortinbras** – the 'born leader' (leadership, motivation, personality).
   (i) **The Ghost of Hamlet's Father** – is he there at all? (perception, attitudes, personality, paranoia?).
   (j) **'Something is rotten in the state of Denmark . . .'** (organisational misbehaviour!).

Try it with Ibsen, The Ring Cycle or Peter Rabbit – it throws a whole new light on them!

[1]You need a long memory or SKY TV for these two.

2 Learning

 ## The sense of learning

Background

You are a member of the Training Department of Dassan Ltd, a manufacturer of domestic 'white goods'. The company employs some 5,000 staff at seven locations spread throughout the country. The company has pursued a policy of decentralisation over the past ten years and each site operates as an autonomous business centre with its own manufacturing, administrative, finance, personnel and sales departments. There is also a small head office located on the west side of London near the M25 where the company's corporate departments are based. In line with the policy of decentralisation, the main functions of these departments is to develop policy within which the business units are required to operate and to provide advice to unit managers should they not have the particular expertise needed to deal with specific problems.

Each unit has its own personnel manager but there is a head office Personnel and Training Department headed by the personnel director. Within this department is a team of six training officers, including yourself, reporting to the training and development manager. The department has a number of functions including identifying the training needs of all employees, recommending appropriate courses to meet these needs and designing and running in-house programmes for staff nominated to attend by their manager. Where there is no in-house course suitable, the department retains brochures of externally run programmes and arranges the booking of staff onto these. In addition the department carries out a regular evaluation of the courses it offers to ensure that they still meet the business objectives of Dassan Ltd and the business units. This work involves close liaison with the personnel and training managers of the business units who are the budget holders for training received by staff within their unit. A significant demand for training results from the annual staff appraisal process which covers both manual and white collar employees and managers.

The responsibilities of the head office training officers are wide ranging and all are involved in the variety of work carried out by the department. This means that they contribute to corporate training policy, undertake training-needs analysis of groups of employees at a unit and deliver training courses to employees either at head office or, more likely, at one of the business units.

Leading the team

Amongst the portfolio of programmes you and your colleagues have designed and run for staff is a two-day, non-residential course called 'Leading the Team'. This course has been developed for supervisors and first-line managers to enhance their skills and knowledge in order to help them and the groups they supervise become more effective. The objectives of the programme are such that by the end of course participants should:

- Have developed their understanding of the role of the first line manager/ supervisor.
- Understand different leadership styles and their application to managing people.
- Be able to recognise the symptoms of poor motivation and understand what motivates and demotivates employees.
- Have increased the knowledge and skills needed to build an effective team of staff including being able to manage conflict.
- Be able to provide counselling to employees who have personal problems which may affect their work performance.

Since the majority of those attending the course will not be used to the 'classroom environment' or being 'lectured to', the programme is designed to be highly participative. The trainer running the course is expected to provide only short teaching inputs and a number of other activities have been designed to facilitate learning. In addition to plenary discussions led by the trainer, these include:

- Small group discussions on particular topics, during which the participants are expected to note the key points of their discussions on flipchart paper and report these back to their colleagues in a plenary session.
- Individual 'pencil and paper' exercises where the course members complete a questionnaire either by ticking a box to indicate their response to a question or by allocating a score showing the extent to which they agree or disagree with the statement.
- Small group activities designed to explore teamwork; for example, the physical task of building a tower out of Lego bricks against specific design criteria.
- Watching a video and discussing the learning points contained within it and their application to participants' own work roles.
- Short role-play exercises designed to develop interviewing and interpersonal skills.

For some of these activities the trainer will introduce the subject and use viewfoils on an overhead projector or write on the whiteboard, as well as leading a review which may similarly involve noting the points that emerge during the plenary discussions. The training team have also produced a number of handouts to complement the course and relieve the participants of the need to take copious notes.

The issue

Your department has been approached by the general manager of an associated company, Dassan (Applications), with a request to run the 'Leading the Team' course for a group of fifteen of her managers and supervisors. She has written to the corporate training manager stating that she believes the objectives are such that the course will meet the identified training needs of these managers. In addition, two of her current staff attended the course when they worked for your organisation and she has received very positive feedback from them on the course content and the learning methods used.

Dassan (Applications) have developed a range of consumer goods which have been specifically designed to meet the needs of people who are visually impaired. There is a significant demand for the company's products and the associated company is regarded as a market leader in the field. A number of the company's employees are themselves visually impaired and as the general manager's letter requesting the course points out, nine of the fifteen potential participants are visually impaired. Five are described as 'large print users'. This means that they are able to read print provided it is THIS SIZE and are able to see images on a television provided they are able to sit very close to the screen. Of the remainder, four are blind. They are, however, competent braille users and the general manager has stated that she can arrange for all the printed teaching material to be converted to braille provided she receives copies in advance of the start of the course. The blind participants can also take notes during the course, if necessary, using a portable braille writer. This machine needs to be rested on a table since it is too heavy to be placed on someone's lap for any length of time. Obviously, since it produces braille output it cannot be read by anyone not proficient in braille which includes the majority of the other course participants and the team of trainers who might be involved in presenting the course.

 ## Activity brief

The training manager has asked you to plan and deliver this course for Dassan (Applications).

1 What are the particular difficulties you see in presenting this course to the mix of participants from the associated company?

2 How might a knowledge of learning theory be helpful in seeking to ensure that the objectives of the course are met for *all* the participants?

3 What practical steps can be taken by the trainer delivering the course to assist in the learning process?

Case study provided by Derek Adam-Smith, University of Portsmouth.

Learning from others

Managers at Ratchetts Ltd, a dealership for Lifestyle Cars,* were undertaking a voluntary self-assessment programme as part of a training programme. Using an outside consultant, a number of training needs had been identified.

It soon became all too clear to the consultant that the managers knew little of management theory. Management skills such as leadership, motivation and team-building were all tackled by one approach: 'Do it, or else!'. The problem, however, was to let them see it for themselves without them losing face or feeling that they were being patronised.

The managers concerned were the dealer principal (the eleventh in three years), the sales manager, the parts manager and the service manager. The consultant decided to ask them to carry out an exercise whereby they assessed themselves and the dealer principal assessed them as well. At the beginning Ian, the service manager, asked if his part in the exercise could go further because he also wanted his team to assess him as well. He wanted to do this because he had recently been on a four-day management development course and had come back with vaguely completed action plans. He thought that he knew what he should do differently but he wanted to see what the assessment showed him.

When the results were displayed he needed little explanatory analysis and no persuading. Since his feedback he has already drawn surprised comments from other managers about a change in his attitude – 'He just gets stuck into everything now' – and about his commitment to addressing the needs that had been identified, spending two hour sessions with the consultant to try and improve.

 # Activity brief

1 What was preventing Ian from implementing his action plan prior to the assessment exercise?

2 How did Ian come to realise what he needed to do?

3 What enabled Ian to change?

4 How relevant is time to the learning process?

5 Describe a similar example from your own experience. Try to analyse when the initial learning took place and when and how this was confirmed/implemented.

Case study provided by Val Marchant, Ibis Training and Development.

*For a more in-depth description of Ratchetts, see the case study 'Firing on three cylinders' in Chapter 8.

Activity one: Breaking assumptions

For this activity form into small groups of about four people and, if possible, go into separate areas where you cannot overhear the conversations of your colleagues. Each group should be given a bag containing a mixture of letters (those from a Scrabble game are ideal).

Task

Your task is as follows:

- Produce as many four-letter words as you can in a three-minute timed run. The timed run is to commence from the time that the bag is opened.
- There will be three timed runs and you should improve your group's performance on each successive run.
- The results of each run for each group should be written on a board and communicated to the groups before they commence their next run.

 # Activity two: The origami exercise

Materials required

1 Squares of coloured paper.

2 A book on Origami (paper folding) with one exercise copied as follows:
   (a) one picture of the completed article and the written instructions;
   (b) one set of written instructions only; and
   (c) the completed origami item only.

Task

The participants should be divided into three groups and then a trainer chosen from each group. It is the trainer's task to train the rest of the group to make the origami item and therefore trainers should be taken on one side, briefed and given a chance to practice first.

- Group 1 is given the finished item and some coloured paper.
- Group 2 is given the picture, written instructions and some paper.
- Group 3 is given the written instructions only and some paper.

 # Debate one

'You learn more out of class than in.'

Starting points

For

- 'Learning is a feature of all human activity' (Mullins, p. 124). Much more human activity occurs outside class than inside, in consequence so does much more learning.

- A crossword answer comes to you when you are not thinking about it; you can ride the bike today that yesterday you were still falling off. Learning happens unconsciously all the time.

- Experiments with rats in 1930 (Tolman and Holzick) showed them acquiring cognitive maps of their environment in a process of latent or incidental learning while accomplishing other tasks.

Against

- 'Ratology' (generalising about humans on the basis of experiments with rats) is unreliable and the unconscious is undemonstrable.

- Classroom learning is systematically tested and provides distinctions between people (a process that is 'ingrained in our society' - Mullins, p. 119). These distinctions are used in job selection procedures. I sincerely hope my next airline pilot or surgeon has had plenty of formal training and is not just trusting to incidental learning.

Further reading

Kolb, D. A. (1985), *Experiential Learning: Experience as the Source of Learning and Development*, Prentice Hall.

McCormack, B. and McCormack, L. (1994), 'Experiential learning and the learning organisation', in *Cases in Organisational Behaviour*, D. Adam-Smith and A. Peacock (eds), Pitman, 280–7.

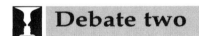 **Debate two**

'Measuring learning leads to strife not knowledge'

Starting points

For

- To help parents and patients learn more about schools and hospitals, the British government began publishing, in the 1990s, league tables purporting to distinguish between the successful and less successful of these institutions. The scheme was widely criticised by medical and teaching organisations. The Bishop of Birmingham publicly preached that patients are people in need of care, not statistics for the accountants to work on. There is no point knowing how long you will have to wait for attention in a hospital if you have no idea of the kind of care you are waiting for. The plumber whose phone rings three times when you call is not *necessarily* less efficient at mending pipes than one whose phone rings twice.

Against

- Measurements give information. Hospital A will see that hospital B is doing better on waiting lists and might try to learn how this is done. Some hospitals really are 'suitable cases for treatment' (*The Times*, 30 June 1994). Refusing information simply because it is incomplete means you will never learn anything.

- If you believe in Individual Differences (Mullins, Chapter 4), you will know that each person has different perceptions, attitudes and motivations, and therefore that they need different learning programmes and achieve different results.

Further reading

Eysenck, H. J. (1962), *Know your own IQ*, Pelican.

Lessem, R. (1991), *Total Quality Learning*, Blackwell, p.1, ch. 5.

Luthans, F. (1992), *Organisational Behaviour*, 6th edn, McGraw-Hill, ch. 8, 218–31.

✓ Look, it really works!

1 Until a few years ago, most organisations came under the auspices of an Industry Training Board: an organisation whose main objective was to ensure that training for their particular industry was not only carried out but that training standards were maintained. One of the most popular courses promoted by any training board was the one usually called 'trainer skills' or 'train the trainer'. Ask any senior manager which course has had most impact on them and the chances are they'll say, 'Trainer Skills' rather than 'Advanced Marketing' or 'The business game simulation'.

Why should this be? Why should senior managers remember such a basic course? To try and throw some light on this, let's quickly outline the course programme. First, there would be general introductions – What do you hope to gain from the course? – What problems do you have with training? (Yes, oh cynical reader, we trainers are nothing if not predictable and whilst you're busy doing that, it gives us the chance to work out who the bolshie one in the group is, take a quick trip to the loo, phone the office and work out the next session.) This will be followed by sessions on how people learn, how to structure a training session, some skills work (questioning, listening, etc.) and a demonstration training session by the tutor. Finally comes the chance for delegates to put it all into practice (at least once and hopefully twice or three times) by training another delegate for ten minutes on a fairly simple task like folding a shirt or changing a plug. Because they're very simple tasks, it ought to be easy to train someone . . . not so! Because we do them all the time, we forget to put ourselves in the trainee's shoes and fail to find out enough about their previous knowledge. (If you're not convinced at this stage, ask a child to show you how to do something you haven't been able to master – like setting the video or getting your watch to stop 'bleeping' on the hour – or alternatively try teaching a four-year-old how to tie a shoelace).

It's only when delegates are put in the situation of training someone that they themselves learn by doing; they learn to find out about prior knowledge, they learn to break assumptions, they learn to make sure that the task is broken down into manageable bits. Some examples we've had on training courses are: changing a motor car wheel and forgetting to put the wheel nuts back on . . . teaching someone to knit without finding out that the trainee was left-handed . . . changing a barrel of real ale without realising that the task was both too complicated for the trainee to absorb and there was no spare barrel for them to practice on . . . and showing someone how to open a bottle of champagne whilst pointing it at the trainee.

This example illustrates a real casserole of learning theory: Kolb can be applied in that delegates were learning experientially and evaluating what was happening; you can also add in a dash of Thorndike (people learn by trial and error, repeating their successes) and finally a soupçon of Skinner (the trainers were trying to shape their delegates' behaviour to the point where a structured training session would become an automatic response for them).

2 Imagine yourself at the end of your OB semester – no more 9.15 lectures on Monday mornings, no more frantic copying of other people's notes because 'the night before' and 'the morning after' had merged into a dreadful blur. There's only one hurdle left to jump: 'the exam'.

This year you decide to get organised and allow two whole weeks for revision. Day one dawns and you sit yourself down and open your notes. Two hours later you're still looking at them trying to make sense of pyramids and chess-boards with numbers like 1:9 and 9:1 in the squares. Where on earth does it all fit in? You begin to feel like the rat in Skinner's Box except that there isn't a lever to press . . .

Still waiting for inspiration to strike, you leave it for a while, watch the lunchtime edition of 'Neighbours' and pop to the pub for a quick one. The afternoon session isn't any better and again you give up early. You've just settled down to the six o'clock News when your partner comes in and says: 'If I give a good presentation tomorrow, there's every chance I'll get the promotion I've been wanting, so I'm going to work on it all night. By the way, how's the revision going?' Pause for clap of thunder and 'Blinding Glimpse of the Obvious'. . . was there ever a case of Expectancy Theory in practice? Welcome to the world of insight learning – you've just experienced Gestalt (remember, the whole is more than the sum of the parts?). You've suddenly made the links which have enabled you to see the jigsaw completed.

 ## Assignment one

In a recent survey of twelve London boroughs carried out by the London University Institute of Education, so-called ethnic pupils (Black African, Indian, etc.) were found to have begun outstripping their so-called white class-mates in GCSE examinations (*The Times,* 27 June 1994). A Labour MP called for detailed research to investigate this apparent disparity of educational achievements.

Task

Drawing on ideas found in Mullins, pp. 115–23, write a 1,500 word essay discussing the kind of factors that would need to be taken into account in embarking on this programme of research work.

Assignment two: An exercise in experiential learning and decision-making

'Change is one of the common features of organisations over the last decade . . .' (Mullins, p. 124).

Task

Design a learning or training programme for your group or organisation that is appropriate to the situation it finds itself in after a significant period of change. This might have been brought about by the introduction of new technology, a merger, a rapid growth in student numbers, the launch of a new product, privatisation, a new management structure, and so on.

The factors in Figure 4 on p. 116 in Mullins will all clearly have to be considered as will alternative strategies arising from this analysis. You will probably find yourself having to make decisions about some of the following issues:

taught courses	–	student-led learning
organisation centred	–	partnership with educational institutions
formal teaching	–	on-the-job training
full-time	–	part-time, day release, sandwich
individual learning	–	group work
grading schemes	–	self- or peer appraisal
punishments	–	rewards
lectures	–	seminars
programmed learning	–	incidental learning
knowledge	–	skills

It could be interesting too to attempt a portrait of an 'ideal' teacher (animator, manager, facilitator, counsellor, lecturer?) for the programme. Remember, also, to present, in some detail, the situation the programme is being designed for.

! Pause for thought

1 A different approach to the whole concept of training, learning and educating has been taken by Body Shop founder, Anita Roddick. The company's training school was started in 1985 because Roddick didn't want staff (or customers for that matter) to stop learning just because they'd started working. Initial courses concentrated on human development and consciousness raising and they've even run a course on management-by-humour.

Roddick feels that education of staff is an important responsibility, particularly since at that time retailing was one of the few growth areas for women. 'Training', however, is a word she professes to dislike, claiming 'that you can train dogs and you can train horses' but the company's aim was to educate people to help them realise their own potential. She claims that the closest the company has ever come to conventional training was a course on customer care, but here again the difference seems to be in the overall approach: employees were told the history of product ingredients, given information and amusing anecdotes to pass on to customers. She says, 'conventional retailers trained for a sale; we trained for knowledge. They trained with an eye on the balance sheet; we trained with an eye on the soul' (Roddick 1991).

Given its huge success, this approach has clearly worked for Body Shop. Could it work for, for example, a high-street fashion retailer? If not, why not? Should it be the responsibility of organisations to train and educate with 'an eye in the soul'? Valid hypothesis or trendy fad?

2 For many years a popular topic for discussion in Management Studies classes has been: 'Are managers born or made?' The existence and growth of manager education and management development supports the hypothesis that, to a very high degree, managers are made.

Wide-ranging changes in the processes of education, training and development and the awarding of qualifications are being forced through the system at an alarming rate. There is an inexorable movement towards National Vocational Qualifications (NVQs) for all levels of achievement in all vocational disciplines, including management.

The making of a manager is a long-term project; 'getting it wrong' has serious and expensive future implications. It would be more appropriate now to consider not *if*, but *how* should future managers be 'made'.

There are claims and counterclaims for the superiority of the two main systems: 'Traditional' management education in centres of further and higher education on the one hand, and vocationally based NVQs on the other.

There are fundamental differences between the two approaches, as the following table shows:

NVQ	Traditional
Based on demonstrating competence	Based on proof of learning
Primarily experiential learning	Primarily teach and test
Candidate-driven (in terms of timescale and speed of learning)	Tutor-driven (in terms of time scale and speed of learning)
Work performance is assessed	Learning and memory are assessed
Assessment based on laid down National Performance Standards with knowledge and understanding as an addition	Assessment based on theoretical knowledge and understanding with performance added in the form of simulations and assignments
Results stated only in terms of 'competent' or 'not competent'	Results expressed in levels of success (pass/merit/distinction)
Uses industrially based assessors and verifiers	Uses academic examiners and moderators

In their work on learning, Honey and Mumford identified four preferred learning styles: activist, pragmatist, theorist and reflector. Which are the dominant styles for managers? Which system is more compatible with manager development?

Quality and credibility are vital in any learning and qualification process. What are the implications for quality control and perceived value of any resultant qualifications associated with the two approaches?

'Pause for thought' provided by David Callas (Development Consultants).

? Still not convinced?

1 One of the authors speaks!

My formative years in the real world (doing a 'proper' job as someone once said. . .) were in the hotel and catering industry. Once you got to the dizzy heights of having the word 'manager' after your name, it accorded you three privileges: to have your surname *and* job title on your name badge; to be able legitimately to carry a briefcase; and to be given a 'bleeper'. This last entitlement meant that when on duty you had to carry this invader of privacy at all times, either clipped to your waistband or carried in your pocket. You could be contacted to sort out a variety of problems from 'Room 407 is complaining (again)', to 'We've run out of bread, can you get the porter to go to Sainsbury/Safeway/Tesco?', or (horror of horrors) 'We've done the alarm call for Room 326 five times and he isn't answering – can you go up and check that he's alright?'. There must be Somebody's Law which rules in this case because the chances were very high that your bleeper would go off when you were sitting on the loo, in the middle of a well-deserved breakfast, answering the phone, or in the pub next door.

Eventually I left the industry and via a circuitous route (a sort of academic M25) ended up in education (don't we all, eventually . . .?). My bleep-carrying days were over! However, about ten years after having ceremoniously handed back my bleep and name badge (I got to keep the briefcase), I found myself giving a presentation in a large London hotel to a group of 'very senior businessmen'. Somewhat nervously I stood outside the conference room, awaiting 'the call'. Very near to me I heard a bleeper going off – automatically I looked to my waistband to see if it was *my* bleeper . . .

Classical conditioning if ever there was?

2 Do students learn or are they taught finance?

In twenty years of teaching finance to university students on non-accounting courses, Jim Logic had come to believe that the tutor made a substantial contribution to student learning and felt that interaction was essential. During the first few years he had believed that the way ahead was to throw a large amount of information at the students during the lecture and ask them to work through questions on the topic before the next session. Fifteen years of working in a financial environment before joining the university had not prepared him for the total lack of numeracy that bedevils many people.

Jim pondered the situation at some length and was struck by the brilliant thought that the way to enable people to learn finance was to interest them in the topic first. Once people became interested in a subject they very quickly learnt about it but the difficulty was to discover which particular aspect of finance they disliked least or enjoyed the most. There were several topics that were found in all basic finance courses and he felt that a scientific approach was called for. Jim chose three basic financial topics and decided to introduce each of his financial courses to the subject using a different topic. Group One would be introduced through the medium of double-entry bookkeeping, Group Two through the profit and loss account, and Group Three through the balance sheet.

Group One started in an encouraging way and several of the students who had good application appeared to understand and enjoy what they were doing. The vast majority, however, were very quickly disaffected with the subject and comments were expressed in loud stage whispers which intimated that the course members were not happy. The more polite comments included, 'Why are we doing this?', 'I'm bored to death', 'I wish I'd chosen another course/university', 'I don't understand what is going on at all'. Jim found that *he* wasn't having a particularly happy time either. Despite his best intentions to the contrary, he found that he was becoming less tolerant as he explained the same minor point for the fifth time. Not only this, but he found his voice was getting louder as he sought to clarify the situation. He reminded himself of the vicar who used to write 'SLAW' at strategic points in his sermons. 'SLAW' meant: 'speak loud: argument weak'! Double-entry bookkeeping did not appear to provide a solution to Jim's problem.

Group Two were initially encouragingly interested in the concept of profit, particularly when it was applied to their favourite football or rugby team. Once this initial interest had worn off, however, and some of the more obscure concepts had been introduced, the group became as disaffected as Group One had been. No amount of cajoling or the introduction of stories about fishermen, men in balloons or women pilots sparked more than a passing interest. The profit and loss account did not offer a great deal of hope.

Group Three were introduced gradually to the balance sheet and Jim was gratified to observe that the initial interest of the students was maintained lecture after lecture; they were able to complete the balance sheet item by item. The two-sided balance sheet was initially used as the learning vehicle as it enabled the students to demonstrate where the resources came from and how they were applied. The interest of the group increased as the size of the balance sheet grew and Jim had a new spring to his step and a twinkle in his eye.

'Pride cometh before the fall!' and the transfer from the two-sided to the narrative form of balance sheet did cause some initial problems, but these were relatively painlessly overcome when the published accounts of companies were produced and discussed. The discussions became quite heated when the accounts of companies for whom the students worked were analysed.

The problem had been resolved: students both learn and are taught finance but they learn it most successfully when the appropriate teaching vehicle is used.

Provided by David Davis, University of Portsmouth.

Afterthoughts

1 'Don't go into Mr McGregor's garden: your father had an accident there; he was put in a pie by Mrs McGregor.' (From *The Tale of Peter Rabbit*, Beatrix Potter, 1902.) Why did Peter Rabbit not heed his mothers' warning?

2 This chapter has talked about learning. Under that heading we've encompassed training, education and development. Is there a difference? Yes, and you can display the three words with careful definitions on an overhead slide which you put up on the OHP and then wait while people laboriously copy it down. Unless, that is, you're the student we had once who simply listed all three titles on the whiteboard, prefaced each one with the word 'sex', looked at the seminar group and asked, 'Which one would you want your child to learn in school?'

First afterthought provided by Val Marchant, Ibis Training and Development.

3 Perception

 The eye of the beholder

In the spring of 1994, two men dominated the headlines in British newspapers: John Major and Nelson Mandela. Major's Tory party had suffered its largest ever defeat at the polls and Mandela's African National Congress party had won the country's first ever non-racial election. In the media the Prime Minister was reported as weak, a wimp, a 'Maybe Man', purposefully vague and wobbling. One wit proclaimed Majorism 'a wasm' and one article even devoted several paragraphs to his trousers' crumpled crotch. The new South African President was called a 'great, great, great man', 'the man of the hour, the decade and the century'.

There is no doubting the poor performance of the British Conservative government on the one hand and the remarkable achievement of Mandela and the ANC on the other. John Major's administration had seemed to make no impact on the recession, unable to check rising unemployment, to keep promises on tax restraint, to agree on European policies, and it had seen too many of its number implicated in dubious moral behaviour, while it urged the country to return to basics (the supposedly rigorous standard of a previous era). Mandela, after twenty-seven years in prison for opposing apartheid, came out to lead the ANC to power through a relatively non-violent and democratic process most would scarcely have believed possible in that bitterly divided nation.

None the less John Major was, in many respects, a demonstrably tough political leader. It is hard to imagine a weak politician rising to the post of leader of his party in the first place, and, once there, he fought a successful election campaign in the face of persistent evidence in the polls that he would lose and, like the 'Iron Lady' he had ousted (and to whom, one genealogist has claimed, he is distantly related), steered the country through a war. He was seen to rebuke dissenting members of his government and impose resignations on them when necessary. Those working with him claimed to believe him to be a good leader ('actually very tough', 'more resilient than anyone had realised', and so on) and even supporters of his predecessor called him a man of steel. Nelson Mandela, on the other hand, at the time of the elections was seventy-six years old and had a team of workers carefully attending to his dietary needs, rest periods, exercise, and his health in general. In public meetings his oratory, so fiery when he was a young lawyer defending himself against treason charges, was now often laboured and stiff. During his election campaign he had to take a whole week off with laryngitis and once inaugurated as President he made it known he would not complete his term.

The differences between the two leaders were manifestly many; they were culturally, historically, socially, politically and personally poles apart. But they did both have very difficult situations to deal with. Major faced mid-term blues with a vengeance: numbers of MPs who saw themselves potentially losing their seats with even a fraction of the swing that had led to defeat in the local elections, European elections coming up with a party deeply divided over the very concept of Europe, a tax programme that left the electorate feeling it had been lied to, and an imminent by-election where this discontent could, with dire consequences perhaps, be expressed. Such parochial matters pale in comparison with the issues facing South Africa it is true. The country had been boiling up over many years to what, it was feared, would be a blood bath as Blacks demanded equality. Such an outcome would inevitably have affected the rest of the world in a way the Tories' plight in Britain could scarcely do. The alternative in South Africa was almost as frightening: that the Whites would depart, leaving the country to face the kind of economic decline being suffered by so many of their liberated neighbours on the African continent.

Interestingly though, both leaders faced difficulties which it was possible to view optimistically or pessimistically, to take a positive or negative point of view about. There is little doubt, of course, that the South African situation had been handled with strategic brilliance by the principal players. De Klerk demonstrated foresight, bravery and great strength when he decided to steer the country to democracy, the United States accelerated progress by threatening significantly increased economic sanctions, White financiers had long been working to bring White and Black communities together, the ANC's policy was founded on equality for all races rather than revenge for the Blacks, and Mandela himself had shown great determination and patience, even refusing release from prison on conditions that would control his behaviour. The way the difficulties were presented, however, played a very important part in the success or lack of it in these two otherwise very different cases.

The morning after the Tories' defeat in the local elections, radio reporters were asking people in the street what they thought of Major and the word 'weak' kept recurring. In the studio a colleague said he was prepared to challenge for the leadership. During succeeding days the papers kept the story of his weakness going: 'he must assert his authority', he needs to 'toughen up a bit', he has to be 'master in his own house', he should 'bang his fist on the table', and so on. Even on election day itself one journalist wrote, 'He gets cross in a middle class kind of way, like a golfer who's not allowed to play through.' (*Guardian*, 6 May 1994). The same paper the next day asserted, 'There is little doubt that his . . . lame perfor-mance on TV and tabloid denigrations have undermined Major's standing.' In fact, the biggest tabloid, the *Sun*, strove loyally to keep a sense of balance but had to cash in on the sales potential of what was assuming witch-hunt characteristics. One political supporter spoke of 'the current febrile atmosphere' and another remarked sadly, 'Most of us think he is a very good leader. The difficulty is that this is not the press perception.'

The Pan African Congress, the revenge on apartheid party, polled 1.25 per cent of the vote. The ANC policy of reconciliation, equality, racial harmony and the peaceful transfer of power was clearly what the country wanted and many different groups worked hard to achieve it. An important part of that work certainly focused on presentation. Mandela himself was constantly in the limelight, a tall, straight, even elegant man, with an engaging smile which vanished only when, at the nominations for parliamentary speaker, he found himself sitting next to his estranged wife. He had distanced himself from her soon after she had been charged with assault crimes. The image of the Nobel peace prize winner would certainly not have been enhanced by such an association and Winnie Mandela's own assessment was that 'the moment he stepped out of prison he was national property'.

Mandela's actions all conspired to enhance his image. His rhetoric was insistent: 'our country . . . common homeland . . . common victory for justice . . . time to build . . . national unity . . . amnesty', and, of course, the moving 'rainbow nation'. His gestures were symbolic: shaking hands with his rival de Klerk after a TV debate, hugging him on inauguration day, crossing the floor of the national assembly several times to greet opposition leaders, doing a lap of honour after campaign meetings, visiting the Johannesburg stock exchange, photo sessions in front of the presidential offices and parliament buildings often with hand on heart – gestures enhanced, it should be said, by those of other figures, such as Archbishop Tutu jumping with joy at events and de Klerk standing in a queue to cast his vote. Churlish though it might seem, commentators, even at the height of euphoria over these exciting and uplifting times, were able to talk of 'carefully crafted gestures of reconciliation' and a 'designer outcome' to the election (meaning that the ANC had obtained less than two-thirds of the vote, legally barring them from changing the constitution unilaterally). The *Sunday Times* (8 May 1994) went so far as to assert the vote had been fixed to achieve this hoped-for result.

Mandela is of royal birth and could give the impression of being born to rule. Major is the son of an acrobat, yet could seem very wobbly. In reality, of course, both men were getting on with their daily tasks as best they could.

 # Activity brief

1 Discuss ways photographs and film can affect the way perceptions of reality are selected, organised and interpreted.
2 The 'wet and yellow whistling of the blackbird' (Christopher Fry) is music to *our* ears but probably sounds ghastly to the waiting worm. List some factors that might lead to a less than universal joy at the presidential success of Nelson Mandela. Do the so-called halo (or rusty halo) effects play any part in people's perception of the two leaders discussed above?
3 In English tennis clubs Muslims have been known to decline playing in mixed doubles and English people returning from France often proclaim that the French do not know how to queue. Do cultural factors play any part in perceptions of the two leaders discussed? (See Mullins, p. 143.)

4 Our interests encourage us to see what we are looking for and this can lead to self-fulfilling prophecies. If people think inflation will rise, for instance, it probably will. Can such a process bring about the fall of a leader?

5 Size, colour, movement, attractiveness and even dress are all said to have an influence on what we perceive. Do such factors play any part in perceptions of Major and Mandela?

A rose by any other name or a thorn in the side?

'Trust me, I'm in personnel' is an oft-heard comment which generally invokes cynical laughter. The perceived role of the personnel department varies from a hard-headed human asset accounting approach through the 'soft' people side to Drucker's (1961) 'trash can hypothesis' where he declares the work to be largely redundant.

The development of personnel management has been described as a history of self-image (Torrington and Hall 1991) – the 'social reformer' of the nineteenth century who, with the backing of such as Robert Owen, sought to avoid exploitation of the masses, followed by the 'acolyte of benevolence', again influenced by such people as the early Quakers and Rowntree where the role was perceived as dispensers of charity to deserving employees. The growth of Taylorism saw personnel classified as a 'humane bureaucrat' when there began the slow change from personnel serving employees' objectives to serving those of the organisation. This was further reinforced following the increase in size and power of the trade unions after the Second World War when the growth of joint consultation saw the role becoming that of 'consensus negotiator'. This shift continued into the 1960s with 'organization man' as the era saw a preoccupation with organisational effectiveness, with, perhaps, ensuring completion of the organisation's agenda rather more important than that of employees. The late 1980s saw the move to human resource management (HRM), to 'managing the context' rather than, some would say, the content of the personnel function.

It is this last rebirth of the 'phoenix' that has given rise to the greatest confusion in the minds not only of employees but also within the personnel function itself. This confusion has probably arisen for two reasons: first, the perception of what personnel actually *does* in return for the salary, and, secondly, the ability to be able to differentiate (or not) between 'traditional' personnel management approaches and the 'new improved' HRM approach.

Despite the supposed growth from welfare officer, dispensing tea and sympathy, to the personnel professional, there still exists the perception that nothing has changed. An assistant works manager in an engineering company was quoted by Karen Legge (1978) as saying: 'They should stick to welfare – that's what personnel's job is – looking after routine welfare matters.' Drucker as long ago as 1955 wrote, 'the constant worry of all personnel administrators is their ability to prove that they are making a contribution to the enterprise. Their preoccupation is with the search for a "gimmick" that will impress their management associates. Their persistent complaint is that they lack status.'

It is this preoccupation with the perception of status which arises from job title that has perhaps given rise to much of the confusion. The person responsible for carrying out the 'personnel' function in an organisation may be called variously a 'personnel manager' in the private sector with 'personnel officer' being generally reserved for lower levels in the hierarchy, whilst the latter term is used to denote a departmental head of some seniority in the public sector. This confusion has been further compounded by the 'new' title of 'human resource manager'; it certainly sounds grand and, if we are to follow the definition of human resource management, would appear to indicate a person of considerable seniority with input and influence in the organisation at a strategic level. However, Legge (1989) found that a close examination of the two models of personnel management and HRM established little difference between them. Indeed, Mullins (1992) writes that 'it is not easy . . . to distinguish human resource management from personnel management. And neither does it follow that human resource management, however it is described, will necessarily lead to a higher level of organisational performance than would be achieved with a traditional personnel management approach.'

We thus appear to have confusion not only as to what personnel *does* but also as to what they should be *called* while they are doing it. Overlaid on this is the further confusion created by the existence, until recently, of two separate professional bodies: The Institute of Personnel Management (IPM) whose main aim can be argued to be furthering the cause of that profession, and The Institute of Training and Development (ITD) whose main focus is as its title would suggest. Whether that part covered by the ITD is a subset of personnel/HRM is arguable depending on which side of the fence you sit. Developments following the recent merger of the two organisations and the proposed new name, The Institute of Personnel and Development, is probably a case of 'watch this space'.

We have, therefore, a situation of 'personnel' concerned with both its title and its status; trying desperately (some would say) to move away from its welfare image to one where it is perceived as contributing to the strategic thrust of the organisation. However, this would now appear to be militating against them. A recent study for the Employment Policy Institute by Professor David Metcalf of the London School of Economics (1994) found that establishing a personnel team seems to be detrimental to the organisation because employees no longer feel that they can take their problems to their line managers: 'Workers see a personnel department as an external agency which distances them from their company and knows little about their work.' Probably more serious is the finding that personnel directors on the board of a company, or even as a specialist resource, produced a downturn in the general management/employee relations climate and an upturn in staff turnover with a subsequent overall decline in organisational performance. Whilst human resource techniques such as encouraging employee involvement, merit pay awards and a blurring of the distinctions between management and the workforce appeared to be successful, this was thought to be 'in spite of' rather than 'because of' the influence of personnel.

Predictably, the IPM were surprised at the results of the findings (*Independent on Sunday*, 5 May 1994) and suggested that John Purcell, a lecturer in HRM at Templeton College, Oxford would support their view. However, he suggested the opposite; the survey results were not a surprise to him: 'people have been getting the same results for thirty years'.

Whether as a result of their own anecdotal evidence or as a result of the current trend towards downsizing and delayering, the 1990s have seen a decrease in personnel/HRM representation on the board of directors to 30 per cent from 70 per cent in the 1980s. Tesco, British Gas and the RAC are among many companies who are reducing or reorganising their personnel departments. The general trend is toward devolution of personnel work to line managers. Presumably HR involvement in strategy is no longer seen as important and the trend towards empowerment will make all line managers a collective company conscience.

Given, then, that industry would appear to be jettisoning their personnel staff but given also that there are currently 100,000 HR professionals in the UK, where are they all going to? The answer would appear to be: back to college! There exists the incongruity that whilst industry is reducing its numbers, educational establishments, who became corporations in April 1994, are increasing the size and scope of *their* personnel departments. Professor Metcalf's survey found an increase not only in the size but also the scope of personnel departments in education. Policies and procedures abound and management/staff relationships appear to be rapidly decreasing. Could this be a final resting place for human resource management?

 # Activity brief

1 People say 'noughts and crosses' even if the order they 'see' them in is actually 'crosses and noughts' (Mullins, p. 137). Is this evidence that our language determines our perceptions or would personnel departments 'smell the same by any other name'?

2 Could changes in the perception of personnel departments be understood in terms of McGregor's theories X and Y? (See Mullins, p. 141 and Chapter 13.)

3 Make a list of tasks performed by personnel departments. Compare your list with others'. Are any differences between lists explicable in terms of theories of perception?

 # Activity one

Introduction

Recent experiments in social psychology have suggested that:

● Happiness makes us more prone to make stereotypical judgements.

● Minority members of high-status groups readily stereotype themselves by reference to that group.

- Males and females both overestimate their intelligence but it is more usually males who overestimate their physical attractiveness.

- New workers stay longer in organisations if they are referred for the job by current workers than if they enter by different routes, like answering a job advertisement.

These rather simplistic, not to say downright misleading, statements are summaries made of reports found in 1994 issues of two academic reviews, *The Journal of Personality and Social Psychology* and *The Journal of Social Psychology*.

Task

Read and precis one such experiment for yourself, then report back to a discussion group to try to assess the value and shortcomings of the experiments. (For example, how many of them use college students as the subjects of the experiments? Do cultural factors limit the applicability of the findings?)

 Activity two

Task

Working in groups of four, study the following four items. They give the results of a management assessment exercise completed by Elizabeth (a managing director) and Andy, Steve and Linda (her three senior managers). All scores were given in confidence.

- Item 1 is an explanation of each management skill which is being assessed (see Figure 3.1).

- Item 2 is an explanation of the rating system to be used (see Figure 3.2).

- Item 3 contains the results (scores) given by Elizabeth on each of her managers alongside their own self-assessment (see Figure 3.3).

- Item 4 contains the results (scores) given by Elizabeth as a self-assessment of her own skills alongside those given to her by Andy, Steve and Linda (see Figure 3.4).

Discussion questions

1 What differences exist between each person's perception of their own performance and their colleagues' perception of them? Why should this be?

2 What feedback would you, as a consultant, give to the management team?

3 How would you organise this feedback? (e.g. Individually? In what order? All together?)

4 Devise a role play scenario to act out this feedback session, concluding with an action plan for each of the managers and Elizabeth.

Fig. 3.1 Assessment of management skills

Management skill	Explanation
Performance appraisal	The ability to review and rate objectively past performance and to discuss and agree actions/objectives for the coming period.
Performance counselling	The ability to help a subordinate identify, explore and own his/her own performance strengths and weaknesses, reinforcing strengths and correcting weaknesses to achieve or maintain a high level of performance.
Objective setting	The ability to define clear, measurable, challenging but realistic results with deadlines for achievement.
Planning	The ability to define how an objective will be achieved, stating or agreeing who will do what by when and effectively anticipating potential difficulties, but can change and adapt plans when required.
Organising	The ability to make effective use of available resources, set and review priorities, make decisions and take responsibility for them.
Problem-solving	The ability to identify the root cause of a problem to permit effective action.
Decision-making	The ability to choose between various options using sound judgement rather than bias.
Leadership	The ability to achieve results through others, selecting the appropriate style for the situation.
Team-building	To develop the ability of working within a team by individual recognition of styles and strengths and to identify the strengths of team members for maximum effectiveness and efficiency.
Motivation	The ability to create in others a willingness and commitment to achieve the best performance of which they are capable.
Time management	The ability to organise oneself effectively and to maintain an efficient control of time.
Delegation	The ability to identify and overcome difficulties of delegation.
Selection interviewing	The ability to extract effectively the necessary information from a candidate to permit comparison with the job requirements and enable a (later) decision to be made; to interest the candidate in the organisation/job.
Assertiveness	To identify assertiveness as a management skill. To distinguish between aggressive behaviour and to give and receive criticism in a constructive manner.

Management skill	Explanation
Developing staff	The ability to assess development potential effectively to train staff.
Letter and report writing	To enable clear, concise and effective communication in reports and letters.
Leading and participating in meetings	The ability to identify specific results to be achieved, defining the appropriate structure, effective involvement of the participants and ensuring that the outcomes are clear and acceptable.
Giving a presentation to inform	The ability to present facts/opinions in a logical and clear way that creates and maintains interest and achieves the level of under-standing required.
Giving a presentation to persuade	The ability to present a proposal that highlights benefits to the receiver, proves the case, effectively handles questions and secures approval.
Influencing	The ability successfully to convince others on the same level (or a higher level) to change/negotiate in order to meet his/her own objectives.
Generating options and creative thinking	The ability to generate a wide range of novel options for evaluation.
Managing change	The ability to identify opportunities for improving standards, to plan and organise change, to develop objectives and systems.
Communication skills: **• To/with others**	The ability to succesfully communicate with others and to encourage others to as well.
• Listening skills **• Questioning skills**	To demonstrate sound listening skills. To identify the varying types of question and which to use in various different situations.

Fig. 3.2 Rating system for management skills

Rating	Explanation
1	Rarely displays this skill, if at all.
2	Occasionally displays this skill but considerable development is required.
3	Moderately proficient in this skill but there is still scope for improvement.
4	Displays strength in this skill on some occasions, but not consistently.
5	Displays significant strength in this skill *consistently.*

Fig. 3.3 Elizabeth's rating of the others and their own self-assessments

Management skill	Andy A	Andy B	Steve A	Steve B	Linda A	Linda B
Performance appraisal	4	3	2	3	3	3
Performance counselling	5	3	2	1	4	3
Objective setting	4	3	2	1	4	3
Planning	4	4	3	4	3	2
Organising	4	4	3	4	3	4
Problem-solving	5	4	4	4	4	4
Decision-making	4	4	3	4	4	4
Leadership	4	3	2	4	4	4
Team-building	5	3	3	3	4	4
Motivation	5	3	2	3	4	4
Time management	4	2	2	3	3	3
Delegation	3	3	4	4	3	3
Selection interviewing	4	3	4	4	4	3
Assertiveness	4	3	2	3	4	3
Developing staff	4	3	3	4	4	3
Letter/report writing	3	2	2	4	3	2
Leading/participating in meetings	4	2	3	3	4	3
Giving a presentation to inform	3	2	3	4	3	3
Giving a presentation to persuade	4	2	3	3	3	3
Influencing	4	2	4	4	4	4
Generating opinions and creative thinking	5	3	3	3	4	4
Managing change	4	5	2	4	4	4
Communication skills: • To/with others • Listening • Questioning	4 4 4	3 4 3	3 3 3	4 5 4	4 3 3	4 4 4

Note: A = Elizabeth's rating.
        B = The manager's self-assessment.

Fig. 3.4 Elizabeth's self-assessment and the others' rating of Elizabeth

Management skill	Elizabeth	Andy	Steve	Linda
Performance appraisal	3	4	4	4
Performance counselling	4	4	4	3
Objective setting	4	4	4	4
Planning	4	4	3	4
Organising	4	4	4	4
Problem-solving	4	4	3	4
Decision-making	5	4	4	4
Leadership	4	5	5	5
Team-building	5	5	3	3
Motivation	4	5	5	4
Time management	3	4	2	2
Delegation	3	4	5	4
Selection interviewing	4	2	4	4
Assertiveness	4	4	4	4
Developing staff	4	4	4	3
Letter/report writing	3	5	4	3
Leading/participating in meetings	4	3	5	4
Giving a presentation to inform	4	4	4	4
Giving a presentation to persuade	4	5	5	4
Influencing	3	5	4	3
Generating opinions and creative thinking	4	5	4	4
Managing change	3	5	4	4
Communication skills: • To/with others • Listening • Questioning	5 4 4	5 4 5	5 4 4	4 4 4

Activity provided by Val Marchant, Ibis Training and Development.

Activity three

See Mullins, p. 161, 'The Stroop effect'.

 # Activity four

See Mullins, pp. 161–2, Assignment 2.

 # Debate one

'Even knowing about the perceptual process doesn't prevent perceptual errors occurring, especially in an interview situation.'

Starting points

For

- The tendency to, for example, stereotype, is innate and is not only bound to occur but will also predispose us to act in a particular way even though we know that it is wrong. In fact this predisposition occurs even before the interview: we start making judgements as early as the application stage.

- Because perception is such an *individual* process, two or more interviewers will probably have different impressions anyway. A knowledge of the perceptual process can, therefore, be argued to be pointless.

Against

- A knowledge of perceptual errors will assist in an interview situation because the interviewer will make additional efforts to overcome them through use of such techniques as questioning and listening.

- If a knowledge of the perceptual process is pointless then why bother with it? The research experiments show that it happens and we therefore need to know about it not only in order to obtain the best candidate but also to improve our own self-knowledge.

Further reading

McCauley, C., Stitt, C. L. and Segal, M. (1980), 'Stereotyping: From Prejudice to Prediction', *Psychological Bulletin*, January, 195–208.

Wexley, K. N., Yukl, G. A., Kovacs, S. Z. and Sanders, R. E. (1972), 'Importance of Contrast Effects in Employment Interviews', *Journal of Applied Psychology*, **56**, 45–8.

Debate two

'There is considerable truth in the commonly held perception that women's motivations and attitudes to work are different to men's.'

Starting points

For

● Women do not perceive themselves as having a 'career for life', rather that a job is only a temporary substitute before starting a family.

● Men are socialised into believing that they should be the ultimate 'breadwinner' and should concentrate their efforts on a 'career for life'.

Against

● Studies concerning this are rare, the proposition, therefore, has not been empirically tested but relies on anecdotal evidence.

● The proposition represents an all-encompassing statement which by its very nature is invalid: both women's and men's attitudes and motivations vary and will change depending on their individual life stage.

Further reading

Alban-Metcalfe, B. (1987), 'Attitudes to Work: Comparison by Gender and Sector of Employment', *The Occupational Psychologist*, **3**, December, 8.

Cooper, C. and Davidson, M. (1982), *High Pressure: Working Lives of Women Managers*, Fontana.

Kanter, R. M. (1977), *Men and Women of the Corporation*, Basic Books.

Marshall, J. (1984), *Women Managers: Travellers in a Male World*, Wiley.

✓ Look, it really works!

1 A student on one of our part-time management courses had recently changed jobs. Previously she had worked for a large organisation as a training officer where her job had involved writing and delivering a variety of training courses. Her new job was as a training and recruitment manager for a much smaller, less structured organisation. Along with her promotion came a lot more responsibility: she was in charge of a whole department overseeing the analysis of training needs, planning, designing, delivering and evaluating training courses. On top of that, her recruitment 'hat' gave her responsibility for recruiting trainee managers and monitoring their progress.

Two months into her new job, we asked her how she was getting on. 'I think I've made the wrong decision,' she replied. 'The training part of the job is going well but it's the recruitment part that's causing me problems. The area managers have made the assumption that "recruitment" means any recruitment and they've also further assumed that "recruitment" equals "personnel", so I'm being asked all sorts of questions about employment law and dismissal and I don't know anything about it. My one ally in the company has told me that the area managers are beginning to say that my appointment was a waste of time.'

Where does perception fit in here? Can you see how perceptions of one word – in this case 'recruitment' – can mean different things to different people? When our perception doesn't match reality, cognitive dissonance sets in (Mullins, p. 114) – can you see it in this case? How could it have been avoided?

2 Consider the following . . .

. . . A housewife looked out of her kitchen window and saw a stranger playing with her neighbour's child outside the house. Alarmed, she was about to call the police when she realised that it was the child's father who had shaved off his beard that morning . . .

. . . A lecturer was in his university library one day during the vacation and noticed a young woman coming towards him with an expectant look on her face. Assuming that it was a student new to the library he began to ask her if he could be of any assistance and then stopped when he realised it was his sister who lived over 60 miles away . . .

. . . In the doctor's waiting room, vacantly looking at the child on the chair next to him, John's thoughts were something like this: 'That boy's got a familiar face. Maybe it's a girl though. It's my Lucy!' Lucy was his daughter. The family's child-minder had a doctor's appointment that day and had brought Lucy with her . . .

How might a study of theories of perception help explain these real incidents?

 # Assignment one

Task

Either

1 During a one-week period, review the media (television, radio, advertisements, films, newspapers and magazines) for evidence of traditional male and female stereotypes.

Evaluate the impact and power of these stereotypes *either* in a group discussion *or* as a written report of not more than 1,500 words.*

Or

2 Here is a list of jobs performed in a secondary school:

teacher	gardener
child psychologist	secretary
governor	inspector
caretaker	groundsman

Adapted from Mullins: Review Question 7, p. 160.

deputy head
peripatetic music teacher
cook
head teacher
dinner attendant

cleaner
maintenance worker
educational welfare officer
non-teaching assistant

Which gender did you intuitively ascribe to each function? Were the people White, Black, handicapped? Did your judgements bear out the theory of stereotyping? How do such judgements match up with reality? (Mullins, p. 157).

Contact a local school and check who does these jobs there. Write a 750-word report with the title 'Who works in our schools?' based on two kinds of research approach: case study and statistical. Use the bibliographical evidence given in Mullins (p. 163, notes 31–6) to get you on the trail of appropriate statistical sources. (Notice, incidentally, that bibliographies tend not to identify the gender of the authors.)

 ## Assignment two

Over a six-week period, interview a selected sample of people about their perception of a particular group (e.g. students, personnel managers, trade union officials, disabled people, ex-offenders). Your sample should include representatives from your chosen group.

Prepare a report and/or presentation which evaluates the perceptions of those interviewed and answers the question: 'Do they conform to the "traditional" perceptual errors?'

You will need to:

● Devise and, where possible, test a questionnaire or other suitable interview method.

● Decide on your sample group and sample size.

● Make decisions and arrangements as to how your sample will be interviewed (e.g. by prior appointment or 'on the street', perhaps).

● Analyse your results using either a quantitative or qualitative approach.

● Evaluate your findings and draw logical conclusions.

Pause for thought

1 In May 1994 Robert Black went on trial in Newcastle upon Tyne accused of the murder of three schoolgirls between 1982 and 1986. Mr Black was a van driver whose work took him all over the UK. The bodies of the girls were found at spots which were close to areas to which Mr Black's itineraries would have taken him.

Mr Black's defence barrister, Ronald Thwaites QC, suggested to the jury that his client's arrest and subsequent charging provided the police with a convenient answer to what was a long-term unsolved problem for six police forces. He further claimed that in order to 'make the case fit' the police had disregarded several significant items of evidence.

Mr Thwaites then employed the relatively rare strategy of admitting to the jury that his client was already in prison, currently serving a life sentence for seizing and sexually assaulting a six-year-old girl in 1990. Further he had twice previously been convicted of 'lewd and libidinous practices' in Scotland. He told the jury that his client may well be a 'pervert and a monster' but that did not necessarily make him a murderer, that there was no automatic elevation from molester to murderer, but that in the eyes of the police he had become 'a murderer for all seasons'.

- What is the role of perceptual closure in this case?
- Was Thwaites justified in attempting to change the perception of the jury towards his client?
- Do you think that Black is guilty?

2 Over the last three years the wearing of a small red ribbon has become increasingly popular and people sporting this emblem can be seen everywhere from provincial high streets to public ceremonies – indeed at some of the latter, notably those conferring film or television awards, it has become *de rigueur*, often being included with the invitation. It is even considered in some circles to be churlish, at the very least, not to be wearing one.

The red ribbon vogue began life in America three years ago where it symbolised the red tape surrounding the help and benefits provided for people with AIDS. It is now seen as an emblem for raising awareness of HIV/AIDS, either globally or on a more personal level when it might be worn in memory of a friend who has died of AIDS or an AIDS-related condition.

The wearing of symbolic coloured ribbons is by no means a new phenomenon but, in fact, dates back to the seventeenth century when folk songs of the time record that wearing white ribbons indicated a married woman. They were further popularised during the American Civil War where a yellow ribbon was worn and this was resurrected in memory of both those killed or lost in Vietnam and also for hostages in Beirut. Gathering awareness since the inception of the red ribbon we now have a whole rainbow of colours: blue (unborn children), black (for Black people who have died of AIDS) and pink (for breast cancer).

The red ribbon, however, has gone from strength to strength: not only is there now a metal version but limited editions, using precious metals and gemstones, have raised it to the level of designer fashion accessory.

Distasteful as this glamorisation of a dreadful disease may be, at the very minimum awareness *must* be being raised and the AIDS charities *must* be receiving valuable revenue from the sale of ribbons, particularly the expensive versions. Or are they? There is no one specific campaigning organisation behind the red ribbons although in the past their sale has proved to be an effective fund raiser by AIDS charities. However, it is difficult to copyright a twisted length of red ribbon and, it has been claimed, it is now being incorporated as a fashion accessory rather than a statement of individual attitude: the finale of a recent show by designer Moschino featured dozens of children wearing red ribbons.

- How will the red ribbon be perceived in the next few years?
- How will reading this affect *your* perception of the next person you see who is wearing one?

? Still not convinced?

Consider the following scenarios:

1 It's Saturday evening and Cilla has 'gorralorra' contestants for 'Blind Date'. The programme follows its usual format: three people hidden behind a screen and another of the opposite sex on the other side of the screen who poses questions aimed at finding out which of the three will make the perfect blind date partner.

The audience in the studio and at home have the advantage over the hapless contestants, we can at least see what they all look like and we can make our choice based on this. Usually we decide by applying such scientific criteria as 'She looks like Julia Roberts', 'He looks like Patrick Swayze', 'She seems a fun person', or 'He's got a big ego'. In other words we apply our own perceptual criteria based on our attitudes, personalities and assumptions.

The contest is over and the 'winner' walks around the screen to meet his or her blind date . . . next time you watch, look for the expressions on each face – that'll tell you a lot about how perceptual processes work. Watch the programme the following week, hear how the 'date' worked (or didn't) and look again at the role of perception.

2 A research student of our acquaintance had got to that part of her Ph.D. which involved the actual collection of evidence – a series of semi-structured interviews with various people. She followed all the rules, explained the purpose of the research, how the interview was going to be conducted, and so on, and everything went well. After the interview was over, the respondent asked her about her background. When she replied that her first degree was in psychology, he said, 'I'm really glad that I didn't know that beforehand – I'd have been convinced that not only were there hidden reasons behind your questions but also that you were going to psychoanalyse all my answers.'

- What does this indicate about how we stereotype people?
- Have you ever avoided telling people (such as landlords or bank managers) that you're a student?

4 Personality

Out of the frying pan ...?

(The following are extracts from transcriptions of imaginary interviews in May 1994 with candidates wishing to join the Fire Brigade.)

Interview 1

INTERVIEWER. Miss Seles, this is a very dangerous job.

SELES. So is sport. Ask Nancy Kerrigan . . . ask Ayrton Senna. During the course of the war in my homeland, Yugoslavia, I received death threats and in April last year I was stabbed on court.

INTERVIEWER. The difference is that firemen take the risks again the next day. You still haven't returned to tennis.

SELES. The knife just missed my spinal cord. I'm sure I'd worry if I sat again with my back to the crowd. That might be difficult for you to grasp but you haven't been stabbed, I guess.

INTERVIEWER. Would you say, then, that your equilibrium has been disturbed by the experience?

SELES. Restored I'd say. By the time I was nineteen I was the world's Number One women's tennis player and only one title short of Billie Jean King's grand slam record which took her twenty years to achieve. I played tennis from the age of seven and although my parents never drove me, the system does take you over. It's hard to grow up in public, to be going through all those normal, teenage physical and mental changes but not having any privacy. I've even had a helicopter hovering over my practice court recently. So this thing may have been a blessing in disguise. I was getting distant from my parents. Watching myself on film I see only a part of me, a part I call my 'second personality'. Now I've been hiking, canoeing, fishing; I've been to the movies with my friends . . .

INTERVIEWER. And tennis? Your work; what you're good at?

SELES. I practise a lot still, running, the gym . . . not bench presses though, like Martina. I don't want – you know – bulging muscles.

48

INTERVIEWER. You practise in secret, though, and you didn't stand up very well to the concerted campaign against your grunting in '92. Also you cried on TV recently when the sound of an ambulance coincided with a question on the stabbing.

SELES. Listen, that man stabbed me because he had a crazy thing for Steffi, and he got what he wanted – getting her back to Number One – and the law turned him loose . . . Look, read my references. They tell you I'm physically fit, inexhaustibly energetic, and have a phenomenal work-rate. What sort of a person do you have to be to fight fires? Hell!

Interview 2

INTERVIEWER. Hello Miss Capriati, do sit down. Why is that ring threaded through your nostril?

CAPRIATI. All the kids wear them. It's, like, trendy.

INTERVIEWER. Firefighters don't wear decorations, it would be too risky. They wear a practical uniform.

CAPRIATI. Gee, I can handle that. We wore, like, all the right gear to play tennis.

INTERVIEWER. I'm not talking about fashion. I mean helmets, protective boots . . .

CAPRIATI. That's cool, we had sweat bands, you know, elbow supports, reinforced panties. You should see the photos of me playing. A nightmare: sweating, straining, exhausted, in pain . . . like I'd just been fighting a fire.

INTERVIEWER. But have you got staying power? You get hurt in our job and carry on, but you pulled out of tennis last year after an injury. Why?

CAPRIATI. To chill out and have fun. I started playing when I was four. My father had big ambitions for me and by thirteen I was coached by Chris Evert's father and contracted to The International Management Group. By fourteen I was the youngest player ever at Wimbledon and at fifteen the youngest ever semi-finalist. Even Seles wishes she hadn't started young. There's, like, a Commission just started to see if girls should be made to start later. Remember what happened to Tracy Austin, Andrea Jaeger, and now Seles maybe. They call it burn-out, you know. [*Giggles*] I want to finish school, go to college, I'm real interested in, like, psychology.

INTERVIEWER. I hear you're estranged from your family now. Is there a psychological explanation for your shoplifting last year?

CAPRIATI. That's unfair. I've already explained that was an accident.

[*Phone rings*]

INTERVIEWER. [*answering*] Yes . . . yes . . . Oh . . . right, thanks. Miss Capriati, I've just been informed you were charged yesterday with being in possession of cannabis. I'm afraid that alone means that we won't be able to consider you for the Force.

Interview 3

INTERVIEWER. Miss Navratilova, you are the most successful woman tennis player ever. What motivates you to keep playing at your age, and when there's no prize you haven't won?

NAVRATILOVA. That's never true. There's always something to prove. For instance, the oldest lady champion at Wimbledon was thirty-seven. I'd like that record. I'm fresh, eager, and feel about twenty-three. OK, I get my butt kicked more these days but I still have a great time. I'll scratch and scrape, and even crawl out there if there's a win in it for me.

INTERVIEWER. But where does this resolution come from? You've had plenty of set-backs to overcome: early fame, separation from your family and country, excessive media interest in your lesbian affairs, a stressful court case . . .

NAVRATILOVA. My parents divorced when I was three but my stepfather was really sensible about bringing my tennis along. These young American girls are pushed along too much by their parents. I didn't play at Wimbledon till I was sixteen. Remember, too, I was brought up in a Communist country, sport was a very respected activity. When I defected to the States in 1973, I was eighteen, successful and knew my own mind. I *do* hate the media knocking on my door all hours of the day and night to ask about my love life, but people like me owe a lot to them too. Being interested in both sexes gives you not only variety, you know, but gets you involved with some pretty interesting issues that are important too. And as for the court case, well Billie Jean coped, and so do I. These things can affect your performance temporarily but you can bounce back with hard training, good diet and the determination to win.

INTERVIEWER. You rely a lot on yourself. This job depends on the team. I see you having difficulties fitting in.

NAVRATILOVA. What about doubles, what about playing in your national team?

INTERVIEWER. Well, in your book, *Being Myself*, you do say that you play your worst matches when you smile and start feeling companionship with your opponents. And that once things got competitive with Chris Evert, playing doubles became a problem. It's probably true to say that you haven't always taken the decisions of the authorities in a very disciplined way – umpires, linesmen, tournament organisers . . .

NAVRATILOVA. Well, I know people don't like to hear women talk assertively about themselves. Maybe firefighters still think they're in a male preserve . . .

INTERVIEWER. In your palimony case . . .

NAVRATILOVA. Don't you guys talk plain English in the Force? It'll be 'galimony' next.

INTERVIEWER. Miss Navratilova, you're very rich. Why would you want a job like this?

NAVRATILOVA. I intend to die old, get a degree, maybe have a baby and careers other than tennis. I want to work towards ending world hunger, help preserve nature and wild life, clean up the environment. This job would get me started.

Activity brief

1 Can you situate any of these tennis players on the Myers-Briggs grid in Mullins (p. 108)? If not, why not? Is it your lack of understanding, their uniqueness, the inadequacies of the test itself, or something else?

2 Which candidate would you appoint to the job, if any? Give your reasons.

3 According to Sheldon, Stevens and Tucker (1940), personality is connected with body shape: fattish (even-tempered), thinnish (shy etc.) or muscly (extrovert). Does this account adequately for these sportswomen?

 # All the world's a stage ...

Just last week a professor friend of mine asked me if it was my interest in theatre that drew me to the field of organisational behaviour. Mulling it over, I realised that, yes, they *do* have a lot in common. Hamlet turns up in the first chapter of this book, after all, and I think it's high time he made another entrance.

In reality he is never very far away since most of us quote the play often, whether knowingly, (*'To be, or not to be'*, *'Alas, poor Yorick'*) , or unknowingly, (*'perchance to dream'*, *'brevity is the soul of wit'*). Shakespeare, like cricket, permeates the English language. But when Hamlet says *'the play's the thing'* or *'God has given you one face and you make yourselves another'* and decides himself *'to put an antic disposition on'*, then Shakespeare is doing more than adding colour to our language. He is commenting on human behaviour and, in particular, the complexity of human personality.

Mullins makes the point, in a rather more prosaic way of course, when he remarks (p. 111) that 'in a selection situation candidates may indeed consider the "type" of personality they wish to fake'. He is referring here to the way certain psychometric tests may be manipulated by those taking them, one of the many fears expressed about tests by union officials at Anglia Water when, in 1994, that company decided to use them to help it identify which 900 of its staff it would make redundant. Other fears included the inappropriateness of using personality tests (which are descriptive rather than predictive) to assess job suitability, suggestions that psychometric tests discriminate between races and gender, opinions holding that, of the 2,000 on the market, only about twenty seem reliable, and that buying them off the shelf instead of having them, expensively, made to measure means their validity becomes highly questionable. In short, they might be said to be *'more honoured in the breach than the observance'* (*Hamlet*, I. iv).

Faking it, though, is a problem affecting personality tests rather than aptitude ones. This capacity we have to exert control over our personalities rather than just be in receipt of them is perhaps, as Shakespeare, the theatre director/actor/author, well knew, most strikingly to be witnessed in the acting profession.

Anthony Hopkins, whose acting style seems to convey this sense of control, was voted London Theatre Critics Breakthrough Actor of 1971 and in 1992 was knighted after more than twenty years at the top of his profession. Many of the characters he played during that period were divided souls, split, often, between guilt and innocence, as in *Guilty Conscience*, *QBVII* and *The Lindburgh Kidnapping Case*. In *Magic*, he played the part of a ventriloquist being taken over by his dummy, and in Jean-Paul Sartre's *Kean*, went deeply into the split personality phenomenon by playing the part of a famous actor who confuses acting with life: 'he is his own victim', wrote Sartre, 'never knowing who he really is, whether he's acting or not'. Many people would recognise this syndrome from meeting with actors who seem to be putting on a show all the time. As Marlon Brando is reputed to have said: 'An actor is someone who, if you ain't talking about him, ain't listening.'

Sociological role theory suggests that we are the dramatis personae of the social play:

> 3M 'All the world's a stage
> And all the men and women merely players:
> They have their exits and their entrances;
> And one man in his time plays many parts . . .'
> *(As You Like It*, II. vii)

Peter Berger in *Invitation to Sociology* (1963), amusingly points out that we all use the same script when, for instance, courting, and, as everyone knows, we put on the appropriate costumes and accents for our roles as interviewee, bride, professor and so on. The problem is to discover the real self amongst all these roles and the danger is to lose that core personality, *'ay, there's the rub'* (*Hamlet*, III. i). This is the point of Sartre's play: like actors, we run the risk of being at the mercy of the audience whose acceptance we depend on for our sense of being. 'I have become a spectacle down to the last detail of my private life,' says Kean. We rely on others' views of us. 'Hell is other people', says a character in another of his plays. Berger adopts Sartre's existentialist escape from this trap by insisting that the self is that entity that chooses which roles to play, how and when to play them, thereby exercising personal freedom.

Anthony Hopkins, the man, has this relationship with his acting roles. Roger Lewis in *Stage People* (1989), presents him as a hard-working, level-headed man whose job is to play roles. He does have personal characteristics of course: 'I've always been a little self-involved, private, a loner' (p. 289), a man who, despite his accent and origins, is far from being the stereotypical Welshman: 'I've never been interested in rugby; I can't sing . . . and I cannot speak Welsh' (p. 287). And though, like Richard Burton, he has finally done a Dylan Thomas show, and does come from the same part of Wales, he has managed to avoid the trap of alcohol and has had the quality career that star never achieved. Hopkins, then, is a family man who loves his job and works very hard at it. Not really material for the gossip columns though anyone with as high a profile as this will be someone's target, to wit the rather bitchy item (*Sunday Times*, 26 September 1993) implying he was two-faced about his knighthood, when claiming that, while he was not interested in it, his wife was. *'Frailty thy name is woman'* (*Hamlet*, I. ii).

Theatres are organisations where being two-faced (or more) is a requirement for the key job. One could be forgiven sometimes for thinking that there are many other such organisations.

One case study on leadership in Chapter 7 suggests Bernard Tapie's reputation in France as a rogue may even be a contributory factor in his success. In Britain, less than two years after Michael Mates was reprimanded by the House of Commons Committee on Members' Interests for failing to declare, as the chairman of the Defence Committee, his consultancy with a military equipment supplier, he was given a cabinet post. He was forced to resign ('*hoist with his own petard*' (*Hamlet*, III. iv)?) when, in 1993, he was found to have links with Asil Nadir, a highly success-ful businessman who had been accused of stealing over £20 million mainly belonging to the company Polly Peck. And the rather gruff and grumpy-looking Alan Sugar finally sacked one of the most engaging smiles in football, Terry Venables, who had been suspected of abusing his managerial position for his own financial gain. But in January 1994, Venables was honoured with the most prestigious job in English football, manager of the national team. You might think it's not cricket but in July 1994 the English cricket captain was fined £2,000 for being less than forthcoming over a charge of cheating.

The Solicitors Complaints Bureau in Britain receives 17,000 complaints per year about lawyers, and solicitors pay as much a £1,000 each to a fund that compen-sates their profession's victims. Malcolm Edwards, for example, solicitor and MP for Christchurch, was struck off by the Law Society, and his ex-clients were paid £250,000 compensation. He and his wife left for Southern Spain where they launched a successful chain of shops selling baby clothes and toys. As I write, two MPs have been suspended from their junior government posts, suspected of taking money in contravention of Parliamentary conventions, and the President of the United States is trying to raise funds to pay lawyers to defend him in fraud and sexual harassment cases.

Playing a role for the politician, then, or for the lawyer or business person, may be the way to success. It may be for the Navy, too, if my five-year-old neighbour is right. When asked what an admiral is, he replied, 'A sort of good pirate'. It certainly *is* for spy organisations and Hopkins made an excellent job of Guy Burgess in the 1986 TV film, *Blunt*. Actors themselves cross the divide too, per-haps, when they perform in advertisements, but acting in the theatre is the lie told to reveal the truth. The audience is aware and participates in the make-believe. For the individual actor, play-acting can have salutary effects. An actor can escape from shyness by hiding behind the mask of assumed personalities. But though that seems like running away from problems, in fact it takes a certain kind of courage to let go of one's personality: 'I am always trying to conquer my cowardice', said Hopkins. In his career, many of his parts have been a long way from his own quiet and private personality. Thinking of Lear, he said 'I've been lucky to be offered monsters', but in 1990, of course, his role in *Silence of the Lambs* topped them all. One columnist claimed the actor had to dine facing the wall in restaurants because people would back away from him if they saw his face. So, it is perhaps ironical that just as a politician, say, might climb the ladder to power through dissembling, so the mild-mannered Hopkins won an Oscar for playing the most vile of all his creations, a psychologist who is also a serial killer who eats his victims.

Films seem to have abandoned the convention of bringing baddies to book. Hannibal the Cannibal is preparing to carry on killing and eating at the end of the film. And if Oxford University finals exams in English Literature in 1994 are anything to go by, Shakespeare himself might follow the fashion. One question demanded: 'Make out a positive case for the witches in *Macbeth*' and apologies were sought in other questions for Malvolio, Claudius, Goneril and Regan. A great many British leaders are nurtured at Oxbridge, of course, and sometimes traitors too. Recently an auction of some of Kim Philby's effects fetched surprisingly high prices, including £2,200 for a briefcase and £26,000 for eleven letters. There is hope yet though. Alan Sugar's football club was heavily fined, Venables was not tried, lawyers do take responsibility for their own bad eggs, Nadir is not welcome back in Britain, and the current Prime Minister has successfully fought off any attempt to blacken his name. Furthermore, Cabinet Secretary Robert Armstrong invented a piece of English that has entered the language with all the authority of a Shakespearean phrase: 'being economical with the truth'. And Sartre himself has explained that we are all inveterate story-tellers. So, as Hamlet (who else?) says: '*Use every man after his desert, and who should 'scape whipping?*'(II. ii).

Activity brief

1 How does the paradox of an actor showing off on stage because he is fundamentally shy seem reminiscent of Eysenck's introvert/extrovert continuum?

2 The acting profession is often perceived as having many homosexuals in it. Ingenious explanations for this include the idea that, being generally childless, they choose creative work to compensate; that being skilled at disguise ('in the closet') they are well prepared for the job; that, without the responsibilities of raising a family they are more prone to 'play' than other adults. On the basis of this argument, or any other, can you think of any other profession homosexuals might be suited for? Or is this to take stereotyping too far?

3 Hopkins has said 'We are all of us stuck with the same personalities', but Mullins suggests in Figure 4.1 (p. 99) that though our personalities are given in the nomothetic sense, we none the less do change them by adopting roles and that our life experiences can change them too. What anecdotal evidence does the above case provide for either of these views? You might like to try them out on your own character by talking through with a friend how roles you adopt affect your personality. Does your experience support the nomothetic or the idiographic approach?

Activity one: Role-play exercise

In groups of three (one candidate, one interviewer and one observer), role play interviews for the following jobs:

- a commission in the armed forces

- a secondary school teacher

- a TV researcher

- a personal secretary

- a graduate management trainee in a bank.

Discuss any assumption made about personality in terms of the theories you have studied. Discuss their applicability or otherwise to the job in question.

 # Activity two: Graphology exercise – you are what you write

Introduction

Graphology is the technique of interpreting personality traits from analysis of movements in handwriting. Its use in Europe is widespread, particularly in France and Switzerland where over 75 per cent of companies use this technique to assist in personnel selection. However, in Britain graphology has been the subject of much controversy and scepticism, although the number of businesses using it currently is growing.

Handwriting evolves and develops from the rigid style we were first taught at school. It is the differences from the 'copybook' model that the graphologist studies in detail and to which he or she assigns interpretations. Each of the particular handwriting movements may affect and modify interpretations of the next handwriting movement, and so subtleties of character emerge. Professional graphologists undergo a minimum of three years' training to understand and interpret the nuances of handwriting analysis and to reach The British Institute of Graphologists' qualification standards.

It is very difficult to change one's handwriting without losing its natural spontaneity, its rhythm and speed. Many handwriting movements are unconscious and the writer may not be aware that he or she may be forming a particular letter or stroke quite differently to someone else. To become aware of the differences between styles, try copying a sentence or two of someone else's handwriting. Even if you manage a convincing copy, the concentration required to do this can be very high. Imagine trying to fill in a whole application form in someone else's handwriting.

The following short self-administered test was designed for sessions to help individuals who were facing job change, either through choice or redundancy, to help them focus on their 'selling points' and to home in on particular areas where they would do well. It gives a superficial glimpse of some of the positive aspects that can be gleaned from handwriting, without going deeply into the modifying or contradictory factors in handwriting that can alter interpretations.

Task

Write a letter applying for a job and spell out your good points. Then try out the following test on yourself, or on a colleague. Does it work? You be the judge. (Some guidance notes as to how the test should be interpreted are given in Appendix 1).

Look at a sample of your handwriting and use the examples as a guide:

1 Is the middle zone of your writing
(a, c, e, m, n, o, r, s, u, v, w) measuring
from top to bottom:
(a) large – over 4mm high;
(b) small – under 3mm high; or
(c) mixed?
See Figure 4.1.

Fig. 4.1 Size of writing

2 Are the letters in the words:
(a) all joined up;
(b) all disconnected; or
(c) a mixture?

See Figure 4.2.

3 Is the shape of your writing:
(a) loopy; or
(b) loopless?

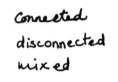

Fig. 4.2 Letter connections

4 Is your writing:
(a) rounded;
(b) angular;
(c) stretched; or
(d) mixed?
See Figure 4.3.

5 Are your m's and n's:
(a) humped;
(b) angular;
(c) pointed; or
(d) mixed?

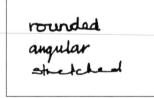

Fig. 4.3 Overall shape of writing

6 Are your left and right margins:
(a) about equal;
(b) wider on the left; or
(c) wider on the right?

7 When you write 'I am', is the capital 'I':
(a) as large as the other capitals;
(b) larger than the other capitals; or
(c) smaller than the other capitals?

8 Is your signature:
(a) larger than your writing;
(b) smaller than your writing; or
(c) the same size as your writing?

9 Are the words in your writing:
   (a) fairly close together;
   (b) fairly wide apart; or
   (c) a mixture?
   See Figure 4.4

Fig. 4.4 Spacing in writing

10 Is the slant of your writing:
   (a) vertical;
   (b) right;
   (c) left; or
   (d) mixed?
   See Figure 4.5

11 Is every letter:
   (a) clear and easy to read; or
   (b) some letters skimmed over, but generally legible?

12 Are the lines in your letter:
   (a) going up;
   (b) going down;
   (c) forming an arc; or
   (d) horizontal?

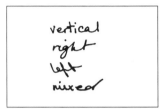

Fig. 4.5 Slant in writing

Activity provided by CB Graphology Consultants, Chandlers Ford, Hampshire.

 # Debate one

'Interviews are preferable to psychometric tests in the recruitment process.'

Starting points

For

● Everyone uses interviews for selection – it is so universally accepted that candidates would be suspicious of any firm not doing so.

● A survey has shown that managers have little faith in tests (Mullins, p. 625).

Against

● Interviewers are generally untrained, reliant on their intuition and, like everyone else, subject to perceptual errors.

● If an interviewer's time etc. is costed, selection tests are much cheaper than interviews and enable an objective comparison to be made between candidates.

Further reading

Bertram, D. (1991), 'Addressing the Abuse of Personality Tests', *Personnel Management*, April, 34–9.

Fletcher, C. (1991), 'Personality Tests: The Great Debate', *Personnel Management*, September, 38–42.

Goodworth, C. T. (1993), *Effective Interviewing for Employment Selection*, Business Books.

Mullins, L. J. (1993), *Management and Organisational Behaviour*, Pitman, 624–31, 640 (n. 30).

Debate two

'Freud's personality theories are of no use to the organisation.'

Starting points

For

- Freud's id, ego and superego are hypotheses that cannot be tested.

- Dreams and Freudian slips are glimpses only of the subconscious. We cannot, and should not, delve into them when considering employees for promotion, transfer, training, and so forth.

Against

- Freud was trying to understand the whole human being rather than individual personality traits, attitudes or any other little fragments of a person.

- Freud's account of our fundamental drives helps us to understand such organisational behaviour as power struggles, attitudes to leaders and conflict.

Further reading

Eysenck, H. J. (1972), 'The Experimental Study of Freudian Concepts', *Bulletin of the British Psychological Society*, **25**, 261–7.

Kline, P. (1972), *Fact and Fantasy in Freudian Theory*, Methuen.

Mullins, L. J. (1993), *Management and Organisational Behaviour*, Pitman, 106–7.

 # Look, it really works!

1 Sunnyside Hotels is a medium-sized group of three-star hotels which annually takes ten to twelve graduates on its management training programme. The programme is a very concentrated one with graduates taking six-month supervisory positions in a variety of functions in a number of hotels. Thus a graduate trainee may find themselves working as a reception supervisor in Barrow in Furness for one module and then as a restaurant supervisor in Torquay for the next. As well as job competence, this calls for a high degree of flexibility and mental, emotional and physical toughness.

Over the years Sunnyside have found that, on average, only 20 per cent of graduate trainees make it through the training programme to their first junior management appointment. For the company this doesn't represent a good return on their investment and they began to look at their recruitment process. They've decided to institute a series of 'open days' for up to a hundred applicants at selected hotels which will involve presentations on the company and the training scheme together with a personality test which the personnel officer has seen advertised in a training catalogue. All this will happen in the morning and whilst the potential recruits are having a buffet lunch, the personality tests will be scored and, from the results, a short list drawn up. Successful candidates will go forward to a formal interview in the afternoon from which a final choice will be made.

All seems OK, doesn't it? They've chosen a relatively scientific approach to their recruitment and tried to limit subjectivity. Why, then, did they find no improvement in their retention rates of graduates? Look at example two, below, and see the difference.

2 UK Leisure plc are a broad-based company with interests in hotels, holiday centres and pubs. Like Sunnyside they, too, have problems in recruitment, both in making up short lists from a first sift of applications and in retaining graduate trainees. Also like Sunnyside they have opted for a 'scientific' approach and have decided to use a psychometric test. However, it is at this juncture that all similarities disappear. UK Leisure are using a test which is validated, approved by the British Psychological Society and is administered and interpreted by a trained consultant. They are also not using it to obtain their first short list but as *one part* of the final interview process.

Their 'open day' policy is similar to Sunnyside but final choices are not made at that stage. Instead, a further short list is drawn up and candidates attend an in-tensive two-day assessment centre which includes a series of group and individual exercises, presentations, the personality test and an in-depth interview. It is at this latter event that the results of the test are shared with the candidate who can comment on the interpretation. After all this, the assessors sit down, compare their results from each activity, the test results and the interview, and a final decision is made. It is interesting to note that *their* attrition rate is very low: many of their graduate trainees complete their programme and go on to take up junior manage-ment positions.

Can you see the differences in the two approaches to the use of personality test-ing? Sunnyside used a statistically unproven test and used it as the only basis for selection without sharing the results. UK Leisure used an approved test as *one part* of the whole process and shared results with the candidates, thus giving them the opportunity to comment on the findings.

 ## Assignment one

In order to undertake this assignment, you will first need to complete 'Activity two'. Using the results from this activity, try to analyse your own and others' handwriting.

Your results can be used as a basis for group discussion and/or written up as a report.

Some discussion points could be:

● How predictive and reliable is graphology as a recruitment tool?

● Whilst graphology is widely and openly used in many European countries, its use in the UK is thought to be more covert. Why is this? What are the implications for, for example, perception and attitudes?

Assignment two

Take a significant period of time (five or ten years) and look at how your personality has changed over that period. What has occurred during that time that might be the cause?

In not more than 2,000 words, prepare a case to support either the nomothetic or idiographic approach to personality.

Based on Review Q2, Mullins, p. 124.

! Pause for thought

1 We have heard much about the subjective, inaccurate nature of the selection interview and yet it still remains one of the most popular methods of recruiting people. In the past, emphasis had been placed on improving the reliability of the selection decision by underpinning it with such instruments as personality tests. Other elements came into vogue for short periods of time including graphology and phrenology. Now there is yet another medium by which companies can determine business and organisational compatibility: astrology.

The California based Triangle Group are marketing a computer disk called 'Seer' which, for about £60 will evaluate the compatibility of two people on a rating of 0–30. The owner of Triangle, British-born Peter Mackeonis declares that the disk calculates the conjunction of planets and stars which astrologers believe determines individual characteristics and patterns of behaviour. Triangle already claim to have signed up Pizza Hut and Motorola as customers (*Sunday Times*, 15 May 1994).

Perhaps in future we will be analysing our teams according to astrological compatibility rather than by Belbin's team types – Mercury rising and the Sun in Pluto rather than Completer–Finishers and Plants?

Could this be the *real* dawning of the Age of Aquarius?

2 In January 1994 Southwark Council, as part of its preparations for competitive tendering for the Revenues and Benefits Service some months hence, decided to carry out a skills audit. The audit included a personality test in which staff were asked to agree or disagree with 462 statements including: 'Women should not be allowed to drink alone in pubs' and 'I would like to see a bullfight in Spain'. The audit also included ability tests, interviews and individual assessment.

The results of the audit left nineteen finance staff facing redundancy or redeployment.

Reaction to the use of the test was sharply divided: Unison, the public service union called it 'a pantomime: racist, sexist and irrelevant', while Professor Clive Fletcher of Goldsmith's College, London, said that 'It's a long-standing and well-researched test. Although many of the questions appear to be meaningless, they might reveal something about the personality of the individual' (*Personnel Management Plus*, January 1994).

It appears, therefore, that we have bi-polar views concerning not only this personality test in particular but personality tests in general.

Is it ethical that a test perceived as racist and sexist should be used to determine not only the future careers but also the futures of people?

? Still not convinced?

1 In the case in Chapter 3, 'The eye of the beholder', you will have read that John Major was frequently referred to as a 'wimp', a 'grey' or 'colourless' man, a man who Eysenck might have classified as a 'stable introvert'. (Eysenck's early research, incidentally, indicated that these personality types were often the ones to make successful businessmen.) We are told that family circumstances for the Prime Minister took a somewhat dramatic and drastic downturn with financial losses, a move to a smaller house in Brixton and the urgent need for the young John to get out into the world and start earning a living. Not the most auspicious start, you might think, for a future Tory Chancellor and Prime Minister.

During his time as PM he has instituted numerous campaigns variously entitled 'back to basics/family values', 'the classless society', and a series of Citizens' Charters. He is well known for his love of cricket and would almost seem to be advocating a return to the Britain that existed prior to 1939 where, according to our perceptions, the summers were always long and hot, the hero always got the pretty girl, the local squire always hosted the harvest supper and the 'baddies' always got their come-uppance to cries of 'jolly good show'. (If, dear reader, you are too young to remember all this, watch any black and white Ealing Studios film on a rainy Sunday afternoon and you'll get the general drift . . .)

If we take an idiographic approach to this, we can, perhaps, begin to put some interpretations on this behaviour. Remember the idiographic approach (pp. 102 and 105 in Mullins if you don't)? This is the one that says that personality development is not static but is open to change: people respond to other people, events and environment surrounding them. Consider the background of the young John Major and his subsequent campaigns – can you see where this approach fits?

2 On any Tuesday afternoon during a parlimentary session turn on the television at 3 o'clock and tune to BBC2 for a quick look at Prime Minister's Question Time in 'Westminster Live'. For those of you who normally switch off after 'Neighbours', let us set the scene . . . Imagine a great barn of a place, longer than it is wide with a corridor down the middle and men and women of all ages, dressed in business suits, seated either side. At the top end sits the Speaker, an imposing figure who is dressed as if she's just come off the set of a BBC production of any Dickens novel.

After a certain amount of pomp and ceremonial, the proceedings get off to a relatively leisurely and polite start. People on the left of the corridor stand up to catch the Speaker's eye and are nominated to put a point. The situation is reversed on the right-hand side of the corridor and the point is answered (or not, depending on your political leanings and perception).

Suddenly there is a stirring in the ranks . . . the Prime Minister enters and makes ready to answer apparently impromptu questions. The scene now changes from one of almost mundane sedentary to one which resembles a cross between the first day of Harrod's sale and a verbal loose scrum at Cardiff Arms Park. People pop up and down like hyperactive jack-in-the-boxes in vain attempts to catch the Speaker's eye (watch their facial expressions when they don't . . .). Expressions of agreement or disagreement are manifested in loud cheers or boos and everyone seems intent on scoring points (with self-satisfied expressions if they succeed), temper tantrums occur, and the scene quickly becomes one which resembles Grange Hill rather more than the Mother of Parliaments.

You may be asking yourself at this stage whether this has got *anything* to do with personality. Trust us, dear reader, *it has*! Let's look at Freud for this one – remember he said that under stress we regress into habitual ways of responding that worked for us as children. Think about how *you* behaved as a child when you couldn't get your own way – can you see a correlation?

5 Attitudes

 ## Broadheath District Council

Introduction

This case is about the attitudes of a small group of managers working for a large district council during a period of political, managerial and social upheaval. It is based on real events but incorporates material gathered from a variety of sources.

Background to the organisation

In the late 1980s the government passed legislation with the twin aims of making local authorities more accountable to the people and bringing them more firmly under central control. The old rating system was abolished and replaced by the unpopular community charge. Local authority spending was drastically curtailed through 'rate capping'. Councils were also forced to expose many of their traditional services to compulsory competitive tendering. Many workers lost their jobs as a result. 'Getting closer to the customer' and 'becoming more businesslike' became the main themes of local government philosophy.

Broadheath District Council's initial reaction to this onslaught was both unexpected and drastic. In 1989, after a vote of 'no confidence' by his chief officer's management team (COMT), David Armstrong, the council's chief executive since 1974, took 'early retirement'. Shortly afterwards, the personnel manager (who reported to Armstrong) and his two senior personnel officers also left. No convincing explanation was given to the staff for their departure. The former treasurer, George Harvey, was appointed chief executive. Harvey immediately recruited a new, professionally qualified personnel manager, Susan Cole, from a large engineering company. Cole's brief was to change the culture of the organisation and make it more like a private sector company.

Susan Cole's first move was to engage a firm of management consultants to advise on a remuneration strategy. After considering the consultant's report, the council introduced a new recruitment and retention package aimed at attracting and keeping high-calibre managers. Benefits included extended pay scales with accelerated progression for outstanding performance, free private medical insurance and fully funded lease cars for senior managers. To qualify for the package staff were required to sign new contracts of employment which released them from the nationally negotiated scheme of conditions of service.

The council's chief officers were redesignated 'directors' and put on three-year, fixed-term contracts. The membership of COMT was extended. It now comprised chief executive, director of finance and administration, director of planning, director of technical services, director of health and housing, director of leisure services, and director of personnel.

The environmental health section

To discharge their statutory duty to enforce legislation on food hygiene, health and safety at work, pollution control and housing standards, local authorities employ professionally qualified environmental health officers (EHOs) and technical support staff.

From 1974 to 1983 Broadheath District Council's environmental health section was organised on a generalist basis. Each EHO was responsible for the whole range of duties within a group of parishes. The officers worked in four divisions, each of which was responsible for approximately a quarter of the Broadheath district. The environmental health section was headed by a chief environmental health officer (CEHO), Derek Lloyd, who reported to the chief health and housing officer (CHHO), Don Wilson. Wilson was himself a qualified EHO who was widely experienced in all aspects of environmental health. He was also a qualified housing manager. A senior divisional EHO (SDEHO), Ian Palmer, deputised for the CEHO and headed one of the divisions. The other three divisions were each headed by a senior EHO (SEHO). The section was managed from the council's headquarters at Dunford but two SEHOs and their divisional teams were based at the branch offices in Moorfield and Beckton, eight and twelve miles from Dunford respectively.

As environmental health legislation became more complex and public expectations of the service rose, a reorganisation on specialist functional lines became necessary. This was carried out in 1993 with the creation of four specialist divisions: pollution control and housing were both based at Dunford; commercial (south) operated out of the old Town Hall at Moorfield; and commercial (north) worked from the former Rural District Council offices at Beckton. The SDEHO Ian Palmer was made responsible for health education, pest control and student training but his main role was to deputise for and provide close managerial support to the CEHO.

In 1987 Derek Lloyd was hospitalised for three months and Ian Palmer managed the section in his absence. Palmer enjoyed being in charge and was complimented on his performance in the role by Don Wilson. To support Derek Lloyd on his return to duty, two new management posts of assistant chief EHO were created. Ian Palmer was appointed to one of them and Reg Newman was recruited externally to the other. The environmental health section was split into two new groupings: 'domestic services' brought together the pollution control and housing divisions and was based in Dunford under Reg Newman; 'commercial services' combined the former commercial (north) and (south) divisions. These latter two remained at Beckton and Moorfield respectively but were managed by Ian Palmer whose office was at Dunford.

Shortly after this reorganisation the CEHO had to retire early on medical grounds. Both Ian Palmer and Reg Newman were interviewed for his post but it was offered to an external candidate, Richard Headley. Ian Palmer and Reg Newman jointly managed the section while Headley worked out his three-months notice. When Richard Headley took up his new post in September 1991 he made it clear, to the relief of all his staff, that he would not be making any further changes to the management structure of the section.

Don Wilson, the director of health and housing, trusted his senior managers and left them to do their jobs with the minimum supervision. He encouraged them to experiment and find new and innovative solutions to problems. He was quick to support them when things went wrong. Wilson's staff respected him both for his vast knowledge of housing and environmental health and for his professional integrity.

Changes are announced

In the week before Christmas 1991 the chief executive called a meeting of all the council's senior managers supposedly to 'celebrate the achievements of the past year'. The health and housing and leisure services directorates were each nominated to give presentations on this theme. Don Wilson asked Ian Palmer to represent health and housing. During his presentation Ian Palmer was aware that the chief executive was not listening. Harvey sat at the back of the Council Chamber making notes. He seemed very preoccupied. When the presentations were finished, Harvey addressed the meeting. He told the managers that no matter how well they thought they were doing now, there was no room for complacency. Everyone must work harder to achieve the council's business objectives. He added that further, perhaps painful, changes would have to take place if the council were to survive the government's proposed boundary changes and become one of the new unitary authorities. There was no air of celebration during the buffet that followed.

After the Christmas break Don Wilson broke the news to the health and housing management team that he was leaving the council. Wilson refused to elaborate but it was clear from his tone that he had known for some weeks and that he was not going willingly. Wilson explained that health and housing was being combined with leisure services under Jack Croft, the leisure services director. The new directorate would be called 'community services'.

While Don Wilson was working out his notice, Jack Croft began to network among the health and housing staff. Croft had gained a reputation for ruthlessness throughout the authority during the five years he had worked there. He was also very friendly with the chief executive. It was with some trepidation, therefore, that Ian Palmer found himself summoned to a private meeting with Jack Croft.

After some small talk Croft told Palmer that he thought of him as a key manager within his new directorate. Jack Croft then began to ask sensitive questions about environmental health staff. Who could be trusted? Who could not? Who were the team players? Who were the loners? Who were the troublemakers? What did named EHOs think about recent developments? Whose support could he rely on? Ian Palmer gave evasive answers to all the questions and was relieved when the meeting ended. Croft made it clear that their discussion was to remain strictly confidential. During the following weeks Ian Palmer learned that other managers in health and housing had also been interviewed by Croft. All were worried about the implications.

The management meeting

When Don Wilson vacated his office, Jack Croft and his secretary immediately moved in. Don Wilson's secretary was transferred to an administrative post in the branch office at Moorfield. One of Croft's first actions was to call a meeting of all the senior managers in his new directorate.

At the meeting Croft told the managers how excited he was at the prospect of working with such highly qualified people. He made the point that, while he was totally unqualified, he believed in surrounding himself with more intelligent people and using them to achieve his own objectives. 'That's what management is all about,' he said. Using sporting metaphors, he emphasised the need for everyone to work together as a team to achieve the council's goals.

Jack Croft then invited questions on the changes within the directorate. Reg Newman asked if it were true that an administrative assistant from leisure services was being promoted to a vacant post in the domestic division in preference to a member of his staff who had been doing the job competently for three months. Newman explained that his staff were very concerned by the rumours that were circulating and morale was suffering. Croft confirmed that the rumour was true. Reg Newman commented that in view of the council's much vaunted policy of 'openness and trust' perhaps it would have been courteous to have discussed the matter with him first. The implications for his staff were serious. 'While I'm in charge of this directorate I'll decide who does what,' barked Croft. 'You'd be better advised to concentrate on your own work and not to meddle in things that don't concern you.' The colour drained from Newman's face. He folded his arms across his chest and kept his eyes fixed firmly on the floor for the rest of the meeting.

Jack Croft then showed a video about management in British companies since the Second World War. The video discussed management styles in successful and failed companies and then compared them with Japanese management practice. When the video ended, he invited comments. Ian Palmer (whose Master's degree in Business Administration dissertation had been on this very subject) said he felt that the examples given in the video were simplistic. He suggested that it was unwise to assume that management initiatives taken in the private sector would work in the local government environment and culture. Jack Croft was furious. He thrust his hand out towards Palmer, palm outwards in a dismissive gesture. 'That's being negative,' he shouted, 'I only want to hear positive comments!' Croft then turned his back on Palmer who was allowed to take no further part in the meeting. The other environmental health managers were visibly shaken by what they had just seen and said nothing.

After the meeting everyone went to the local recreation centre where a buffet lunch was provided. 'I want you all to mix and get to know each other,' said Croft. It was a vain hope. The six environmental health managers sat huddled together in a corner. Dick Headley sat with Jack Croft, the housing manager and their opposite numbers in leisure services. Only Mike Malone, a senior manager in the housing section approached the EHOs' table. 'I'm not sure I should be seen talking to you two,' he said to Ian Palmer and Reg Newman. 'Croft has marked your cards now. You'd better start clearing your desks.' When they could, the environmental health managers made their excuses and left.

Later that afternoon Richard Headley called Ian Palmer and Reg Newman into his office. He was shaking with anger. 'I expected you two to set an example for the others,' he said. 'You've embarrassed me and let me down'. 'On the contrary, Dick,' replied Reg Newman, 'we and our staff think you've let our section down. You've let Croft walk all over you.' 'He's nothing more than a jumped-up swimming pool manager,' added Palmer. 'How the hell are we supposed to motivate our staff now? You and Croft have made our jobs impossible.' With that both stormed out of the room.

 ## Activity brief

1 What were the environmental health managers' attitudes towards the creation of the new directorate of community services?

2 What key factors influenced Ian Palmer and Reg Newman's attitudes towards the merger of health and housing and leisure services?

3 Taking the role of Jack Croft, what alternative strategies might you have adopted to ensure that the merger of the two directorates was a success?

Case study provided by Brian Thornton, Southampton Institute of Higher Education.

 ## An attitude of mind?

The following cases, based on real-life situations, illustrate some of the problems which a lack of understanding of HIV and AIDS can cause in workplace situations.

Case one

John works as a sheet-metal worker for a medium-sized engineering company. When he cut himself he told the company first-aider who attended him, in confidence, that he might be at risk of having contracted the HIV virus. Later in the week two of John's fellow shop-floor workers started to abuse and insult him, accusing him of being a 'disease-spreader'. Although John's life was being made a misery by this persistent bullying, he was reluctant to report it, or the obvious breach of confidence by the first-aider, to higher managers because he was unsure of how they would respond, and feared that he would lose his job.

Case two

June worked for three months as a part-time counter assistant in a small butcher's shop. In conversation she mentioned that her son had recently died from AIDS. The following week her employer told her that her services were no longer required. When she asked why she was being dismissed the owner eventually explained that he feared that his customers might find out about her contact with someone with AIDS and that he would lose customers as a result of their fear that she would contaminate the meat.

Case three

George managed a chain of retail shops for a small independent charity. A main part of his job was recruiting salaried managers for these shops (which were otherwise staffed by volunteers). Because of difficulties in providing cover, the reliability of these managers was extremely important. George was worried that if he employed someone who was infected with HIV this would inevitably cause problems because of time off through illness. He was wondering whether it would be possible to ask potential recruits to take a HIV test prior to employment.

 Activity brief

Consider each case individually and write brief notes under the following headings. Do not consult the guidance notes in Appendix 2 until you have written your answers. In a group discuss your answers and compare them to those of the other group members. Reassess your answers in the light of the guidance notes.

1 What is the difference between HIV and AIDS, how is it contracted, and what are the risks of being infected by, or infecting, another person?

2 What do you think about the attitudes and responses of the people described in the examples?

3 Put yourself in the position of each of the people in the cases and consider how you would have responded.

4 What do you think are the main workplace implications of HIV/AIDS and how should managers respond to these (both as individuals and organization policy-makers)?

Case study provided by Dr David Goss, University of Portsmouth.

Activity one

Recent research on attitudes has suggested that

● People who are against the transportation of nuclear waste also oppose capital punishment, that those who support it tend to be apolitical or conservative, and that such attitudes are not easily changed by means of information packs, community involvement or persuasion.

● Vivid messages (using colourful language, striking metaphors, etc.) have a less persuasive effect on inattentive audiences than do pallid messages.

● Women are more in favour of equality in sexual behaviour, marriage and vocation than men.

● Men are more competitive and money-centred than women.

● People holding pro-leisure attitudes may also be strongly pro-work.

● Almost everyone rates themselves above the mid-scale point for intelligence, since ego-preservation is a basic need leading individuals to present a rosy picture of themselves.

Decide for yourself or in discussion with others the extent to which these suggestions confirm the account of attitudes found in Mullins, pp. 111–15 and p. 159.

 Activity two

1 Most of us belong to a number of organisations (college, firm, church, etc.) and a number of groups (family, hockey team, drama society, etc.). Make a list of yours and alongside it try to sum up in a short phrase or sentence why each one is important to you. Do this part of the exercise before reading on.

2 One of the difficulties in theorising about attitudes is their close connection with values and interests. Going through your list now, which of the three are you stressing each time?

3 Considering next your attitude to work in particular, which of the following do you want from it:

autonomy	authority
variety	status
money	stimulus
challenge	to be creative
excitement	to be useful
social interaction	

Do your answers change if you ask the question of any unpaid or voluntary work you have or intend to do? Do they change again if you think in terms of a temporary post only?

Activity three: Personal construct grid

See Mullins, p. 125.

Using 'Assignment one', complete your own personal construct grid and then discuss each grid with the rest of the group. Discussion could focus on:

● The importance of constructs, goals and priorities in people's life.

● The meaning of work to each individual: whether it is a central or peripheral goal.

● The satisfaction of individual needs at work.

 # Debate one

'The task of assessing students' work at post-secondary school level should be transferred from the staff to the students themselves.'

Starting points

For

● Stress, which can have 'an adverse effect on individual performance' (Mullins, p. 191), may be relieved if workers are given 'greater discretion in how their work is performed' (Mullins, p. 487).

● Such delegation of power would help change students' attitudes towards teachers and knowledge for the better. 'Beware the boss who walks on water' (Mullins, p. 532).

Against

● According to McGregor's Theory X, the average person is lazy, has an inherent dislike of work, avoids responsibility, and prefers to be directed (Mullins, p. 400), so students will resist self-assessment.

● Transferring the task of quality control to the worker, or indeed the customer, is simply a cost-cutting exercise by managers looking for an easy life.

Further reading

Fox, S., Caspy, S. and Reisler, A. (1994), 'Variables affecting leniency, halo and the validity of self-appraisal', *Journal of Occupational and Organisation Psychology*, March, **67**, 44–56.

Glen, F. (1975), *The Social Psychology of Organisations*, Methuen, ch. 2.

Debate two

'Managers don't need to waste time and money conducting attitudes-to-work surveys in a recession.'

Starting points

For

- Widespread unemployment makes it easier to replace employees holding unproductive attitudes to work.
- Recession has a way of reminding workers of the fundamental importance of work.

Against

- Public attitudes often conceal contrasting private ones (Mullins, p. 112). Flexing your economic muscle in the short term could have repercussions in the long term.
- The time and money spent firing an employee, then employing and training a replacement, are too significant to make this attitude to staffing a profitable one.

(See Mullins, p. 80: a diagram showing environmental influences on the organisation as being far wider than the economic one alone.)

Further reading

Brown, J. A. C. (1980, 1954), *The Social Psychology of Industry*, ch. 6.

✓ Look, it really works!

1 Alison, always with an eye for a bargain, haunts local antique fairs in a quest to expand her collection of blue and white china. Antique fairs are not as cheap a source of this china as car boot sales but she doesn't have to get up at 6.00 a.m. on a Sunday morning to get the bargains and they're certainly easier on the pocket than the Olde Antique Shoppe found in small, usually thatched, villages.

Over the years Alison has perfected what she considers to be a pretty good technique for getting the prices down. She would pick up, say, a cup and saucer, 'hum and hah' for about fifteen minutes and, if she was lucky, the stallholder would knock £1.00 off the price. (The cynical amongst you are no doubt saying that it had probably been added to the price for that reason in the first place, but no matter, she felt that she had got a bargain and honour was maintained on both sides.)

Now Alison has a close friend, Anna, a Greek woman who, having totally bare walls in her kitchen, decided to enhance them with decorative plates (of the willow-pattern kind rather than the Sunday supplement 'special offer' type). Alison suggested that they went together to the next antique fair to see if any bargains could be had. Aware that there may well be cultural differences, Alison decided to initiate Anna into the art of bargaining by showing her how it was done. Standing by a stall in the customary position with blue and white gravy boat in hand and with a suitable 'do I want it or not' expression on her face, Alison looked around to smile encouragingly at her friend, only to find that she was nowhere to be found. Hastily putting down the china, she eventually found her at another stall with a plate in her hand. 'How much is it?' enquired Anna of the stallholder. '£7.00' came back the reply. 'I think that's rather expensive, don't you?' Anna asked. 'How much can you reduce it to?'. '£6.00' was the answer. 'I think that's still too expensive, I'll give you £4.50.' 'OK, done,' said the stallholder. Triumphant, Anna looked around to find her friend adopting an 'I've never seen her before' expression.

Sitting in the pub later, inspecting their purchases over lunch, Alison asked, 'Anna, how could you *do* that to me in there? How could you be so blatant? I was *so* embarrassed.' 'Why?' her friend replied. 'Where I come from, that's how you do business, it's a way of life. And besides, I got a lot better deal than *you* did – when is the next fair being held?'

Can you see how the general influence of national culture might affect the attitudes that we have towards certain situations? Is there a role here, as well, for considering our *perception* of other people's attitudes?

(*Note:* Alison never did learn to barter and Anna continued to get better deals . . .)

2 One of our hotel and catering students had been offered a place on a graduate training programme with two different companies and couldn't decide which one to choose. She came to us for advice and to see if 'we knew anything she didn't' about the two organisations in question. Company A was larger and positioned in the three- and four-star market, whilst Company B was smaller, positioned in the two- and three-star market but was expanding steadily and had a reputation for promoting from within. After much soul searching she eventually chose Company B, largely on a 'feel good' basis rather than using any rational criteria. She came to tell us of her choice: 'I hope I've made the right decision. I know Company A have a better reputation and have been training graduates for longer but I just felt that Company B might have more to offer.'

Six months into her training she came back to see us and to give a talk to the current final year. She was full of praise for her new employers: they were giving her challenging assignments and had identified her as a 'fast track' trainee, someone who would be a future general manager in a short period of time. She also mentioned that a friend of hers had gone to Company A and had so far spent her first six months in charge of the pot-washers. The training programme was slower and not, as had been promised, tailored to individual needs. Furthermore, it was reported that that particular company was in financial difficulties and may have to make some of their trainees redundant. 'I'm so glad I chose Company B,' she said. 'They're brilliant – poor old Lizzie is having an awful time with Company A.'

What is happening here is post-decisional dissonance (Festinger 1957). Decision-making almost always produces dissonance and when we're forced to make a choice between alternatives we have a tendency to forget the good aspects of our discarded choice and accept the less good aspects of our actual choice (in this case, a small, less 'upmarket' company). Having chosen, our student, in order to reduce the dissonance, had to justify her behaviour. This she did by increasing her attraction to and re-emphasising the good points of her chosen company, becoming more negative to Company A.

Another interesting point to note here is that when post-decisional dissonance sets in, our attitude change occurs *after* the behaviour. In other words her behaviour (choosing Company B) had caused the attitude change. This new attitude will then influence later career choices she might make. In this case, behaviour causes attitudes which will, in turn, cause behaviour. (For a description of cognitive dissonance see Mullins, p. 114.)

Still to be convinced? Apply the above principle next time you buy something major – see how your attitude to it changes and affects your future overt behaviour.

 ## Assignment one

Write a 1,500 word report of a survey you have conducted in your organisation to discover any differences between younger and older workers in attitudes held towards work.

This task is probably best done by a small group and you will need to remember the following:

- First, establish in discussion an appropriate hypothesis to examine (e.g. older people value work more highly than younger ones).

- Construct a series of questions which give rise to clear differences between respondents (i.e. where they can reply 'strongly agree' sometimes rather than 'neither agree nor disagree' most of the time).

- Select respondent groups which not only have a certain homogeneity (e.g. one between 18 and 21 and another between 25 and 35) but also a certain representativeness (e.g. a reasonable mix of men and women, doing a range of tasks, etc.).

- Remember, too, that such work is beset by rogue variables: asking questions before lunch might give different results from asking them after, allowing different questioners to adopt non-standard approaches to respondents could confuse outcomes, etc. Try in discussion to spot as many of these potential problems as you can. If you have time it is a good idea to conduct the survey again with the same people but at a later date.

In your report remember clearly to state your hypothesis, the design of the survey, the make-up of the surveyed groups, and the raw results *before* evaluating the findings. It is worth assessing the validity of your work too (What flaws did it have?, How could it be improved next time? etc.).

Alternative surveys could investigate differences between male and female attitudes or between native and foreign workers.

Assignment two

Some research has suggested that negative attitudes to homosexuality correlate with an authoritarian outlook (see, for example, Haddock, Zanna and Esser; 'Assessing the structures of prejudicial attitudes', *Journal of Personality and Social Psychology*, December 1993, for a brief account of this work). In June 1994, the debate in the British House of Lords concerning the reduction in the age of consent for homosexuals from 21 to 18 revealed some very strong negative attitudes towards homosexuals: 'an unnatural abomination . . . a terrible handicap . . . one more nail in the coffin of the fabric of society . . . a departure from the norms that make up decent and upright society . . . etc.' Prominent in the debate were a leading Catholic and a rabbi.

Preferably using Hansard but also newspaper reports of this debate and the equivalent one in the House of Commons in February 1994, write a 1,500 word essay that both sums up the debate and discusses the extent to which it would seem to confirm or disconfirm the correlations suggested by the research.

Pause for thought

1 The date 6 May 1994 was officially proclaimed the third Annual 'No Diet Day', a day when rallies and picnics across the world would protest against what the organisers, Diet Breakers, termed 'the tyranny of thinness'. Protesters in the USA, Canada and Australia were urged to wear pale blue ribbons (yes, it's those ribbons again) to celebrate 'size diversity'.

Behind this somewhat eccentric notion, however, is a serious theme: a call to curb the diet industry. Although there is little evidence that diets result in long-term weight loss, the estimated 47 per cent of British women who are size sixteen or over do not see themselves as desirable Marilyn Monroe lookalikes. Dr Bridget Dolan, a member of the European Council on Eating Disorders said, 'The diet industry has got the perfect product: it doesn't work but the consumer blames herself, not the product', and Alice Mahon, Labour MP for Halifax, said, 'The diet industry is getting away with murder . . . dictating that all women have to conform to a certain body shape. We have an epidemic of eating disorders in this country, and people's fears and vulnerabilities are being exploited' (*Guardian*, 5 May 1994).

The increase in self-imposed eating disorders has largely been confined to Western societies and has been attributed to the attitudes of these societies towards women. Professor David Haber of UCLA said, 'The "ideal" image of women got thinner and thinner in the 1960s and now it's a sociocultural phenomenon beyond the bounds of rationality' (*Sunday Times*, 8 May 1994). At the forefront driving this pressure to conform is the media: not only in the form of the gaunt supermodels but also mainstream television and film actresses who have become role models for women – they are either depicted as Michelle Pfeiffer types (desirable) or Roseanne Barr types (undesirable). The last five years has also seen a veritable plethora of aerobics and exercise videos and 'beauty secrets' books of the 'this will change your life' genre, all endorsed and some even written and performed by these wafer-thin role models.

All the classic ingredients of the model of attitude change (Mullins, pp. 114–15) are demonstrated here: why the attitude should be changed, the benefits (and penalties) if it isn't, the characteristics of both persuader and audience, how the issues are presented and the influence of peer groups.

Where is this now leading? Have our attitudes towards body size and shape changed from a health perspective to a beauty perspective and have they now become beliefs and, even, deeper-held values?

2 It's early morning and the village is just waking up. Shutters are being drawn back, children are being got ready for school and the little harbour is beginning to bustle as the fishing *caïques* return with the day's catch. The only place open on this tiny island is the *kafeneíon* the local coffee shop which, at this time in the morning is full of local workmen watching cartoons on television and drinking coffee before going off to lay a few more bricks on a villa which will bring an ever-increasing number of tourists to this largely undiscovered and poor island. Through the day the men will gather to drink thick Greek coffee or an ouzo, gossip, put the world to rights and single-handedly solve both the Macedonian and the Albanian problems. Sometimes towards evening the local priest will tether his donkey to a nearby olive tree and join them in their leisurely discourse. It is a scene unchanged in Greece for centuries . . . the menfolk traditionally sit together in cosy camaraderie, for this is a male-dominated society. Indeed, on some of the smaller, tourist-free islands not only the *kafeneíon* but also the village *tavérna* would be a male preserve – a place where no self-respecting husband would be seen taking his wife.

The scene now changes to Athens where the *kafeneíon* setting, although urban, is essentially the same ... except for one crucial difference: the customers of *this kafeneíon* are all women. Fed up with the traditional attitudes of male chauvinism and female exclusion, Athenian women have decided to fight back and have created their own women-only *kafeneíon* where they, too, can discuss politics, books, music and exchange gossip.

Does it always have to be the case that when faced with such a situation, the automatic answer is to apparently apply Newton's Law – for every action there is an equal and opposite reaction? Will we ever successfully *change* attitudes this way or will we merely engender and preserve two opposing attitudes? Is there a case to be made for an integrated male and female *kafeneíon*? Given these two apparently entrenched attitudes, what, if anything, could be done to change them?

? Still not convinced?

1 Jonathan is the son of a friend of ours. Two years ago he completed a Zoology degree and since that time has been working for the Forestry Commission at a research station which monitors wildlife, plantlife and the environment. Having been unemployed for six months, Jon got this job through a government initiative and, as his friends would say, 'Since then he's been counting moths and greater spotted liverworts for £50.00 a week.' Whilst meant partly in jest, there is also a degree of incomprehension underlying their comments. Friends from his university days are well fixed with their feet on the second rung of the career ladder, most are earning competitive salaries and many have company cars and mortgages. They can't understand Jon's value system and he can't understand theirs. When they ask him, he says, somewhat flippantly, 'I want to save the planet – simple as that!' Underlying this apparently glib reply is a serious assertion – he cares deeply about environmental issues and really does want to do something which will be a useful contribution. That matters far more to him than material gains and comforts.

To this end, Jon has now decided to do a PGCE course so that he can qualify as a secondary school science teacher. He says he realises that at this stage in his career he isn't going to discover a particularly rare breed of lesser-spotted fruit fly nor is he set to become a latter day Richard Attenborough. However, he feels that he can make a mark by trying to impart his knowledge and enthusiasm to young people in the hope that some of it will rub off.

Pleased with his decision, he tells his friends, assuming that their approval would be gained – at last he's on the 'approved' way. 'Oh, Jon,' they all said, 'why on earth do you want to be a teacher – it's poorly paid, career paths are slow and the kids are awful. Haven't you ever watched Grange Hill?'

Can you see the differences here not only in attitudes but also in underlying values between Jonathan and his friends? Notice again how the role of perception fits in here in terms of trying to understand other people's attitudes. Looking ahead, you could also look at this scenario in the light of motivation theories – where, for example, do Maslow and Porter and Lawler fit here?

2 Take ten minutes or so to review your music collection (those of you in the authors' age group will have to review singles, albums, tapes and CDs, so you might need a little longer). You'll probably find that you can categorise your collection in one of two ways: either as your tastes have changed with changing musical tastes (up to a point, chronologically challenged readers, when you called a halt and went back to Bob Dylan – see 'Afterthoughts' at the end of this chapter to cheer yourselves up), or you can evaluate your collection according to people who have been important to you (particularly partners). As you look back at the titles, you wonder what on earth could have possessed you to buy the Greatest Hits of Sid Snott and the Kick Starts – until you remember that hot summer of several years ago when you were in love with . . . now what *was* their name? No matter, you *do* remember their penchant for this particular group.

Can you see where Heider's Balance Theory fits in here? If we can't match our attitudes to those of others, cognitive dissonance sets in and we either change our attitude to the thing or the person. How else could you explain why you've got the complete boxed set of Wagner's *Ring* cycle but have never listened to it?

Afterthoughts for the chronologically challenged

1 On the twenty-fifth anniversary of Woodstock recollect the saying of the time: 'If you can remember Woodstock, you weren't there.'

2 One of our colleagues, becoming increasingly annoyed at a student who was drumming his fingers on the desk, said, 'OK, Ginger Baker, put a sock in it, would you?' The student replied, 'Who's Ginger Baker?'

6 Motivation

 ## Midshires University: motivation or abdication?

The organisation

Midshires University is one of the 'new breed' of universities: formerly a successful polytechnic it, like many others, received its new title in June 1992 following changes to government policy. The university has approximately 15,000 students, 75 per cent of whom are full-time. Although the majority of students are studying at undergraduate level, some 20 per cent are registered for postgraduate qualifications either through taught courses or by research.

Like similar organisations, the university, in its polytechnic days, acquired its reputation primarily through the delivery of teaching, with research activities, although important, taking a somewhat second place. Since its change in status, changes in funding have meant that student numbers have escalated and increased competition for research funding has meant that much more emphasis has not only been placed on quantity but also on quality of research delivery and publications. One senior academic was heard to remark: 'We've got to make our minds up whether we're a teaching or a research institution. All this "fence sitting" is wrong: not only are we being pulled both ways, we're not being given any additional resources to cope with it. How can I teach fifteen hours a week, supervise projects for twelve final-year students, be an admissions tutor for one of our biggest courses *and* be expected to undertake research work?' These rumblings of discontent were not confined to isolated departments but were apparent throughout the institution.

As with many organisations of a similar size and diversity, its structure is almost guaranteed to create bureaucracy and, to some extent, distance and divisiveness. The administrative core of the organisation (known officially as the senior management structure but unofficially as 'The Centre') is headed up by the vice-chancellor (although the titular head is the chancellor – a well-known industrialist and public figure); underneath him is a deputy vice-chancellor and four pro-vice-chancellors who are each responsible for a specific area (for example, academic affairs). These six, together with the deans of each faculty form the executive board whose main responsibility is to 'provide corporate leadership'.

In addition, there exist administrative support functions such as personnel, marketing, finance, estates and academic registrar.

The academic core of the university is grouped into five faculties: Engineering, Science, Humanities, Built Environment and a Business School. Each faculty is headed up by a dean and subdivided into a number of specialist schools or departments. The hierarchy within each department is loose in nature: although there is a head of department, several principal lecturers, with the remainder being senior lecturers, there is no real emphasis given to job title. Any bureaucracy which exists in the departments is perceived as originating either from 'The Centre' or from department administration staff whose loyalty to the department rather than 'The Centre' is open to debate.

The department

Within the Engineering faculty lies the department of mechanical engineering with some forty staff, most of whom have been at the university for at least eight years and 90 per cent of whom are 'career academics' who have not held posts in commercial organisations. All are male.

The head of department (who is also the Wallace-Price Professor of Engineering) leads the department in a relatively informal and relaxed manner. Like the majority of academics he is an 'ideas' man rather than an administrator and dislikes formal policies and procedures. Frequently heard to remark, 'I don't like tying things or people up in red tape, I prefer a democratic approach', he has been accused in the past of inconsistency by his staff, of never treating two people in the same way. However, it is true to say that, in general, academic staff are left to organise their lives as they want within the constraints of their teaching schedule. Their research work is highly respected, several innovative engineering designs have been patented and sold on the open market, and there is a well-established programme of industry collaboration.

Whilst the climate of the department is outwardly relaxed and informal, there is very little interaction among staff, particularly outside working hours. Each academic has his own room, there is no central staff room and many staff work from home, only coming into the department to teach and undertake their administrative duties. Gossip is rife, as is professional jealousy, particularly in terms of gaining research funding.

An increase in student numbers, successful franchise arrangements being made to deliver postgraduate courses in China and the Far East and an attempt to reduce teaching loads has led to the department advertising a vacancy for a senior lecturer. Ideally the preferred candidate will have experience of research work, good external business contacts and will want to travel. As is usual in academic institutions, very little, if any, thought is given to the personality of the successful candidate or to the desirability of them fitting in to the rest of the department.

The candidate

Anne Henderson was one of the first women engineering students at Midshires. Graduating in 1975 with a first class honours degree she immediately continued her studies with an M.S.c programme, gaining recognition for her work into environmentally friendly car engines, a largely untapped field in those days. On completion of her Masters degree she was offered a post as a research assistant where she could have developed her Masters research and worked towards her doctorate. However she decided that she needed to gain some commercial experience and joined Wallace-Price, a blue-chip engineering consultancy where, apart from a sponsored year out to study for an MBA in the USA, she has remained ever since.

Her tenacity and loyalty to Wallace-Price have paid off and in 1986 she was made a partner in the firm, primarily responsible for bringing in work to the consultancy. With the promotion came various executive privileges including an annual salary of £80,000, a chauffeur-driven car, free use of one of the company-owned London flats, a non-contributory pension scheme, various gold credit cards and first-class air travel. Anne herself would not describe these as benefits, however, but as necessities to enable her to do her job properly. Last year, in order to meet her business target of £2 million of work for Wallace-Price she spent forty weeks overseas, working an average of ninety hours a week. She can't remember the last time that she had a weekend when she was not entertaining clients or travelling but was totally free to indulge herself.

During her time with Wallace-Price she has earned a reputation both as a formidable but honest negotiator and an innovative engineer, often finding seemingly impossible solutions to problems. Known for her single-minded dedication to her job, she does not suffer fools gladly. She is frequently approached to work for rival firms with promises of even greater privileges and has been the subject of numerous magazine profiles, some concentrating on her work and reputation as a high flyer but the majority focusing on her gender.

Her fortieth birthday last year was spent alone in the Emergency Room of a Los Angeles hospital where she had been rushed with a suspected stomach ulcer. Deprived of her portable telephone, fax and computer she had little else to do but to reflect on her life thus far. On her return to health she was working her way through the pile of technical journals which had accumulated during her absence and there she saw the advertisement for Midshires – an institution which had close links with her company and whose Professor of Engineering she knew well. Ignoring the instructions relating to applications she put through a telephone call to the University . . .

 ## Activity brief

1 Making reference to the appropriate theories, what do you consider to be Anne's main motivating factors? Do you believe that her motivation has *actually* changed on a long-term basis?

2 If you were head of Engineering would you appoint Anne to the position? Why or why not? If you did appoint Anne, how would you motivate her during her first year of employment?

3 A year from appointment, what issues do you imagine might be raised at her annual appraisal and how should they be dealt with?

The 'name' of the game

In April 1994 the first round in a major legal battle against Lloyd's of London on behalf of 20,000 of its Names began in the courts. They were suing for hundreds of millions of pounds on the grounds that their underwriting agents had been negligent and ignored the principles of the reinsurance market.

The main reinsurance principle involved here is to spread the risk round a large number of people by insuring the insurers. The QC representing the Names argued that the underwriters had bought 'inadequate reinsurance protection' with the result that his 3,095 clients had suffered losses amounting collectively to some £850 million. Ironically enough, the day the case opened saw an advertisement in the *Financial Times* (p. 17) seeking a general manager for the newly created Central Services Unit, which was one of the many reforms promised in the business plan of April 1993, the first ever such plan in the organisation's 305-year existence. It was part of the effort to placate members, who were not, however, satisfied. They felt it was inadequate and feared that the decision to allow corporations, as well as individuals, to become Names, would create a two-tier system working to their disadvantage. They even voted to turn down the £900 million Lloyd's offered them in compensation in December 1993.

Lloyd's had certainly not had the best of luck since the late 1980s. Hurricanes Hugo and Andrew, the San Francisco earthquake, the Piper oil rig disaster, the war in Iraq, the Alaska oil spill, and increasing numbers of pollution and asbestosis claims from the United States had put unusually great strains on the organisation. Not surprisingly the advertisement explained that the general manager appointed would have 'energy and drive to quite extraordinary levels' and be in 'a critical and high profile position'. With Names deserting this distressed ship in numbers, David Rowland, Lloyd's chairman from January 1993, came into the frame at just such a critical moment then, and with his chief executive Peter Middleton, energetically attempted to turn the situation round. In addition to the new unit and the plan to introduce corporate Names, over which they threatened resignation if it were voted down, their business plan also promised to cut underwriting fees, raise performance standards, increase accountability, reinsure Names' liabilities for all policies before 1986 and resort to a more directive and centralised management to replace the traditionally loose-structured approach. A pay freeze was one such firm action. None of this managed, however, to deter the Names' resolve. One might be forgiven for thinking that the advertisement made a Freudian slip, rather than a typing error, when it talked of putting in place 'remediable measures'.

However, it is hard to imagine Lloyd's ever going under. With the Bank of England and the Stock Exchange it gives the City of London its worldwide reputation and no government is likely to stand by and watch the demise of such an important image. Particularly perhaps since forty-seven of the Names facing such huge claims were, when litigation began, Members of Parliament who would, by law, lose their position if they were bankrupted. The Establishment in general has, moreover, had very close connections with the matter. Names claiming included royalty, eleven judges, three cabinet ministers and many prominent figures such as

Jeffrey Archer, Camilla Parker Bowles, Edward Heath, Melvyn Bragg, Henry Cooper, Virginia Wade and Winston Churchill Jr. Quite a select group to belong to, it might seem. True, many of them, like Nick Mason of Pink Floyd, and tennis players Mark Cox and Buster Mottram were now facing, it is believed, losses of as much as a million pounds. But in the past, a modest investment would result in a £3,000 return in a good year, and only a £2,000 loss in a bad one. In 1986 and 1987 the Names were breaking even but by 1989 the spectre of the million pound loss was looming.

Of more concern maybe was the fate of the smaller people involved. People running small businesses such as the woman selling vending machines from the front room of her house for whom £750,000 would mean bankruptcy; for the many also who would have to sell their homes to cope. It was often alleged too that many had committed suicide under the strain, leaving their families in terrible debt. The writer, Adam Raphael, a Name himself, described the harm done to so many of them in a book published the week the case opened. The sense of injustice reached a peak in September 1993 when the remunerations paid to underwriters were revealed: a number of them receiving £150,000 per annum, with one at least getting well in excess of £200,000, while hundreds of their Names were losing money.

The débâcle affected the rich and not so rich, the knowing and the naïve, those who refused the compensation offered in order to give Lloyd's a bloody nose and those who for whom this prevailing stance spelt ruin and despair. There were all kinds: from the stockbroker who actually urged his agent to sign him up for too many high-risk policies in the hope of exceptional gains, to the woman whose husband persuaded her to sign for some of the worst-hit syndicates before running off with his secretary, leaving his wife to face bankruptcy, to Edward de Bono, whose lateral thinking can offer little solace when such a complex organisation gets out of control.

Ironically, as litigation was taking its course, premium rates were rising and claims were falling. Just the moment to become a Name?

 ## Activity brief

1 Using Maslow's theory of motivation as a starting point, could the Names be said to be satisfying any other than the most basic of needs? Do you consider that their main motivation was merely greed for money and the perceived status of being known as a Name?

2 How helpful are Equity and/or Expectancy Theories for understanding the Names' refusal to accept the compensation offered?

3 In 100 to 150 words draft a person specification for the general manager *you* think Lloyd's of London needs to motivate its underwriters, agents and Names for the future.

A nasty shock for Eric Evans

ABC Ltd: a study in (lack of) job satisfaction

ABC Ltd is a private sector organisation which manufactures air conditioning systems and sell them worldwide. Its head office is located in the north of England, although there are outposts of ABC in Spain, Norway, Australia and Japan.

ABC has always been run as if it were a small organisation even though its founder sold it to a big electronics concern some five years ago and it has grown from an original staff of twenty at the outset to employ 500 people at head office and something of the order of 3,000 across all locations. It has never had a personnel department, therefore there are very few policies and procedures governing the organisation. Decisions regarding employees (for example, hiring and firing) are usually taken on an *ad hoc* basis by the relevant manager(s), with the particular circumstances of the case being taken into account. Furthermore management have always refused to recognise trade unions, believing that relations within the organisation are good enough for employees to be able to air grievances without the need for formal representation.

Indeed employee relations have never been seen to present a problem for ABC; the only area that management sees as cause for concern is the shopfloor where the systems are actually manufactured. The unskilled and repetitive nature of the work in this department is recognised to make unrest more likely and indeed several attempts to unionise this staff group have been launched in the past. Other sections, by contrast, are considered not to be in any need of special monitoring – the service maintenance department, for example. The staff in service maintenance are highly skilled engineers who are employed to maintain and repair the systems that ABC sells. They are available between 6.00 a.m. and midnight should any of ABC's customers require them. Everyone in this division has personal pagers and takes turns being 'on call' which, in the main, means attending to out-of-hours calls as the pager records them and telephoning the relevant client to give them advice. If the problem cannot be solved over the phone and it is urgent (for example, the air-conditioning system in a hospital has broken down), the engineer will have to go to the client. Because of the breadth of ABC's market, the job also involves a good deal of overseas travel. The service maintenance department is considered to be one of ABC's selling points, as the cover provided by the team enables the company to promise all their customers a five-year warranty. Recently it has also been necessary to provide cover for the overseas branches of ABC – there has been a secondment to the Norwegian office for the last six months and Japan have also requested that a UK engineer go out there to work until they can recruit to their several vacancies. There are twenty engineers in the service maintenance department, as well as the manager and his secretary. All but one are male.

It was only when Eric Evans (the service maintenance manager) realised that he had recruited no less than five engineers in the previous two years, three of whom had left after a very short time and who he was still trying to replace, that he began to perceive that all was not necessarily well among his team. When he thought back to those who had left he realised that all of them had gone to jobs elsewhere in the local area. In other words, his staff were leaving because they were dissatisfied with the company, not because they were moving away, or retiring, or any of the other reasons why people leave employment.

'Well, it can't be the money,' he thought. 'Those guys get a good whack out of this place plus a company car. Other places don't pay so well or offer cars. It must be something else. I'll have to have a chat with them, see what's going on.' At this point, Eric was interrupted in his reverie by his secretary reminding him of his 10 a.m. meeting with the company directors. He made a note to himself to look into the matter before gathering up his files and leaving the office.

In fact Eric didn't need reminding of the problem he had been considering that morning. He returned from the meeting in the early afternoon to be told that a local customer had called, furious because they had had to wait three hours for an engineer to repair their system. The client's offices had grown so hot in the meantime that they had had to let their staff go home and by the time the system was fixed it wasn't worth calling everyone back in. So they had ended up losing a day's work and were blaming it on ABC.

'But I don't understand!' he protested to Carl Peters, who had the unfortunate task of breaking the news to him. 'We've got enough people in, haven't we? Why were they kept waiting?'

'Well, we've got four people sick, Eric, and there's about five others abroad. We need five people to stay here and cover the phones, so that only leaves three to go out to calls. And it's been manic these last couple of days 'cos the weather's so hot. Martin had to drive from here to Glasgow and then on to Manchester yesterday to answer urgent calls. The call from Barnes Brothers just got shoved to the back of the queue. It's not our . . .'

Eric broke into Carl's explanation: 'Four people sick! Have they called in? I haven't been told about this, otherwise I would have tried to arrange cover'.

'I dunno if they called in or not, Eric, but I know we've been down on staff constantly recently. There's always someone off, and it's usually two or three.'

'Right, OK, Carl, I'll ring the customer and eat humble pie. But I want a meeting with the lads tomorrow, 9 a.m. sharp, and we're going to get to the bottom of this. Can you let them know for me?'

At 9 a.m. the following morning, the service maintenance staff began to gather in Eric's office. Eric opened the meeting by telling them that he was concerned about morale in the department and would appreciate any comments they had regarding their own job satisfaction. At first they were reluctant to say anything but Paul Feather, one of the longest-serving members of staff, eventually got the ball rolling: 'Well, what I hate is never knowing what we're up to, Eric. I'm getting sick of being called out to places, then having to work really late 'cos the client's left it till the last minute to call. The times I've driven back from London at 2.00 in the morning – and I've got a sick wife, as you well know.'

'Yeah, and we never know how far ahead we can plan our social lives and stuff,' broke in Carl. 'The only way to ensure not being called away is to book holiday time. I remember when I was due to go and see my parents and you wanted me to fly off somewhere – I'd had the trip arranged for months and suddenly find out the day before that I'm supposed to be going to Switzerland. Then when I wouldn't go, you got really mad with me'.

'Speaking of being called out, I got a page the other night at 3.30 a.m. I didn't turn my pager off 'cos I was on again at 6.00 and one of the customers thought he'd chance his arm. So I got woken up in the middle of the night. It's not on – they know when they can get hold of us, and to leave a message if it's an emergency. This wasn't even urgent – he was just working late and got a bit warm. It could have easily waited till the morning,' added Paul.

'Plus the salespeople always make rash promises to the customer – they say they can get the system installed in such and such a time. They never consult us – they just come back and dump the order sheet on us.' This came from George Browne, who went on: 'And what's more, the job's actually quite dull, you know. I know it's good money and everything, and we get a car, but we always go to the same companies, here and abroad. Also there's very little opportunity to train on any system that you don't already know. So you end up doing the same work, the same installations and the same repairs, week in, week out. The only training that seems to go on here is for people who come in from outside! Another thing – if we were trained in other systems we could fill in for people more easily'.

At this point Robert Fields was heard to mutter, 'Yeah and the car thing . . . that director who bought the flash new company car for herself, fifty grand or what-ever it was, when we just got told we had ten grand to spend on our cars, take it or leave it. She doesn't have to do thirty thousand miles a year for the company, it's just for posing.' Everyone murmured in agreement.

'I'm with George on the stuff about the training – I've not been here long and I'm bored of the same round of places. There's something else too,' said Sarah Jones. 'It's true about the money being alright but if you look at other departments, they're getting more money than we are, even if you take the car into account. Look at pre-sales – they're all on at least five grand more than we are. The only way to get a rise around here is to threaten to leave, like Carl did that time.'

'Now that's not fair,' Eric burst out. 'What about appraisals? You get an automatic increment after your appraisal, if it's been OK.'

'I can't remember the last appraisal I had – and anyway, when I did have it you'd forgotten to fill out the form, so it wasn't much of a discussion. You just sat there and told me I was doing OK and not to worry, you'd do the form soon. Anyway, those increments are only in line with inflation, so we'd kind of expect them anyway – they're not really because you're working hard or whatever. We haven't had a proper performance-related rise in three years,' Sarah replied.

'I never even got my increment after my last appraisal – you sent me a letter saying I hadn't been awarded one, but you never said why! You said at my appraisal that my work was good and you were pleased with me, so I was expecting one,' chipped in Colin Sanderson, who hadn't spoken up until then.

'And you said that I had to improve, and then I got an increment anyway – which I thought was kind of daft. Then you sent me to America to do that really big job, booked me away for a week and totally ignored me when I said I'd never get it done in that time. You had to send John Carter out to help me,' Carl commented.

There was a brief silence as Eric took all this information in, and the group wondered if they'd gone too far. When he didn't say anything for some minutes, George leapt in to fill the gap: 'Can I just say something else? It's too bloody hot in here most days in the summer 'cos of the great big glass windows – they let all the heat in and then when you open them, papers go everywhere. For an air-conditioning company, we've got rubbish ventilation up here. I had to go home early last week because it was so warm – you just can't concentrate'.

Finally Eric spoke: 'OK, OK, I get the gist. There's quite a lot here needs dealing with, it seems. Can we just summarise what the grievances are and I'll make a point of trying to deal with them as soon as I can.' Eric was starting to feel somewhat beleaguered. He had had no idea that things had got this bad. He made a resolve to act as fast as he could – it seemed that he would have no staff left at all if he did not.

 ## Activity brief

1 There are some obvious indicators of low job satisfaction in the text. What are they? What other factors should managers look for which may demonstrate that morale is low?

2 At the meeting the staff are encouraged to air their grievances. Summarise the points they raise.

3 How would motivation theory explain the various grievances? (For example, George's complaint about the heat in the office in summertime could be described as the absence of a hygiene factor (Herzberg). According to this theory, the role of hygiene factors is to provide a foundation upon which motivation can take place – in their absence, the motivation of staff is said to be difficult if not impossible.)

4 Bearing in mind what the theory says, what action would you recommend that Eric takes?

5 What does the existence of several different points of view as to the negative aspects of the job tell us about the nature of human motivation?

Case study provided by Joanna Brewis, University of Portsmouth.

 ## Activity one: The work hard/harder exercise

Either individually, in groups or using a combination of both, list your answers to the following questions:

● What motivates you to work at all?

● What motivates you to work harder?

Can you relate your answers to one or more of the motivation theories?

 # Activity two: Motivation feedback exercise

See Mullins, pp. 476–8.

 # Debate one

'Money is the only thing that motivates people in the real world – all the theories that abound are redundant when it comes to basic issues.'

Starting points

For

● Money acts as an exchange medium which allows people to 'buy' things which satisfy their needs.

● Money is used as a 'symbolic temperature gauge' by which employees can assess or perceive the organisation's opinion of them.

Against

● There is no guaranteed link between money and higher performance unless it is perceived as a direct and significant reward for performance.

● Motivation is not just about economic rewards, it is also concerned with intrinsic satisfaction and social relationships.

Further reading

Guest, D. (1984), 'What's New in Motivation?', *Personnel Management*, May, 20–3.

Herzberg, F. (1987), 'One More Time – How do you Motivate Employees?' *Harvard Business Review*, **65**, Issue 5, Sept./Oct., 109–20.

Kovach, K. A. (1987), 'What Motivates Employees? Workers and Supervisors Give Different Answers', Business Horizons, Sept./Oct., 61.

Locke, E. A. *et al.* (1980), 'The Relative Effectiveness of Four Methods of Motivating Employee Performance' in *Changes in Working Life*, K. D. Duncan, M. M. Gruneberg and D. Wallis (eds), Wiley, 363–83.

Mitchell, T. R. (1982), 'Motivation: New Directions for Theory, Research and Practice', *Academy of Management Review*, **7** (1), January, 80–8.

Sievers, B. (1986), 'Beyond the Surrogate of Motivation', *Organization Studies*, **7** (4), 335–51.

Debate two

'In a recession you can motivate employees to do anything as long as they feel that their job is under threat.'

Starting points

For

- What *actually* motivates at the end of the day is the satisfaction of basic/lower order needs – in other words, Maslow and Alderfer.

- In times of economic crisis managers need to have flexible staff in the organisation – people may have to do the work of two employees and the business is more concerned with staying in business than bothering with ensuring that higher order needs are satisfied.

Against

- How long is the recession likely to last? Organisations which survive are not likely to be the same (in terms of design, culture, etc.) at the end as they were at the beginning. They will need committed and loyal employees and this is not likely to happen if a 'climate of fear' has reigned in the interim.

- Consider McGregor's Theory X and Theory Y: how effective is 'management by fear' likely to be? To enable the organisation to survive it needs employees who are 'singing the same song', in other words who are committed to survival. This will involve flexibility and adaptability (not to mention excellent customer care skills) – qualities which are unlikely to be produced if people are in fear of their jobs and, as a consequence, hate both their jobs and the company.

Further reading

Locke, E. A. (1976), 'The Nature and Causes of Job Satisfaction', in M. D. Dunnette (ed.), *Handbook of Industrial and Organizational Psychology*, Rand McNally, 1297–349.

Steers, R. M. (1977), 'Antecedents and Outcomes of Organizational Commitment', *Administrative Science Quarterly*, **22**, 46–56.

 # Look, it really works!

1 One of our students once remarked: 'This business of motivation theory is OK and I understand what they're trying to say but I don't see how I can relate most of it to my job – they just don't work in the real world.' The student was a civil engineer responsible ultimately for the work of up to 200 short-contract labourers involved in a variety of projects including road building, bridge and office block construction. She said, 'I can see where Maslow fits, but at the end of the day all my lot want to do is to earn enough bonus each week to go out on a Friday night, get blitzed and wake up somewhere strange on Sunday morning with a monumental hangover and no memory of the intervening thirty-six hours. Don't tell me that I'm being a harsh judge of them because I see it happening every week and 90 per cent of the time I'm proved right. Where do your airy-fairy process theories fit into that then?'

If, for example, Expectancy Theory is simplified into the proposition that the degree of energy/motivation expended is dependent on the likelihood and attractiveness of an outcome happening, we can translate our student's situation into 'real life' as shown in Figure 6.1.

Fig. 6.1 'Real life' analysis of situation

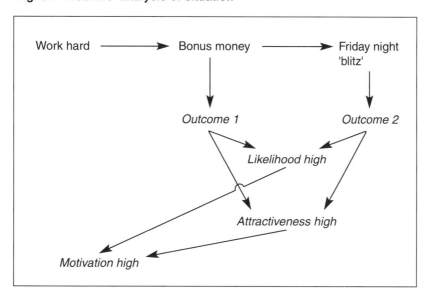

One of the most frequent comments that we receive from students when we return marked assignments is (with varying degrees of politeness): 'I don't understand why you've only given me 52 per cent when I worked myself stupid over this essay – I know that Chris didn't spend half the amount of time in the library that I did, they skipped your 9.15 lecture to write it and you gave them 61 per cent. It isn't fair – if that's all the thanks I get, forget it – I've never liked OB anyway.'

Equally Chris may come to us and say, 'Thanks for my assignment mark, I wasn't sure if I'd taken the right approach – I know a lot of people spent all their time in the library but I thought the question was more concerned with what I thought rather than repeating all the theories word for word. I know that I missed your lecture but I'm really bogged down with assignments at the moment and although I stayed up most of the night I still needed some extra time to put the finishing touches to it.' (*Alright, we weren't born yesterday but it does sound fairly plausible*) 'I wasn't sure about OB but it's more interesting than I thought.'

For this situation, let's look at Equity Theory and remember that this theory revolves around *perception* of inputs and outputs and the consequences of that perception on individual behaviour. The first student equated quantity time (*inputs*) with an assumed high mark (*outputs*) and used this equation as a comparison with Chris. When it didn't compute, the restoration of equity was achieved by condemning the subject itself – in other words, cognitive distortion.

 # Assignment one

Using *one* of the models of motivation, test it in practice by designing and carrying out a small research study using either work or college colleagues.

You will need to:

● Decide which motivation theory you are going to use.

● Design a questionnaire based on what the theory says.

● Decide on your sample population and your sample size.

● Describe the characteristics of your sample.

● Administer the questionnaires.

● Analyse the results.

● Link your results back to the original theory.

● Decide on your conclusions – for example, did the theory apply to your sample population, if not, why not?

● Decide on your recommendations and how you would implement them.

Your assignment can either be written up as a report, presented verbally to the rest of the year, or a combination of both.

 # Assignment two

An article with the following title has recently appeared in *OB Quarterly*, a behavioural science journal aimed at both academics and practitioners: *'At the end of the day, competition is the only thing that motivates – the theories revisited.'*

In *not more* than 2,000 words, complete the article as if you were submitting it for publication. You should bear in mind the following:

● Your target audience will be both academics who know the theories in detail and practitioners who probably won't have the same understanding but will have a basic knowledge (in other words, you don't need to redraw Maslow's Pyramid and describe it in detail).

The non-academics who read your article will be practising managers and you will therefore need to relate your theoretical arguments to the workplace.

- As with all academic journals, your article will be sent to at least two people with a knowledge of the area in order to obtain their views prior to it being accepted for publication. Your arguments, therefore, must be clear, logical and lead the reader to an obvious conclusion (a one-sentence statement beginning 'Thus it can be seen that . . .' will not only be unacceptable but also indicates that you haven't really thought the issues through).

- Your work must be referenced (for an example of footnotes and references, see the final pages of any chapter in Mullins, 'Notes and References'). There is nothing wrong in quoting other authors' views or opinions but at least give them the credit for having stated the point before you did!

! Pause for thought

1 Increasingly we are told that the traditional organisational configurations which have endured for decades will have to change to meet the challenges of the future. Organisations will be 'leaner and fitter','downsized', 'upsidedown', shamrock-shaped or will even resemble that often neglected plant which graces most office windowsills, the spider plant (see, for example, Handy 1989 and Morgan 1993).

The words by which we describe traditional procedures have changed and continue to change: control and delegation are out, empowerment and ownership are in.

The nature of jobs themselves are changing; we have already witnessed an increase in job-sharing and we can look forward to more teleworking via home-based computer workstations. We are told that employees of the future will have not one but several jobs, some paid, some unpaid – they will become 'portfolio people'.

How will the 'manager' of the future (assuming that such a person will still exist) motivate these employees? What roles will, for example, Equity and Expectancy Theory play in these new organisational forms?

2 In the fifty or so years since Abraham Maslow suggested his theory of individual development and motivation, we have seen the various theories build, develop on each other and finally divide into two schools of thought: content/behaviourist and process/cognitive. With the exception of Maccoby (1988) who suggested that motivation of individuals should be linked to social character types, the last twenty years has seen a scarcity of new approaches.

- Does this mean the end of innovative motivation research as we know it?

- Have we finally exhausted all the possibilities, probabilities and suggestions as to how to get that extra ounce of effort from employees? Is a discussion of 'what's new in motivation' now meaningless?

- How would *you* undertake the next research study into motivation?

? Still not convinced?

Look at the following two scenarios.

1 You are a first-year student at the Fresher's Ball. You've enjoyed your first week so far and this is a good party. Across the room you see someone who you noticed in your Study Skills lecture and they appear to be on their own, which could be a point in your favour. However, you've also noticed that they're already very popular with other students while you know yourself to be a bit reticent and sensitive, always fearing the 'brush off'. If you ask them for a dance what is the likelihood that they will accept and what is the further likelihood that you may get to see them again?

Can you see where Expectancy Theory comes into play? Think about first- and second-level outcomes, the chance of them happening and their attractiveness – how does this affect your motivation to ask for the dance? (Consider also that there may be an intervening variable coming into the picture here: the DJ may suddenly switch from 'Lady in Red' to 'Guns 'n' Roses' – ask yourself about the timing of the motivational drive.)

2 As a new second-year student you've had to move out of Halls and into your own accommodation. You have taken great care to team up with like-minded people for a house-share and after many hours of scanning the local newspaper, networking with final-year students and pounding the pavements, you've finally found the perfect place. There are students in the houses on both sides (so noise won't be a problem), there is a take-away and pub within a two minute walk, the house has central heating, a washing machine, TV, video and telephone and the landlord lives several miles away. Congratulating yourself on your good fortune, you move in and proceed to enjoy your second year away from some of the constraints of the Hall of Residence.

Several weeks go by and your parents pay a 'surprise visit' early one Sunday morning. You proudly give them a grand tour of your new house but to your disappointment your mother remarks on several things: the kitchen in general is dirty and the grill pan in particular has a mixture of toast crumbs and last week's bacon sandwich congealing together; there seems to be an inordinate amount of empty coffee cups and beer cans all over the sitting room; the bathroom has mould on the walls; there is a large burn hole in the settee and there appear to be at least two 'extra' people who have clearly not only just got up but also appear to be somewhat disoriented.

In despair, your mother remarks, 'For goodness sake, how can you *live* like this – it's total squalor. I can't believe that a child of mine has these values.'

Can you see where Goal Theory might apply? Is there a place here also for Maslow? (Think about differing perceptions of what 'basic needs' actually *are*.)

Afterthought*

When asked the question, 'What do you understand by the word "motivation"?' a senior manger within an international manufacturing company said, 'Well, I don't like to give my staff a bollocking every time . . .'

This particular franchise had the worst record for customer satisfaction in the whole group.

*Provided by Val Marchant, Ibis Training and Development.

7 Leadership

 ## A French Berlusconi?

Silvio Berlusconi built up a business empire that made him the second richest person in Italy. By 1993 his holding company, Fininvest, owned three Italian television channels, shares in two others and interests in several overseas stations. Its publishing houses sold a third of Italy's magazines and a quarter of its books. It controlled the country's biggest advertising agency, its biggest supermarket chain and, arguably, its finest football club, AC Milan.

A man of great self-confidence (his communication skills owed something, perhaps, to his experience of singing in night clubs), he decided, in 1993, at the age of fifty-seven, to use his powerful position to launch a new political movement and rescue Italy from the deep crisis caused by revelations of widespread corruption at the heart of the traditional parties. Ironically, nearly the worst case was that of his friend, Bettino Craxi, a Socialist and the longest serving of post-war prime ministers. However, the Left still looked like winning the 1994 elections since Communist hands seemed to be relatively clean. Astonishingly though, Berlusconi's three-month-old Right-wing party gained the highest number of parliamentary seats and the president asked him to form a government. A quite unparalleled feat. How had it been achieved?

Undoubtedly his charisma, entrepreneurial fame, and gift for rhetorical language, all contributed and he was, moreover, a self-made man in a country that boasts the highest number of small concerns in Europe. The deep disillusion the country felt about its traditional leaders and the disarray of the old political parties certainly made it a propitious time for new figures to emerge. His platform, too, was simple and clear: lower taxes, deregulation, curbs on public spending and immigration, and aversion for the bureaucrats of Brussels, the Social Chapter and moves towards a centralised, unified Europe. This programme along with his self-belief, patriotic claims and conviction that the country needed strong leadership were not unreminiscent of another famous Prime Minister, Mrs Thatcher. But, despite the undoubted contribution of Saatchi and Saatchi, even she had to take the conventional route to political power – for Berlusconi's trump card was surely his control of the media, still not possible in a Britain of the 1990s.

Indeed, one explanation for Berlusconi's decision to enter politics was that the Left was threatening to control the media more along British lines, not a welcome future for someone whose empire is built on the communication industry. The Saturday after he announced his intention to enter politics, two of his channels changed their schedules to give him a slot the length of a football match to present his plans – his 'Freedom Crusade' as he liked to call it. In the run up to the election, numerous attacks were made on the man and his new party: suggestions of involvement with the Mafia, criticism of his top-heavy management style and his links with neo-fascists (he was to invite the National Alliance into his coalition government in fact). But most complaints were about his unfair use of the media to further his cause: a top sports programme presenter finished one show by informing the viewers he was voting for Berlusconi, his famous footballers went on shows to back him, party candidates were given professional media training, he avoided confrontations on the screen and 'produced' his own appearances to spread the image of the man of providence. The audience for his three channels was 40 per cent of all viewers. Not for nothing is Berlusconi called *Sua Emittenza* (Your Broadcasting Highness). Finally the TV ombudsman stepped in . . . the day before the election.

Berlusconi's other trump was his football club. Italy has more sports papers than most countries and Italians adore soccer. One of their chants to encourage their national team is *'Forza Italia'* (Play up Italy!), the name of the new Prime Minister's party.

Mrs Thatcher could not play the football card either, of course. But in France, an entrepreneur of almost Berlusconian proportions, bought l'Olympique de Marseille in 1986 and did not hesitate to exploit soccer's popular appeal to advance *his* political ambitions too.

Bernard Tapie is a self-made man. The son of a heating engineer and a nurse, he had a technical training and, although it is said he had hopes of being a singer, he started work in 1963, at the age of eighteen, in the car industry. He soon went into business on his own, however, and embarked on a series of acquisitions and sales (Addidas being perhaps the most celebrated) that rapidly made his fortune. By the 1980s his holding company owned the textile firm with the highest turnover in France. In 1989 he became a Member of Parliament and in 1992 Minister for Urban Affairs.

Though lacking Berlusconi's singing experience, Tapie is a showman of talent: during his political campaigns he fearlessly confronts his opponents in the public arena. He is boundlessly charming, eloquent and energetic, and, it is said, capable of outbursts of anger and haughtiness that are also effective weapons in his arsenal. Unlike Italy, France could not be said in the 1990s to be in crisis, but both soccer and the media do have the power to persuade. So, when standing for Parliament in 1988, Tapie chose to fight the constituency around his Marseille stadium and was given to mentioning his new signings in his political speeches. He had already had media training in 1986 as host of a successful TV show, suitably called 'Ambitions', and his appearance on TV guarantees good ratings. When TF1 was privatised in 1987, Tapie became one of the shareholders and served on the planning committee.

Tapie, too, attracts much criticism. As a business man he has been accused of being unproductive of anything other than money, often selling an acquisition as soon as there was a profit to be made in doing so. It seems he never injected the money he promised into Addidas, his early involvement and enthusiasm evaporated, there were redundancies, loss of sales to Nike and Reebok, and, after three years, he sold the company he had promised to keep for ten. As a football boss it is said he can be ruthless with both players and opposition, in favour of the early crunch tackle and putting winning before all other considerations. After a sortie into Belgium to negotiate a deal with Donnay, he was written off by one journalist there as simply a media cowboy.

There is a theory (Hoffmann 1967) that explains the success of leaders such as Pétain and de Gaulle in terms of French society and its predilection for bureaucracy. It *can* be an efficient organisational system but is prone to hinder innovation. In France this has meant that modernisation comes with a rush after a crisis, and it requires heroic leaders to achieve it. Such leaders are therefore, by definition, anti-establishment: indeed, there exists no equivalent French word for 'leadership'. Bernard Tapie has not infrequently been accused of having his 'hand in the till', most spectacularly in 1993 when his colleagues voted to lift his parliamentary immunity to enable proceedings to be taken against him for misuse of public money, forcing him to resign his ministerial post. Even more attention was given to the part he played in his football club's alleged bribery of an opposing team. The French football authorities relegated the team and struck off its management, Tapie included. Astonishingly, the setbacks seem to have fuelled his fame and fortune to such an extent that the French President shook his hand for photographers after the football scandal surfaced. He has obviously retained his friends in high places, then, and opinion polls show his popularity remaining high. He was a candidate for the European parliament in 1994. His candidacy was a resounding success and the judge in charge of his case saw fit to order a dawn raid on his home when she believed he was planning a temporary absence from the country until the immunity granted to him as a European MP came into force. Robin Hood is alive and well and living in France.

Although both Tapie and Berlusconi are anti-establishment figures, an important difference between the two men is their political platform. Tapie set out not to save, but to defeat the Right wing by attacking the country's National Front leader, Jean-Marie Le Pen, whom he did not hesitate to confront in an American-style TV debate. Some say he will be President of France, let alone Prime Minister. It could be an omen that Marseille actually beat Berlusconi's AC Milan in the final of the European Cup.

 # Activity brief

1 With reference to definitions of leadership in Mullins (pp. 229–34), argue that Berlusconi and Tapie may be justifiably thought of as leaders.

2 'I had six honest working men, they taught me all I knew,
Their names were What and Why and When
And How and Where and Who.'

This little rhyme might be used as a way of remembering the five approaches to leadership which Mullins identifies on p. 234:

(a) Traits – *Who* are the leaders?
(b) Functions – *What* do they do?
(c) Style – *How* do they do it?
(d) Behaviour – *Where* is their focus?
(e) Situation – *Why* do they behave that way?

See if the trick works by asking these questions of Tapie's and Berlusconi's careers and then see if your answers match the corresponding approaches Mullins identifies.

(If you're wondering where '*When*' went, try Clark and Pratt and Rodrigues – Mullins, pp. 256–7.)

3 If you find Bernard Tapie's career interesting, find out about another Frenchman: Jacques Médecin, one-time mayor of Nice. Question a French person you know about him or interrogate a national paper on a CD–Rom database. Alternatively, if you read French, try one of the weeklies like *L'Express* (e.g. 11 August 1994) or *Le Point* (e.g. 4 December 1993).

 # Mr Prince, chairperson of NA – a man for all seasons?

All members of the Republican Party in government were in agreement: Mr Prince had been the correct appointee as chairperson of National Airlines (NA). They had chosen him because he was a strong supporter of private enterprise. He also had a reputation for reversing the fortunes of ailing or stagnating companies by providing strong leadership and taking responsibility for directing all areas of the policy of the companies under his charge. At the time of Prince's appointment, NA was still in the public sector. However, the newly elected Republican government believed privatisation to be the panacea of all the country's (and the company's) economic ills. Consequently, the Republican President, Marshmallow, had asked Prince to take whatever steps were necessary to reorganise the company in preparation for its transfer to the private sector.

When under state control, NA had grown through a vertical expansion of its operations. It organised the management of airports, scheduling of air time, maintenance, repair and flying of civilian aircrafts, running of duty free shops and provision of on-board catering. Additionally, a wide range of other services that supported these operations were now being provided in-house. NA had its own fleet of staff cars and a number of garages to service them, a tailor and a dry cleaner to make and clean staff uniforms, and a complex of different catering services providing meals in different environments for the different grades of its own staff. As one journalist commented: 'NA organise themselves according to the principle of "If we need a glass of milk, we'll go and buy a cow"'. By the time Prince took over, the company were employing 60,000 people. Unfortunately, the organisation's growth had not been accompanied by the introduction of adequate measures for monitoring the financial viability of each initiative, nor by the adjustment of the existing management structure to accommodate the new operations. No one was really sure who was responsible for, or the actual cost of, the increasing number of supplementary services. Previously, this had not been a problem for the company. They had simply subsidised any unprofitable subsidiary operations with their earnings from their highly profitable civilian air transport. Now licenses to organise flights were being granted to small independent airlines who were without the burden of large subsidiary operations and were able to charge their customers cheaper fares.

Marshmallow had given Prince a free rein to appoint any new director that he felt would allow him to carry through the privatisation that the government desired. Prince knew the people that he wanted and he knew their price. He also wanted to be sure that he had full authority to organise NA as he saw fit. So, by threatening to tender his resignation, he obtained from the President the right to pay any appointee a salary that was higher than the norm in the rest of the public sector. Prince had then systematically dismissed or cajoled into early retirement any dissenters amongst the existing executives. Those who remained from the old board were in agreement with Prince. They were joined by a collection of people who, like Prince, had made large fortunes in private industry and had reputations for not standing any nonsense from subordinates. Each had been selected for both their willingness to accept Prince's authority and for their ability to put into practice Prince's plan for the organisation of NA.

This plan involved either selling or dismantling any part of the organisation that he considered was not integral to the firm's main business of maintaining and flying a fleet of aircraft – subsidiary services were to be purchased from outside suppliers and contractors and Prince instructed that the remaining operations should be broken down into divisions such as air transport, maintenance and airports. Each division was to have its own clear chain of command and a new accounting system. That, Prince believed, would enable anyone higher in the organisation to know who below them was responsible for what, and how well they were doing. Improvements to the profitability of all operations were to be sought by increasing the working hours of some staff and by putting on to short-term contracts all those staff who had low levels of skills. They could then be laid off if the company had to prune its operations in the face of competition. Prince estimated that by these changes in employment policy and the sale of some parts of the corporation, the size of the workforce could be halved. Everyone of the directors was each given responsibility for implementing different parts of this plan, with the instruction to check with Prince about any divergence that might compromise the implementation of the remainder.

When these changes had been instituted, Prince informed Marshmallow that he thought now was the time for the privatisation of the industry. The President agreed and organised a share issue.

Prince believed that his work was completed when the company was transferred into the private sector, so he retired. Many thought that Ray Gunn, the deputy chairperson, was the natural successor. Gunn had been one of the people that Prince had recruited because of his expertise in the private sector and, like the retiring chairperson, he had a reputation of being a firm leader and a strict disciplinarian. However, other members of the board questioned, when in private, whether those characteristics were the ones that would help them in what they hoped would be a period of consolidation. The impact of deregulation continued to offer price advantages to smaller competitors with limited overheads. As NA continued to employ a higher number of administrators than any other company in the sector, there were future threats to its profitability. It also operated most of its business from premium cost sites.

Informal discussions between two directors, Knight and Jones, led the latter to suggest that the best way to reduce costs would be to set up the different divisions of the corporation as stand alone companies who would interact with one another through the external marketplace thus enabling the corporation to reduce the number of middle managers that it employed at present to coordinate the operations of the different divisions, as the new companies could interact with one another through the external market. Knight responded by adding that if some of the divisions were relocated away from their present premium-rate sites, they could take advantage of cheaper rents. The directors decided to raise this at the next board meeting.

At the next meeting, Knight conveyed the content of his and Jones's earlier discussion to the board. Gunn, who felt his position as heir apparent was being undermined by other board members' suggestions of the way forward for the company, questioned whether the costs of removal to the other sites would not outweigh any savings that might accrue in the first fifteen to twenty years afterwards. Smith, who had been on the board longer than any of the others also raised the issue of staff morale. Would another set of redundancies not ruin staff morale, particularly if it affected the middle managers who had been loyal supporters in the upheavals that had already taken place?

At this point, Marble intervened. Like Smith, he was a long standing member of the board, having been appointed prior to Prince's arrival. Towards the end of Prince's reign, Marble had privately questioned the wisdom of some of the then chairperson's initiatives and his style. He knew that the waves of redundancies and Prince's style of leadership had left most low-level employees dissatisfied and afraid for their jobs. He had misgivings about the possibility of Gunn's succession. Marble also felt that he did not owe the same debt of loyalty to Gunn as he had owed to Prince. Furthermore (unlike when Prince was appointed), he was now in a position to vote for whoever the next chairperson would be. He started by pointing out that if the new companies were set up on new sites, they would be eligible for a range of government grants. Also, staff morale in those companies might be improved by introducing systems of total quality management. This would entail organising the workers at every level of each company into groups. Each group would be made responsible for deciding how work would be organised between the members of the group. They would also be responsible for monitoring both the quantity and the quality of the work and they would decide what changes to make to improve their performance. That way, not only would the employees' creative abilities be used for the full benefit of the company, but also morale would be raised by giving to the workers a sense of the intrinsic value of their work.

These initiatives, Marble argued, would allow the corporation to rid itself of a large part of its managerial hierarchy and redeploy those affected in productive work to increase the profitability of the company. Marble concluded by saying that he knew of somebody called Joan Prudence who had overseen the successful installation of such arrangements at her own group of companies, and he believed that the board should invite her along for an informal interview, to establish whether they thought she could do a similar job for NA.

Just then, Gunn spoke. He could see that his chance of becoming chairperson was receding and so he raised a whole number of objections to the proposals that were coming forward. How would the board monitor the performance of personnel at the new subsidiary companies without the apparatus that their existing levels of middle management provided? How would the board ensure that the different companies stuck to a corporate strategy if they became independent? What type of motivation would be offered to individual employees to work for the company when the career ladder into middle management that now existed would disappear? All these questions required answers, Gunn argued, before the company decided whether or not to change its present structure and pattern of leadership.

At this point the board adjourned their meeting to reflect on the issues raised.

 ## Activity brief

1 What are the characteristics of Prince's style of leadership that suggest he is a transactional (or authoritarian) leader? How do these compare with characteristics of transformational (or democratic) leadership?

2 On the basis of this case study, do you consider a single leadership style to be applicable in every situation?

3 What were the bases of Prince's power?

4 In your opinion, what would be the pros and cons of working under: (a) Mr Prince; (b) Ms Prudence?

Case study provided by Dr Bill Lee, University of Portsmouth.

Further reading

Bass, B. M. (1981), *Stogdill's Handbook of Leadership: A Survey of Theory and Practice*, Free Press.

Bass, B. M. and Avolio, B. J. (eds) (1994), *Improving Organizational Effectiveness Through Transformational Leadership*, Sage Publications.

Gordon, D., Edwards, R. and Reich, M. (1982), *Segmented Work, Divided Workers*, Cambridge University Press.

Mullins, L. J. (1993), *Management and Organisational Behaviour*, 3rd edn, Pitman.

Pate, L. E. (ed.) (1988), 'Developing Leadership Excellence', *Journal of Management Development*, **7** (5), special issue.

Sadler, P. (1994), *Managing Talent*, Pitman.

Smith, P. B. and Peterson, M. F. (1988), *Leadership, Organizations and Culture: An Event Management Model*, Sage Publications.

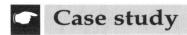
Case study

See Mullins, pp. 262–3.

Activity one

Assume that you or your group are management consultants whose main area of expertise is leadership training.

Design a leadership training programme for middle managers in a work organisation of your choice.

You will need to:

- Specify the objectives of the course.
- Detail the timing of the course (number of days etc.).
- Outline each day's training in detail, including any tutor input, exercises, etc.
- Prepare an evaluation sheet for delegates.

This activity is adapted from Mullins, p. 260.

Activity two

See Mullins, pp. 264–5.

Activity three

See Mullins, p. 265.

Debate one

'Leaders are born to be so: it is impossible to train a person to become a leader.'

Starting points

For

- A glance at the world's great leaders shows that they have one thing in common: charisma. This cannot be instilled into a person through a training course, you either have it or you don't.

- The skills associated with leadership can be trained (delegating, influencing, etc.) but the underlying 'leadership personality' must be there to start with; how else can you explain such leaders as Ghandi, Thatcher, Hitler or Churchill?

Against

- The question is only concerned with charismatic leadership: most organisational leaders do not need this ideological approach to be good 'solid' leaders.

- Given this comment, the nature of a leader can, therefore, be broken down into attributes and skills which can be given and/or improved through training.

Further reading

Caulkin, A. (1993), 'The Lust for Leadership', *Management Today*, November, 38–43.

McElroy, J. C. (1982), 'A Typology of Attribution Leadership Research', *Academy of Management Review*, July, pp. 413–17.

Meindel, J. R. and Ehrlich, S. B. (1987), 'The Romance of Leadership and the Evaluation of Organizational Performance', *Academy of Management Journal*, March, 91–109.

Roddick, A. (1991), *Body and Soul*, Ebury Press.

 # Debate two

'Organisational success depends on the qualities of its leaders.'

Starting points

For

- The organisation/environment-fit equation is important: leaders need to be able to have strategic vision, to anticipate change, to look for and take advantage of opportunities, to motivate their followers.

- Leadership is an integrating activity ensuring organisational coordination and control through the ability to make rapid and decisive decisions which are not constrained by bureaucratic policies and procedures.

Against

- Leadership behaviour is constrained by the demands, pressures and boundaries imposed by others. There is not as much unilateral power vested in the leader as is usually perceived.

- Many factors affecting organisational success are outside the leader's control: labour markets, economics, legislation, etc.

Further reading

Jennings, E. E. (1961), 'The Anatomy of Leadership', *Management of Personnel Quarterly*, **1** (1), Autumn, 2.

Kellerman, B. (1984), *Leadership: Multidisciplinary Perspectives*, Prentice Hall.

Kotter, J. P. (1990), 'What Leaders Really Do', *Harvard Business Review*, May–June, 103.

Smith, J. E., Carson, K. P. and Alexander, R. A. (1984), 'Leadership: It Can Make a Difference', *Academy of Management Journal*, December, 765–76.

✓ Look, it really works!

1 The hotel and catering industry relies to a very large extent on the employment of casual staff to cover seasonal peaks and troughs in its business. This is particularly true of the banqueting and conference department where labour demand can fluctuate rapidly – sometimes in a matter of hours, particularly if a 'Dinner and Dance' originally booked for 200 guests suddenly increases to 250 during the afternoon of the event. In operational terms that means finding space for at least another five or six tables and conjuring up five or so extra casual staff at short notice.

In general terms, these casuals (or 'black and whites' as they are sometimes known after their usual uniform) consist of two main types: catering students who are trying to pay off their overdrafts under the guise of 'gaining valuable industrial experience' and mature women who have been doing the job for years and whose main motivation appears to be primarily to satisfy social rather than monetary needs. It is this latter 'breed' who give rise to the second nickname: 'ducks' (as in, presumably, 'Hello, ducks, how are you?').

One of our Hotel and Catering Management students had, during his industrial placement year, been given the job of banqueting supervisor and, halfway through the training, it fell to one of the authors to visit the student to discuss progress etc. On arrival, the lecturer was greeted by Tom, the student, with the words: 'Can you find me another placement, I'm sick of this one. I'm not getting anywhere and nobody takes any notice of me.' Further questioning revealed some interesting comments from Tom including: 'I'm trying to change the whole department and drag them into the twentieth century. The older women won't listen to anything I say and go off and do their own thing; you need to follow the young kids around all the time otherwise they'll just skive off.'

Now let's try and apply this to a leadership theory by using House's Path Goal Theory. This is the one which is linked to Expectancy Theory of Motivation and which says that leader behaviour should depend on the personal characteristics of the subordinates in terms of how much they will look at Tom's behaviour as a source of satisfying their own needs together with how routine and structured the task is.

In this case the task (laying up, waiting on and clearing down tables) is highly structured and certainly routine; the personal characteristics of the staff and their needs have been recognised by Tom. He should, therefore, adopt a style which is more participative than directive: sell and share rather than tell and do. In this way also, Tom will have a greater chance of success at driving through any changes he might want to make.

2 Let's go back to Midshires University – the organisation we first met in Chapter 6 – for this one. Kathryn Kennedy has recently been appointed as the faculty administration officer for the faculty of the Built Environment. In this particular job, she reports to the dean and is responsible for all administration from managing a large budget to devising exam timetables to initiating administrative policies and procedures.

The Engineering faculty academics we met in Chapter 6 are broadly similar to those in Built Environment (we're the same the world over, unfortunately); they see their main role(s) as teaching and/or researching – anything else has a very low priority on their list. However, whether they like it or not (and most of them don't) they are also required to undertake some form of administration. This can range from managing a very large course to being a schools' liaison officer.

As well as all the other changes which have happened since Midshires became a 'new' university, academic staff have also had changes to their employment contracts which have affected, among other things, their holiday entitlement. Previously some teaching staff had been known to disappear on the last day of term never to be seen again until the first day of the next term; what happened in between, whether it was genuine holiday leave, study or research time was usually left to an informal, *ad hoc* agreement between each lecturer and their individual head of department. The new contract changes require that some degree of formality is introduced in the form of . . . shock! horror! . . . a 'holiday request form'! (Those of you, dear readers, who are practising managers in the 'real world' are probably raising a quizzical eyebrow at this stage: you have to remember that, to most academics, the words 'administration' and 'control' are synonymous and, when used in conjunction with the term 'management', are akin to the equivalent of a mental and creative straitjacket.)

The design and implementation of this system fell to Kathryn as one of her first big jobs. Tackling it with relish, she designed a form for academics to complete which detailed start and finish of the proposed holiday, number of days actually taken, number of days remaining, a holiday emergency contact number and various signatures for authorisation, including her own. The distribution of a sample form was accompanied by a four page, closely typed document on the procedure itself.

After a three-month period had gone by, Kathryn was lunching in the Staff Bar one day when her opposite number from Engineering passed by. 'Hi, Kathryn, how're you getting on?' he said. 'Still enjoying the job?' 'No,' replied Kathryn, 'in fact I'm thinking of leaving. Trying to manage academics is like trying to herd cats – on principle they all go in opposite directions to the one you want. Take this holiday form business – no one sends one in and they've all "lost" the procedure I sent out. When I query them on it they all look blank and either say "What form?" or "I don't understand it – *you* sort it out".'

Let's look at Hersey and Blanchard's Model of Situational Leadership for this one. Kathryn's group's readiness level was one of 'able but unwilling' to perform the task. They therefore need to be allowed to share ideas and participate in decision-making so that they feel a greater sense of 'ownership' – a much more participative approach than Kathryn had taken. Perhaps if she had taken note of people's views, explained what was happening and invited suggestions she would have got a more positive outcome. (OK, we're not hiding behind rose-tinted glasses here, we know that, given the 'nature of the beast' she would never have achieved *total* success but it would have been a starting point for her to build on.)

Unfortunately Kathryn hadn't heard of Laurie Mullins (now *he* would have gone along with her ideas because he's that sort of guy . . .) and was last heard of heading for the Job Centre, having locked a lecturer in the stationery cupboard after he had forgotten to sign a requisition form . . .

 ## Assignment one

When emphasising transferable skills, employers often say that they are looking for leadership qualities in their recruits. In not more than 300 words describe an event in your life which could be used to illustrate this quality in yourself and which you could use in an interview or on a CV.

 ## Assignment two

Take any two of the leadership theories or models and apply them to a leader, either in the workplace or a public figure in whom you're interested. You should bear in mind the following:

● You will need to thoroughly research the theories and choose two which appeal to you.

● Look at your chosen leader as objectively as possible, identifying situations and incidents which mark them out as a leader. (If you have chosen a public figure you may need to do some library research at this point.)

● Using your two chosen models, lay them like a template on your leader and see how good the 'fit' is.

● What conclusions can you draw? Does the leader you have chosen 'fit' the models you have selected? Why or why not?

Your assignment can either be written up (in not more than 2,000 words) and/or presented to the rest of the group.

Pause for thought

1 Attribution theory can be applied to leadership as well as perception. It deals with how people make sense of relationships: when something happens, there is a natural tendency for someone to attribute it to something. In the context of leadership, the theory simply says that leadership is an attribution they make about other people.

Using attribution theory, researchers have found that people characterise leaders with traits such as intelligence, an outgoing personality, aggressiveness, strong verbal skills, understanding and industriousness, who are consistent, committed and unwavering in their decision-making and goal-setting (Lord, DeVader and Alliger 1986). Research shows that a 'heroic' leader is perceived as being someone who takes up a cause which is difficult or unpopular and who, through determination and persistence, succeeds (Staw and Ross 1980).

We can probably perceive all these attributes in both Silvio Berlusconi and Bernard Tapie (see the first case study in this chapter) – but how does attribution theory affect our perception of John Major? Would it change if he were to show himself to be more ruthless, authoritative and even immoral?

2 Organisation Yin and Yang

A rather different view of leadership has been provided by Anita Roddick, founder and managing director of the hugely successful Body Shop chain. She suggests that leaders should have both flair and a sense of fun, should not adopt a 'holier than thou' attitude reinforced by artificial status, elevated titles, allocated parking spaces or separate dining rooms. Indeed, leaders should be entrepreneurs who create new rules, discard stereotypes and succeed for themselves. It is this high need for personal achievement, for a person she describes as 'marching to a different drumbeat', who is essentially an outsider with a total belief in what they are doing, that characterises a successful leader.

A further point she stresses is the need for organisations to stress both masculine and feminine values, whereas currently too much emphasis is placed on male-dominated culture that not only sets up hurdles for women but also results in hierarchical structures based on authority.

How appropriate is this style of leadership to running, for example, the civil service? Is it only appropriate for an entrepreneurial business?

? Still not convinced?

1 It's Stardate 23 30 21 and the Starship *Enterprise* is still 'boldly going' its merry way through outer space. All is peace and calm on the bridge: Ohura has managed to find the galactic frequency for One FM; Spock is tuned to 'Intergalactic Test Match Special'; Mr Sulu is midway through 'The Hitchhiker's Guide to the Galaxy (revised edition) and Captain Kirk is surreptitiously practising his sardonic eyebrow lift and wry smile. He knows that his crew are self-motivated, enjoy their job and are happy to work together as a team, contributing to the smooth running of the *Enterprise* – a typical Theory Y approach, in fact.

Suddenly Ohura loses Steve Wright and in her right ear she picks up a message delivered in a flat Bawston nasal twang: 'Now let's go through this keyhole and see what we have . . .' 'Captain,' she says urgently, 'prepare for possible invaders: starboard bow' (why do they never appear on the port bow – are they all right-handed?). All eyes turn to the huge plexiglass awareness panel as, floating into view, comes Lloyd Grossman and a team of invited panellists. 'Activate shields, phasers on stun and ahead Warp Factor 12,' barks Kirk. 'Aaaw, Captain, I canna get that much power out of the old girl so quickly,' complains Scotty. 'I'm not asking you, Mr Scott,' replies Kirk, 'I'm telling you. Now get on with it.' The SS *Enterprise* streaks off leaving our hapless quiz show host floating in space.

What happened to our Theory Y leader? Nothing, really, except that he became a Theory X leader when the situation demanded it. If you were on board a Boeing 747 midway across the Atlantic with two engines on fire, what type of leader would *you* prefer at the controls: Theory Y or Theory X?

(It's leadership, Jim, but not as you may have thought about it . . .)

2 Let's go back to our hapless student from Chapter 6. He's still in his first year and coming to grips with such diverse issues as launderettes, union bars, OB lectures and the potential boost to his social life he was hoping for. In terms of lectures, he's discovered the lecturer's secret weapon: group assignments. Now, dear readers, you may think we invented 'the group assignment' in order to reduce our marking levels. Not so, oh cynical ones! We invented it to 'facilitate student learning/interaction/interpersonal skills . . .' Honest! (trust us, we're lecturers; would we lie to you?)

At the start of term a particular lecturer has set an OB seminar on some particularly obscure subject and three of you have got to present it at the end of term. You don't really know the other two students very well (that serves you right for having a lie-in the day that seminar topics were chosen) and nothing much has been done so far.

The day of the presentation is looming (Monday, in fact, and today is Thursday) and panic is setting in. You bribe (sorry, motivate) the other two into a meeting by offering to buy them a drink (on second thoughts, for 'panic' substitute 'desperation'). You're sitting round in the Union Bar, clutching your respective pints of Old Thumper, looking at each other and not saying much. Desperate times call for desperate action . . . 'Right,' you hear yourself saying, 'we've got to do this by Monday, so if you, Rick, do the first part, I'll do the second bit, and Neil, you do the conclusions and the overheads because you've got the neatest writing. We'll meet again on Saturday morning before the match and go over it and then have a practice on Sunday evening before we go to the pub. OK?'

What does this tell you about leadership style, the situation and the followers? Can you see where, perhaps, Tannenbaum and Schmidt fit in? What about Action Centred Leadership?

8 Groups

 Firing on three cylinders ...

Lifestyle Cars Ltd, as is general amongst car manufacturers, distributes its vehicles through a series of authorised dealerships all over the UK. In order to successfully qualify for such authorisation, each potential dealership has to undergo rigorous vetting procedures to ensure that Lifestyle's quality standards will be adhered to. Competition for authorised dealerships is always fierce, never more so than when, as with Lifestyle, the products are popular and sell well. Dealers are expected to meet sales and growth targets laid down by the manufacturer – in trade jargon 'to move the metal'. Rewards for success are not just monetary: dealers who are performing well are awarded a variety of other prizes, from holidays to extra deliveries of new models into their showroom. Out-of-date models are obviously not as easy to 'move' and no dealer wants deliveries of these cars in favour of new or improved styles.

Once accepted as an authorised dealer, the symbiosis between dealership and Lifestyle is not always an easy one. The two organisations must live side by side for as long as the contract lasts. Lifestyle have no direct authority over a dealer but indirectly have great power.

To understand this situation more fully, let us look at a typical dealership, Ratchetts Ltd. Founded more than twenty years ago by Alan Ratchett, it has seen steady growth over that time from its humble start as a vehicle repair shop to the present day which sees it as a Lifestyle authorised dealer. Founder Alan Ratchett, managing director of his own company is also the Lifestyle 'dealer principal'; the organisation chart is shown in Figure 8.1.

Overlaid on this is the Lifestyle organisation of two regional managers, responsible for either sales or service. Thus the car sales manager reports directly to Alan Ratchett and indirectly to his Lifestyle regional manager who has his own company targets to meet. Equally Ratchett, whilst being managing director of his own company, is also equally accountable to Lifestyle Cars via the two regional managers and *their* bosses. Failure to meet standards and targets set could well result in the loss of the franchise.

It would appear from Figure 8.1 that the dealership falls naturally into two distinct areas: Sales and After-sales. Even if this were the case, it would not be a welcome

Fig. 8.1 Organisation chart for Ratchetts Ltd

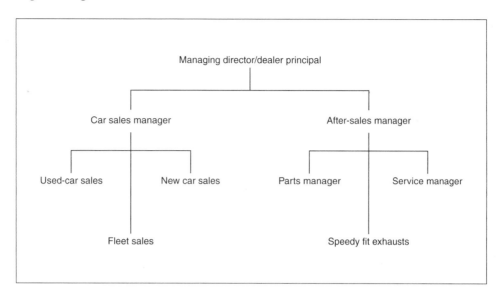

division: profit margins on new cars are low and a dealership relies on the after-market to engender customer loyalty and boost revenue. However, in the case of Ratchetts, the groups divide even further. Let us look at each section separately:

Car sales

The car sales manager is responsible for essentially three separate and distinct areas: new cars, used cars and fleet sales. To take the first two, historically there is always a bigger profit to be made from used cars than from new. 'Used' cars can mean anything from a five-year-old vehicle to one which has only been owned for six months. An unknowing customer, therefore, intending to purchase a brand new car may be successfully 'prospected' by a used-car salesman to buy a six-month-old car before they even get as far as the showroom door. Behind-the-scenes arguments ensue as to the customer's intentions and to whom the commission should go, particularly if the customer has always purchased 'new' before. Similar arguments occur within each team as to who the customer 'belongs' to: comments such as, 'She was *my* customer, I talked to her first but Debbie signed her up on my day off – I deserve a percentage', are frequently heard and in an industry where base salaries are low and made up by commission, are hardly surprising.

Sales techniques can range from the subtle to the not so subtle. Subtle, in that test drives will always take a left-turn route so that the 'prospect' does not feel worried or unsure about how a car will perform if they have to turn right across the traffic. Not so subtle is the use of 'controlled selling' techniques where 'prospects', on a flimsy excuse of taking the used car for a test drive, find themselves minus keys and virtually locked in a room until they sign on the dotted line.

After-sales

This area also tends to fall into two distinct sections: Service and Parts. The Parts department serves two masters: the general public (be it a self-employed motor mechanic or a private car owner intent on doing his own servicing) and the Service department itself. The Parts manager is under increasing pressure to keep his inventory levels as low as possible and is frequently heard on the telephone trying to 'borrow' essential but seldom-used parts from other Lifestyle dealers in the region. The Service technicians are highly trained mechanics who these days have traded in their ring spanners for state-of-the-art computer diagnostics. They are paid by the number of jobs they complete. Taylorism is alive and well in the motor industry: each job has a set time allotted to it and listed in the job book. Therefore if a technician can 'beat the book', not only are they paid for the number of hours that it should have taken but they can also go on to another job. It is not unusual, therefore, for a technician to be paid for seventy-five hours having only physically worked for thirty-nine. Clearly, therefore, there is tension between workshop and Parts: the former don't want to be held up waiting for a part which the department is trying to locate at another dealership.

Against this general background we then have the manufacturer imposing strict controls in all areas from the showroom layout to the procedure for warranty claims. As mentioned, the car industry is a competitive one and Lifestyle have decided to introduce an even greater element of competition by introducing a set of 'customer care principles' against which each dealer will be measured. Ten in total, five for Sales and five for After-sales (but primarily Service), they detail the main stages in a customer transaction and include areas such as 'manner, tone and attitude of the salesman', 'quality of purchase experience' and 'right first time, every time' for Service. Performance against standards will be measured by customer questionnaires and each dealership will be given their results in a monthly league table for the whole region. Lifestyle have decided that each dealer who consistently falls below the region average will lose discounts – a not inconsiderable amount of money over the year.

After the first quarter's figures had been issued, Alan Ratchett called a meeting of all staff and explained the results. Overall they were below the group average in the following areas:

- Customers considered that salesmen were too 'pushy' and they felt that they were abandoned once the deal had been done with them.

- Service department was experiencing a high level of repeat repairs. Further analysis showed that this was partly due to standard of work but also due to the fact that the fault could not be immediately rectified because parts were unavailable and had to be ordered.

All in all, if the dealership were to continue on this slippery slope it stood to lose up to £30,000 in the coming year. Asking each of his managers to come up with some solutions 'PDQ', Alan Ratchett then wandered around the dealership where he overheard the following comments:

- *'I don't know why he's getting at us – the customer care principles don't include Parts.'* (Parts manager)

- *'I hope he's not going to change the payment system unless he's going to double wages. 'Beating the book' is the only way I can earn a living wage.'* (Technician)

- *'I try to "move the metal" so that I get my commission and keep Lifestyle happy and now they're saying that I'm too pushy – in this job you have to be, otherwise somebody else gets the deal.'* (New-car salesman)

- *'We'd be a lot better off if Parts got their act together.'* (Workshop supervisor)

- *'We do the best we can and Service lets us down each time.'* (Used-car salesman)

- *'A lot of the problems are due to the Lifestyle warranty procedure – they're just too picky and that's why it seems as if we're getting repeat repairs.'* (Service manager)

Returning to his office Ratchett murmured to himself, 'I just don't know what to do. I read an article recently about 'quality circles' but you need a spirit of cooperation for that – this lot aren't even speaking to each other.'

 ## Activity brief

1 Identify reasons for the breakdown in intergroup communications and suggest ways that they might be overcome.

2 Do you consider that the different departments at Ratchetts are groups or teams? Justify your answer.

3 Taking the role of a management consultant, prepare a report for Alan Ratchett as to how things might be improved in his dealership.

 ## Just another cog in the machine?

Englishmen have been known to behave in a superior way about their cricket: what other country can boast a competitive event of such complexity and which lasts five whole days? 'Le Tour de France', reply the equally smug French, who as good as founded cycling by inventing the penny farthing in the 1860s.

The Tour can last twenty-four days, involving nearly two hundred competitors who endure all kinds of weather from Mediterranean heatwaves to mountain blizzards and cycle nearly two-and-a-half thousand miles, crossing borders into as many as seven countries. Like cricket, its jargon is so impenetrable that books about it need a glossary and the outsider might well be forgiven for thinking that, as in cricket, for hour after hour nothing really happens. When it comes to the Tour, Frenchmen have it in their bones, but the English can find themselves on a sticky wicket. Would *they* know the difference between the yellow, the green and the polka dot jerseys? Or between the general ranking, the team ranking and the points ranking? The standard stage, the time trial stage and the criterium? What *réel, fictif,* and *village* starts are? Do they understand what an escape is? Or a *domestique*? Or a neutralised section? Yet this is the biggest annual sporting event in the world: it is claimed that twenty million people watch it from the roadside and that nine hundred million in more than 120 countries watch it on television.

The event is clearly extremely complex, involving many interacting groups. The *Société du Tour de France*, a body roughly thirty-strong, connected with a company that publishes two sports papers in France, has to coordinate a great variety of groups, all necessary to the operation. There are the local authorities of the towns and counties that host the start of each stage of the race (and who pay tens of thousands of pounds for the privilege), police departments throughout on the route (for shutting off roads, attending to security, etc.), sponsors who make up the huge publicity cavalcade (1,500 vehicles) that precedes the cycle race and who cover 60 per cent of the Tour's costs, the hoteliers who will house and feed the Tour at each stage, journalists who need to follow the race with their cameras and microphones in their shared cars and on motor bikes, medical services, the army of stewards, timekeepers and judges, and, of course, the racing teams themselves, usually about twenty, with nine riders each.

Each of these groups are complex in themselves, of course. Just to take the racing teams, they include the cyclists, their manager, their *soigneur* (who looks after the athletes' physical needs, including their daily massage), their mechanic (an honour and a privilege in the Italian teams, says Laurent Fignon, Tour winner in 1983 and 1984), and sometimes their doctor, whose job is not merely to attend to injuries (falls during races are not at all infrequent) but also to supervise the riders' diet and prescribe the many products riders need to accomplish such a gruelling feat. These include vitamins and minerals and, it is often alleged, stronger fare. Paul Kimmage, a successful Irish racer, has written about such practices in his book, *A Rough Ride* (1990). As well as good-humoured games like 'hunt the syringe' in riders' back pockets, Kimmage also speaks movingly of the pressure he felt to conform with group practices in this illegal and dangerous area. The first ever English rider to wear the overall leader's yellow jersey, Tommy Simpson, died on a climb in the 1967 Tour from a combination of the exertion and drugs.

Inevitably, then, a group with such a variety of roles will have complex dynamics. To look just at the cyclists, it could seem that the key is to blend teamwork and a share of the limelight for each individual. Teams in recent times, however, have been sponsored by commercial firms such as Panasonic, Motorola and Renault who obviously want as high a profile as possible for their products. One result is that the cyclists fall into two categories, the leader(s) and the team riders. The leader is the star and it is the job of his team to do everything they can to help him win. These *domestiques* must shelter him from the wind, if he gets behind, pace him back into the *peloton* (the main pack, a minimum of about twenty riders who spend most of the stage together making the job that much easier for all its members), fetch food and water for him, give him their bikes if needed and even push him while he urinates. In return they get reflected glory and, as a consequence of their efforts, often most of the cash the star wins. All the riders are required to exhibit on their clothing the names of the many subsidiary sponsors who help with the cost of the venture, and are encouraged to wear team tracksuits at all non-racing times. In practice, rooming, planning, eating and, of course, racing together, mean that there is precious little time for partners or wives during the month of the Tour.

112

Clearly the task of the team manager/trainer is a particularly complex one. He has to handle the star, who sometimes demands more control than he should have, the jealousies and disappointments of the team riders, the esteem needs of absolutely vital contributors such as the mechanic, the solicitations from outsiders such as the media and hangers-on, the demands of the sponsors and so on. He needs authority but has to be a friend too, dealing with individuals from different social classes (unlike, say, the medical staff or indeed the first competitive cyclists, many racers come from working class, often rural, backgrounds), frequently many different countries (since teams are no longer nationally representative), and different ages. The Peugeot team of 1982 actually had so many stars (Roche, Millar and Yates) that it did badly because they competed with each other. The new manager had to cut down the number of top riders to get the team back to winning ways.

Launched in 1903, the Tour's history is bristling with stories that add colour to the rather general description above. Racing had begun well before the Tour though, for manufacturers organised races to promote their cycling wares. They found that longer races were more effective for this and an early anecdote concerns the winner of the 1,500 kilometre race in the *vélodrome d'hiver* in 1893, who devised a tube to urinate down while riding, thereby avoiding stops. To motivate racers now, the Tour offers prizes for practically everything: the longest breakaway, the most combative performance, the most elegant rider, the most amiable . . .

It was as prize money grew (well over a million pounds now in the Tour) that more working-class riders were attracted to the sport. One of the first champions actually rode a bike all day as a news courier and the competitiveness is aptly illustrated by the incident where a pretty admirer offered him a rose, which his manager snatched away just in time to avoid his rider being chloroformed by it. The Tour was launched as part of a circulation war between two sports papers and, in earlier races, competing commercial concerns and towns were not averse to scattering glass or nails on the road to halt the show in front of their patch. Even now, a rider might be permitted by his opponents to lead the field as he goes through his home village. But it was not unknown for riders to be deliberately obstructed, even beaten up, or for the riders themselves to take a train to get ahead. One photo of the 1927 Tour shows a group of riders having a break for a cigarette. When urine tests came in, competitors occasionally topped up their sample with someone else's offering. One tested cyclist, relieved to get a negative report was, however, surprised to find that he was pregnant!

Renowned for his aggression ('Being a racing cyclist makes you both aggressive and vindictive'), Bernard Hinault is one of only three riders to have won the Tour five times. His dealings with team-mate, Greg LeMond, were much criticized during his winning years, especially in the 1985 and 1986 Tours ('Americans seem to me to be lacking in humility!'). Less dramatic, but more interesting perhaps, is his reputation for being a highly professional cyclist who knew how to organise his team so that he would win with as little effort as possible. This is one area where the English *do* need tuition if they are to understand how careful planning can produce strategies which slow the race down, impede dangerous competitors, give up small prizes to secure the big one, and so on. It is a highly technical matter but a fascinating example of how the work group can control the job. Hinault took this attitude into the public arena when he led a riders' strike to stop the organisers making the riders take tiring train journeys between Tour stages in search of more demanding, dramatic and therefore lucrative routes. As it is, up to 40 per cent of the competitors fail to finish the race.

Despite his ruthless reputation, Hinault was very team-oriented, insisting on the sharing of plans, giving team riders their chances, seeing they received large parts of the prize money, arguing that rooming arrangements should be on a rota so that everyone got to know everyone else, changing places at the meal table – in other words insisting that the social and the task functions of the group were each attended to. 'You don't win races alone,' he said, 'you win because others help you and sacrifice their own chances.' When he changed to Bernard Tapie's team in 1983 he found there was a financial and public relations manager in addition to the usual mix. To be fair, too, Greg LeMond did win in 1986 and seemed to build on Hinault's example by being even more businesslike and determined. He was shot in a hunting incident in 1987, yet got back to fitness and won the Tour again in 1989 and 1990. The French often found his American approach to the race rather odd, especially the way he frequently had his family with him. But as he said himself, 'I have won for a team of which my family is part.' The 1990s star is not French either. Miguel Indurain, a Spaniard, rode in 1994 to become only the second rider in history to win the Tour four times in succession. Happily for the French, the first was a Norman, Jacques Anquetil.

For the comic writer Pierre Daninos, the Tour is distinguished by the fact that it is the police themselves, some twenty thousand of them, that actually paralyse the traffic. Cricket would hardly cause such a standstill. Twenty times more people watch football matches than cricket matches in Britain. And to some extent the popularity of a sport depends on media coverage. Television gave snooker a tremendous boost and the Tour could not do without such coverage since a spectator at the roadside can see no more than a few minutes of the race a day and needs papers to identify riders and television to understand the overall shape of the competition as it progresses. It was Channel 4 television that started to break down the ignorance of the British with regard to the Tour. Its daily coverage was so popular that it has had to go to repeats and moving the programme to prime time. In 1994 there was still no UK-sponsored team but the reputation of the Tour was considerably enhanced there when two of the stages of the Tour de France were raced in England, one from Dover to Brighton, and the other a circuit starting and ending in Portsmouth.

The Tour's visit to Hampshire was expected to generate between five and ten million pounds' worth of revenue: in the short term (for hotels, restaurants, pubs, cycling shops, £10-a-day car parks, etc.) and, in the longer term, from the countless people who would be introduced to the area's historic sites and beautiful English countryside, hopefully to return as holiday-makers or business investors. But for that prize the local authorities, as well as investing about half a million pounds, had to accomplish a huge organisational feat. They began three years before the event. Technical officers, police officials and newspaper people visited the Tour in action in France several times. A Joint Authorities Panel of Hampshire and Portsmouth was set up; negotiations entered into with other authorities through whose districts the route would pass; and a central project team was formed to coordinate the three big events of the 1994 summer: Portsmouth's 800-year celebrations, D-Day and the Tour. The team comprised a project director and deputy, a coordinator, phone and desk receptionist, and commercial, advertising, hospitality, tourist, liaison, transport and associated events officers. A special booklet of instructions was produced for the one thousand volunteer marshals who were organised into sectors with a supervisor for each section and a key marshal for every twenty or so volunteers. The project also galvanised a multitude of other groups such as the Southern Tourist Board, intercounty police committees and the Greater Portsmouth Hoteliers Association, whose particular job it was to provide hospitality for the visitors and who hit on the idea of representing in their various hotels, food and drinks from various French regions. Businesses combined with local authorities to provide day-long festivities on village greens and in pubs and forecourts all along the race route.

The Tour entered the UK through the Channel Tunnel on 5 July and left on Brittany Ferries on 7 July after two days racing, ready to start again in Cherbourg on the morning of 8 July. However, Bernard Hinault would not have needed to complain: the weary riders travelled from Portsmouth to Cherbourg by plane.

 ## Activity brief

1 The Hawthorne experiments (Mullins, pp. 168–9) suggested how groups can control their work tasks. How do racing cyclist teams illustrate such organisational behaviour?

2 On the basis of this account of the Tour, how far would it be true to say that a sporting group can provide its members with an outlet for high spirits, single gender activities and even violent impulses that families, work and friends cannot? Does this idea help distinguish between the notion of team and group? How far do you think contemporary Western environments (television, feminism, private cars, etc.) might weaken the 'club mentality'?

3 Psychologists studying sport have paid a good deal of attention to the connection between group cohesion and effectiveness. They have suggested that they are causally connected in both directions and that the process changes over time (Lambert 1968). Some experiments have even suggested that social tensions in a group can improve its effectiveness (Lenk 1969). How far do you see the Tour as exemplifying any of these conclusions?

 ## Hovertech plc

See Mullins, p. 197.

Activity one: Build your own dinosaur!

Logistics

The group should be divided into smaller groups of between four and eight. You will require a large picture of a dinosaur, which you will then need to 'slice' vertically so that each group can be provided with their own 'slice' that they have to build.

An observer should be appointed to each group who will give feedback to the group at the end of the exercise.

Task

Using the materials provided (and only those provided) the group is required to build a dinosaur which is:

● recognisable as such;

● creative in use of materials;

● with the maximum dimensions of 18 inches from head to toe and 18 inches from head to tail.

Method

Each group will be briefed as to which part of the dinosaur they will be building.

Materials provided

Plasticine	2 sheets of A4 plain paper
2 sheets of newspaper	Glue
String	Drinking straws
Felt tip pens	Blueprint of dinosaur

Time allowed

The total time allowed for this exercise is forty minutes. At the end of this period each group will take their part of the dinosaur to the coordinator. Groups should then reassemble and take twenty minutes to hear the feedback from the observer and discuss their own group performance. This discussion can be shared with the others if wished.

Discussion points

Discussion can centre around the following areas:

● How small groups work together (or don't).

● The need for communication, cooperation and communication between groups in order to get a task completed successfully.

Activity provided by Beverley Wallace, Gowrings (Newbury) Ltd.

Activity two: Working together

Materials required

One box of Polydron material (a building kit available from the Early Learning Centre) for each group. You will need to check and sort the boxes so that each contains identical shapes and colours. The person managing the activity should use one box to create a structure of their choice but do not allow participants to see what has been created until instructed to do so.

Logistics

Divide the particpants into groups of four, to a maximum of five groups.

Group briefing

- Each group will be given an identical box of building materials.
- Each group of four will consist of two builders and two architects.
- Architects may visit the structure one at a time. Their role is to communicate the design brief to the builders. They may not draw, record or use their hands to help describe the structure. Their communication with the builders is entirely oral.
- Builders may not visit the structure – their role is to reproduce the structure according to the architects' brief.
- There is no time limit to the completion of this activity.

Discussion points

- What was happening during the activity?
- What were the barriers and blocks to success?
- What worked really well?
- What was happening as the group worked on the task together?

Activity provided by Anne Chivers, Defence Research Agency.

 # Activity three: Group role analysis

See Mullins, pp. 220.

 # Activity four: Wilderness survival exercise

See Mullins, pp. 223–6.

Debate one

'Training in group dynamics, whilst interesting, has no practical value as a means of increasing group effectiveness.'

Starting points

For

- Group dynamics can identify and highlight more problems than it can solve and as a result can actually *detract* from performance.
- The group should exist to do, and, indeed, are paid to do, a job of work. They don't need cossetting and pampering – it's a waste of money.

Against

- A manager needs to know and understand how a group functions and how people relate to each other in order to be able to point them in the right direction.
- Knowledge of group dynamics can lead the group towards self-awareness which can result in empowering them to improve their own performance and effectiveness.

Further reading

Campbell, C. L. and Dunnette, M. D. (1968), 'Effectiveness of T-Group Experiences in Managerial Training and Development' , *Psychological Bulletin*, **70** (2), 73–103.

Cooper, C. L. and Mangham, I. L. (eds) (1971), *T-Groups: A Survey of Research*, Wiley.

Luft, J. (1970), *Group Processes: An Introduction to Group Dynamics*, 2nd edn, National Press.

 # Debate two

'Individuals will complete a task more effectively and efficiently than a group.'

Starting points

For

- It takes a considerable amount of time to build a group; it *has* to go through the various stages of development until it completes them – if ever.
- There are too many uncertainties surrounding groups: groupthink, risky-shift, and so on, which make them suspect.
- People prefer to be evaluated on their own performance and to be able to see a direct link between their own effort and outcome.

Against

- In a group there is a greater likelihood of creativity in both problem-solving and implementing decisions.

- Behaviour can be controlled more effectively and commitment gained more effectively through the imposition of group norms.

- Groups will happen anyway, so we might as well harness their strengths.

Further reading

Allcorn, S. (1989), 'Understanding Groups at Work', *Personnel*, **66** (8), August, 28–36.

Grayson, D. (1990), 'Self Regulating Work Groups – An Aspect of Organizational Change', ACAS Work Research Unit Occasional Paper No.146, July, HMSO.

✓ Look, it really works!

1 One of the groups of students taught by the authors are on a one-year full-time postgraduate management course. In one particular year the group was made up of a wide variety of ages (from twenty-one to forty-five), a variety of nationalities, some with no work experience and some with twenty-five years' experience. The group was 70 per cent male.

For their major OB assignment of the year (which carried a 70 per cent weighting towards their final mark), the author decided to set a group assignment which consisted of some research, some analysis, a presentation to a panel of visiting managers and a written report. Normally, at this stage of their studies it would be expected that each group would form naturally but because in this particular year it had been noticed that there was a very definite 'in' group and 'out' group (one academically strong and the other weaker), the lecturer decided to predetermine the groups. Each group comprised a representative sample of gender, nationality, work experience and academic ability because the lecturer thought that this would make things fairer and that the group members would learn more from each other if they were so mixed. Oh, how wrong can you be! There was intergroup and intra-group conflict and rivalry, deputations to the lecturer to change the groups, and complaints about the assignment. Interestingly, although there was no group cohesion towards getting the assignment completed, there was a high degree of cohesion against the common enemy, the lecturer, which continued long after the assignment had been completed.

Can you see how strong the influence of the informal group can be and the problems associated with attempts to break it up?

Can you also see where the power of individual motivation comes into play? It was a final assignment with a high weighting of marks – the drive to succeed was so strong that students didn't want to be associated with others whom they perceived as weaker academically and who might pull down the final mark.

2 For an example of how informal groups govern individual behaviour, have a look at 'Prisoner Cell Block H' (any episode will do – they're all rich in examples). For the purposes of this section we've created a composite scenario.

The scene is set in the prison laundry where tension has been rising. No doubt some of it has to do with those endless blue sheets and overalls but the majority of it is to do with who is to be 'top dog' – the informal leader for the prisoners. Various fights ensue and Bea Smith emerges as victor. From now on the prisoners will take their cue from her and even the warders will take notice (although this occurs in different ways: Miss Ferguson works against Bea, Mrs Morris – representing the 'caring' face of officialdom – tries to work through her). Maybe Bea isn't the staff's idea of the perfect leader but group consensus has voted her in.

Another classic example occurs in the next scene. A prisoner is beaten up (any spurious reason will do) and accuses Bea who is promptly despatched to 'solitary' for forty-eight hours to ponder the error of her ways. The prisoner is beaten up again and warned of the perils of being overaccurate with the truth. The scene cuts to a hospital bed where, when asked 'Who did this to you?', the prisoner replies through suitably swollen lips, 'I didn't see anyone'. Ferguson turns to the Governor and says, 'It sounds like a lesson in "lagging"'. 'I don't care,' says the Governor, 'I shall find out who did it.' What chance do *you* think she has against such strong group norms?

 ## Assignment one

Using the Belbin Self-perception Inventory in Mullins (pp. 220–3) select a group of people to study. Your group could be from an organisation which you know, from an informal group of students or from a 'hobby' group (e.g. a sports club committee).

Explain to the group what you are planning to do (and why) and then administer the questionnaire. Ask individual members to score their own answers. Analyse the results and present the findings:

1 As an oral presentation with appropriate visual aids.
2 As a written report of not more than 1,500 words to be submitted to both the group studied and your tutor.

Remember that, depending on both the group you choose and the results, you may raise more questions than you'll be able to answer. You may need to use a considerable degree of tact and patience, particularly with group members who disagree with their ranking and you'll certainly need to be very fully conversant with the Belbin work in order to present it well and to be able to handle questions.

 ## Assignment two

Mullins (chapter 6) identifies many different kinds of group: formal, informal, defensive, non-defensive, apathetic, strategic, and so on. Working either individually or in small groups use these categories to differentiate any *four* of the groups in the following list, justifying your decisions. Is it possible to use just two categories – social and work groups – to differentiate between these examples? Indicate, if necessary, where the two types overlap within a group.

a semi-professional jazz band	a family
a racing cyclist team	a hikers club
a yacht club	a section of The Women's Institute
a special events project group	a doctors' partnership in a health centre
a street gang	a class of students
a team of workmen	a submarine crew
an amateur dramatics group	a voluntary or charity organisation

Write up your findings in not more than 2,000 words and, if you worked in a small group for this assignment, include a one-page report on how the group worked during the assignment. You may find the following suggestions helpful for this:

● What type of group were you?

● What roles were taken by individual group members? Were these roles chosen by the individuals or given to them by the rest of the group?

● Who was the leader and did they emerge naturally?

● Did the leadership change? Why?

● Did everyone work together or did some opt out? Why?

Try and be as objective and constructive as possible when writing this part of the report. Equally try to be critically analytical about group roles and so forth. Comments such as 'The group worked well together and Matthew did the typing' are not really what is wanted.

 ## Assignment three

Working in a small group, elect an observer and then, starting with a brainstorming session (for an example, see Mullins, pp. 214–15), invent a board game based on the Tour de France.

Present your game to the wider group. Each group will be judged by other groups using the following criteria:

● creativity;

● presentation of the game;

● interest likely to be engendered; and

● simplicity and ease of playing the game.

Have your observer report on the group's functioning throughout the exercise, using theories such as 'groupthink', 'risky-shift', 'interaction analysis' and so on to help with the explanations.

! Pause for thought

1 Once upon a time a British company and a Japanese company decided to have a competitive boat race on the river Thames. Both teams practised long and hard to reach their peak performance. On the big day they were both as ready as they could be.

The Japanese won by a mile.

Afterwards the British team became very discouraged by their loss and morale plummeted. Senior management decided that the reason for the crushing defeat had to be found and a project team was set up to investigate the problem and recommend appropriate action.

Their conclusion: the Japanese team had eight people rowing and one person steering. The British team had one person rowing and eight people steering. Senior management hired a consultancy company to do a study on the team structure. Millions of pounds and several months later, the consultancy company concluded that too many people were steering and not enough were rowing.

To prevent another loss to the Japanese the following year, the team structure was changed to: four steering managers, three senior steering managers and one executive steering manager. A new performance system was set up for the person rowing the boat to give more incentive to work harder and become a key performer. 'We must get it right first time, every time' the British were heard to say.

The next year the Japanese won by *two* miles. The British company made the rower redundant for poor performance, sold off all the paddles, cancelled all capital investment for new equipment, halted development of a new boat, awarded high performance awards to the consultants, and distributed the money saved to senior executives . . .

2 In June 1994 Ray Illingworth, the new, tough manager of the English cricket team sacked the team's chaplain saying: 'Anyone who needs a chaplain shouldn't be in the English cricket team.' However, snooker player Dennis Taylor won the world championship after employing a psychologist to help him. Laurent Fignon, twice winner of the Tour de France, said that his 1993 Italian team, Gatorade, had five doctors servicing it.

The announcement by the BBC that a counselling service was available for employees who might be experiencing emotional difficulties following their involvement with the coverage of the celebrations for the fiftieth anniversary of the D-Day landings was met with much derision.

The Bodyshop head office in Littlehampton, West Sussex, employs an occupational health specialist known throughout the organisation as 'The Company Carer'.

Do we *really* need to attend to the spiritual, physical and psychological needs of groups of employees or is this just another trendy fad for the 1990s?

? Still not convinced?

1 Think back to your first day at college (and some of us have to think back further than others). It's 9.15, you're all in the lecture theatre and the course manager is about to do the 'welcome to the course and have a great time' bit. You listen with one ear and glance nervously around at the people who'll be your companions over the next three or four years. These are the people you'll work with, get drunk with, go out with and perhaps live with (although not necessarily in that order). Surprise, surprise! They're all wearing the same type of clothes: jeans which are just sufficiently worn out to be acceptable and a slightly faded sweatshirt (ideally either advertising a rock band's tour from about two years ago or, failing that, a brand of real ale). Then you notice a lone soul sitting in the corner in *brand new* jeans (with a crease up the centre) and a *brand new* chain store sweatshirt. They look totally out of it and you decide to give them a wide berth: definitely an oddity, that one. Still, the rest look OK.

What has happened here is that you've all been through the process of anticipatory socialisation: you want to be accepted by the group in general and so you start by wearing the sort of clothes which will immediately identify you with that group. Luckily for you, you got it right. Unluckily for the other one, they had the right idea but got it ever so slightly wrong.

(If you want a further example of anticipatory socialisation/group norms, remember back to the same period but a little later into your college life when the groups had begin to form and courses and faculties began to differentiate themselves: the pharmacists always drank more than anyone else; the engineers always wore leather jackets; the computer boffins were altogether different (you know what we mean . . .)

2 **Kirk's Team Saves The World (Again . . .)***
Captain's log: Stardate 8454.2

My senior officers and I have taken command of the new USS *Enterprise*, after six charges against us were dismissed by a Starfleet Federation Court Martial. The court was swayed in our favour because we had recently saved Earth from the depredations of an immense, intergalactic hump-backed whale; armed as we were with nothing more than a clapped-out Klingon bird of prey and Scotty's recipe for transparent aluminium.

This has prompted me to reflect on the qualities which enable my crew and I to function so successfully as a team and have found the writings of a twentieth-century management author, Dr. R. Meredith Belbin, most interesting in this context (as Spock would say). I therefore asked the ship's computer to undertake an analysis of our respective team roles using the Belbin model.

Science Officer Spock's sober logic, his capacity for accurate data-based analysis and his habit of making decisions only when he has fully evaluated all possible options mark him out as a *monitor-evaluator* in Belbin's typology. His somewhat clinical judgements mean, however, that he does not make an inspiring

*Provided by Gill Norris, University of Portsmouth.

leader and his openly expressed criticism frequently causes him to clash with the ship's doctor.

Dr McCoy's outspoken and often argumentative cynicism makes him a prickly, but highly expert, individualist. He is quick to challenge and frequently expresses himself in a provocative, colourful, even hurtful manner. His courage, often born of outrage at stupidity or petty bureaucracy, is also typical of the **shaper's** team role.

Communications Officer Uhura is a popular and friendly crew member; frequently confidante to Scott, Chekov and Sulu, and able to smooth over tensions and conflicts between senior officers. An accomplished singer and musician, she is always ready to entertain her colleagues during off-duty moments and this indicates her role as the sociable *teamworker*.

Chief Engineer Scott is our *specialist*. Devoted to his dilythium-powered engines and knowing every inch of the *Enterprise* like the back of his hand, he is typically single-minded and dedicated, though sometimes too preoccupied with technicalities to bother with overall mission objectives.

Our extrovert **Helmsman, Mr Sulu,** is outward-looking, open to new ideas and experiences, though some of his enthusiasms are short lived. He shows many characteristics of the *resource investigator*.

Navigator Chekov is destined for Starship command. As a conscientious all-rounder, he is meticulous to the point of obsession, rarely leaving any task unfinished. He appears to be a *completer*.

As for myself, **James T. Kirk**, the computer indicates that my maturity and confidence, combined with my capacity to optimise the talents of others, make me a *coordinator*. However, it seems that I also exhibit the unorthodox and creative problem-solving tendencies of the *plant* which have led me into more than one clash with Starfleet Command.

We are receiving news of a hostage crisis on Nimbus III; can Belbin's Team Theory save the world once more? Ahead Warp Factor 5, Mr Sulu, and steady as she goes.

9 The context of the organisation

Changing organisation structures and processes at Northern Taverns

This is a case study in organisational change. It is based upon what has been happening in one of northern England's largest public-house (or 'hostelry', as our preferred term)-owning companies. In order to preserve anonymity the name has been changed, along with certain details which are not crucial for our present purposes; the essence of what has occurred (and is likely to occur) has been retained.

The paper is organised as follows:

1 The organisation is briefly described.
2 The changing external contexts of Northern Taverns are outlined.
3 Certain key objectives set by the company are described.
4 You are provided with an activity brief and recommended reading.
5 A note on methodology provides guidance on how you might proceed to collect the necessary data.

Northern Taverns and Northern plc

The plc has its head office in the north of England, from where it runs a number of businesses in a divisionalised mode: taverns, leisure, soft drinks, wines and spirits, and hotels. It is one of the UK's larger operating companies in this sector, employing around forty-five thousand people. This case study is based upon what has been taking place in just one of these divisions – Taverns, although, of course, it is not possible to entirely divorce what has been going on there from what has been happening in the rest of the plc, for there are a number of links and interdependencies between the divisions, for example between Taverns and Hotels, Taverns and Soft Drinks, Taverns and Leisure. The plc agrees objectives and targets that the constituent divisions are expected to achieve over a given time period.

Northern Taverns runs the hostelries and restaurants business of Northern plc. It makes the largest contribution to the plc's profits (having generated over 50 per cent of total profits for a number of years), employs over thirty thousand people, and has 2,000 managed and 1,000 leased hostelries located throughout the northern UK and the Midlands, which are organised into six regions, each region

125

Fig. 9.1 Structure of Northern Taverns

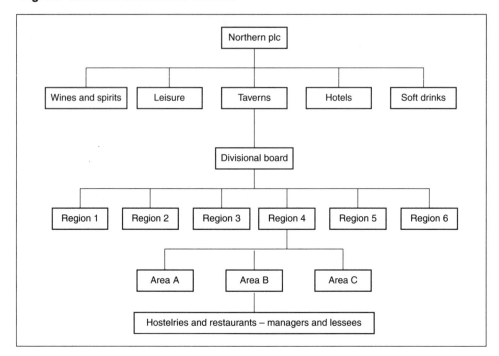

in turn being split into a number of areas; the structure is shown in Figure 9.1.

A variety of specialist services are provided for the staff located at each of these levels, some of them having a presence at just one of the levels, others being duplicated across a number of levels; examples include Acquisitions (for new hostelries or restaurants), Marketing, Construction, Personnel and Training, IT and Finance.

Northern Taverns has recently introduced electronic point-of-sale systems into its outlets to improve control in its hostelries. This has involved substantial capital expenditure, and stock control has shown a marked improvement; however, as yet, the systems are being used less effectively for marketing and business development purposes.

A managing director heads up each of the regions and there exists a strong regional identity – an identity which has been nurtured by Northern Taverns over the years through devices such as distinct trading names reflecting each particular region. Territories and resources are jealously guarded. Risk aversion is the predominant ingredient of decision-making; accountability is thinly spread and this adds up to a conservative orientation. Take the processes involved in identifying and approving a new site for a hostelry, the following specialists take part: Acquisitions, Marketing, Operations, Catering, Personnel, and Finance, and authorisation proceeds from area to region to divisional board to Northern plc. The 'lowest common denominator' rules, and the result has often been, as a member of the company graphically put it, 'cosmic constipation', or 'nothing coming out'.

The predominant orientation to be found in the sector, and Northern Taverns were no exception, can be summarised in the following three phrases:

1 'Hostelry managers are not to be trusted, therefore they must be controlled.'

2 'The hostelry is supply-driven – the "shop window" for a range of ales and lagers.'

3 'Individual outlet performance is the key consideration.'

The social and organisational nature of the company may be conveniently captured along certain key dimensions as shown in Figure 9.2).

On the basis of this overview of Northern Taverns' structure and culture, let us now move on to consider the key ways in which the contexts of its operations have been changing in recent years.

Changing external contexts

Four key contextual influences over Northern Taverns' business in recent years can be identified: (i) changing consumer preferences, (ii) economic recession, (iii) competition, and (iv) state/legislation. Taking each in turn: (i) examples include the impact of the health food and drink lobby, and the shift away from the 'on trade' (buying drink and food in hostelries) to the 'off trade': that is, people buying all or most of their wine, spirits and beer from supermarkets or off-licences for consumption at home; (ii) as a result of the later 1980s and early 1990s economic recession, many people had less discretionary spending power, and the cheaper prices to be found in some parts of the off trade became more appealing as a result; (iii) with respect to competition, examples would include the mergers and alliances which have been formed between brewing and retailing groups, the entry of foreign brewing companies into the UK market, and the regeneration of hostelries by smaller independent companies which have focused upon service, choice and variety of real ales, and a return to the basics of a 'good local'; (iv) finally, as a

Fig. 9.2 Key dimensions of Northern Taverns

Dimension	The existing situation	Your proposed solution
People	were *controlled*	
Structure	was *hierarchically based*	
Business expertise	was based upon *function*	
The manager	was the *supervisor*	
The board	act as *scorekeeepers*	
Senior management's priority	was *control*	
Values	were *defensive*	
A VIP	was a *manager*	

result of the 'Beer Orders' issued by the UK Government in the late 1980s, a ceiling was put on the number of hostelries which could be owned by a brewing group where those hostelries were tied in terms of supply to that particular group.

For Northern Taverns (as a division of Northern plc) this has meant that it has been forced to sell off over 1,000 hostelries during the period 1990–2 in order to comply with the 'Orders', and, although it is now below its ceiling, there is a strict limit on how many more hostelries it can open without simultaneously closing others.

Objectives

In 1994 Northern plc agreed the following objectives with Northern Taverns, to be achieved by 1999:

1 Outperform the 'on trade' competition by 10 per cent.

2 Increase net profit per £ taken from 8p to 16p.

3 Increase hostelry sales volume by an average of 10 per cent.

4 Open one new hostelry every month, and lease at least one hostelry every week.

 # Activity brief

1 Consider the options available to Northern Taverns for achieving the objectives set by the plc, focusing upon the people and organisational issues and possibilities. Outline these in report form, discussing the advantages and disadvantages of each. Make a recommendation as to your favoured option, justifying this choice.

2 Critically outline and discuss the concepts, models and perspectives which can be drawn upon from the behavioural social sciences in order to make sense of the social structures and processes which characterise this organisation.

3 Show how a use of the above (2) could be of help to those managers and other actors who have been given the responsibility for achieving the necessary social and organisational changes.

4 Return to Figure 9.2, take each of the dimensions in the first column and produce a new third column which indicates in summary terms what you think the company should move towards from the present situation as described in column 2 (for example, you might want to recommend that the people dimension moves from *control* to *empowerment*). Write a sentence or two on each of them, explaining why you have made this choice.

A note on methodology

We recommend that students read a sample of the annual reports of the national and regional brewery and pub companies; examples include: (i) under the national banner:

Whitbread, Scottish & Newcastle, Bass; (ii) under the regional banner: Greene King, Wolverhampton & Dudley, Eldridge Pope, Marstons, Wadworths.

It is perfectly possible to answer all the above questions on the basis of knowledge of the behavioural social science literature, and, indeed, it is *essential* that students draw upon and use this understanding in responding to the questions. In other words, it *can* be treated as a library/secondary material-based exercise. However, as strong advocates of fieldwork or 'getting involved in the action', we recommend that, if time and opportunity allow, you visit some hostelries and talk to/interview the bar staff and managers (indeed, if you are an undergraduate student, it is quite possible that you do part-time bar work yourself, thus facilitating the process). You can pick up information simply by sitting in the hostelry or standing at the bar, that is, through a form of participant observation. The better answers will likely be based upon a sound reading around the area *and* fieldwork, where the information and ideas coming out of the former are fed into the latter, and vice versa, in an iterative mode.

So, when you next go down to your local hostelry for a pint or two of real ale, you'll be able to inform your friends and tutor that you have been taking the research for your coursework seriously, and that you got so absorbed in the work that you ended up staying all evening . . . Cheers!

Further reading

Annual reports of regional and national brewery and public-house-owning companies.

Buchanan, D. and Boddy, D. (1992), *The Expertise of the Change Agent*, Prentice Hall.

Carnall, C. (1990), *Managing Change in Organisations*, Prentice Hall.

Dawson, P. (1994), *Organizational Change: A Processual Approach*, Paul Chapman.

Huczynski, A. and Buchanan, D. (1991), *Organizational Behaviour: An Introductory Text*, 2nd edn, Prentice Hall (esp. chs 15, 16, 18, 19 and 20).

Kanter, R. M. (1983), *The Change Masters*, Allen & Unwin.

Kanter, R. M. (1989), *When Giants Learn to Dance*, Simon & Schuster.

Pettigrew, A. and Whipp. R. (1991), *Managing Change for Competitive Success*, Blackwell.

Case provided by David Preece, Gordon Steven and Valerie Steven: People, Innovation and New Technology Research Group. The People, Innovation and New Technology Research Group consists of members from three UK universities (Portsmouth, Coventry and Nottingham) and one of the UK's major brewing and pub retailing companies. It was founded by the authors of the present case and is based at the University of Portsmouth.

 # The organisational setting in Spain

Spain has undergone important changes in business, political and social environments in the last forty years. These changes have been instrumental in helping both public and private organisations make the transition from the authoritarian/bureaucratic style of organisational control to being dynamic and outward-looking. However, this organisational change has not been able to keep up with the pace of change in the external environment, and Spain still lags behind her European partners in many areas, having a negative effect on the competitiveness of Spanish businesses.

Traditionally the culture that has predominated has been characterised by the size and importance of the state sector under the aegis of the Instituto Nacional de Industria (INI), and a rigid, monolithic state bureaucracy which offered civil servants at all grades a job for life; a large number of small and medium-sized firms, many with strong family links that led to a static hierarchical organisational structure; a pool of cheap and compliant labour which removed the impetus to invest in and develop new technologies; and an inward-looking productive structure which was highly protected and therefore denied the challenge of competition. The stability provided by the authoritarian regime of General Franco before 1975, and the cosy relationship between business, banks and government, allowed business organisations and government agencies to forgo long-term planning. Spanish firms thus failed to identify long-term strategic objectives and short-termism, insularity and quick profits for business became the norm.

One significant event which helped force organisations in Spain to change in the second half of this century was the abandonment of the policy of autarky in the late 1950s which led to a partial lifting of government controls on the location and expansions of business and fewer restrictions on foreign investment in Spain. The post-war economic prosperity in Western Europe provided Spain with an influx of tourists and an outlet for workers looking for better pay and conditions abroad. Income from tourism, emigrant remittances and foreign investment led to an economic boom in the country which led to a proliferation of new private business organisations and a more pragmatic approach to the control of the political economy. However the influence of these factors only laid the groundwork for future changes. Foreign investment led to 'a modern, dynamic component of large firms grafted on to the pre-existing world of predominantly small companies' (Shubert 1990), while new ideas on forms of social interaction brought in by tourists and returning emigrants were repressed or rejected by the narrow, authoritarian, blinkered view of the administration and many managers. On the surface at least, there was little movement from the mechanistic organisation and its rigid structures and the organic organisation, more appropriate in a changing environment, identified by Burns and Stalker (Mullins 1993).

Even after the collapse of the authoritarian regime in Spain in the mid-1970s, the political and economic turmoil was not conducive to the introduction of innovative management structures. While the emphasis was on political change, the machinery of state administration changed very little and another layer of bureaucracy was added with the creation of seventeen autonomous communities each with their own regional parliaments and their own administrative structure. The oil crises of 1974 and 1979 left Spanish companies reeling, unable to come to terms with the speed and scope of the changes taking place in the external environment, and unwilling to risk significant changes in internal management structures. This period of crisis led to even greater government intervention in private companies, with the state taking over companies which were in danger of collapse in order to save jobs. This corporatist and paternalistic response from a weak government was allied to a general disenchantment in the business community, which was compounded by the election victory of the Spanish socialist party in the 1982 general elections. There were fears that the government would initiate a policy of nationalisation, support union wage claims and adopt a model of central planning for the economy.

In fact these fears were unfounded. When the socialists came to power 'The Spanish economy was based on an inefficient, backward productive structure. Industry was biased towards consumer goods and traditional sectors, was labour intensive, used outdated technology and had low levels of productivity and competitiveness' (Ferner and Hyman 1994). In order to tackle these problems the government adopted a tight monetarist approach and applied market principles to cut inflation, reduce the balance of payments deficit and promote greater flexibility in business. Another of the commitments of the government was to reduce bureaucracy and initiate a policy of privatisation through a policy of industrial reconversion, that is, restructuring the state sector enterprises to make them more efficient and responsive to market forces.

Not all the government's measures were successful. Public administration fell prey to the party machine and management was again hooked on short-term objectives, governed more by sectoral interests than market principles. On the other hand the adoption of a free market philosophy revitalised the faith in private enterprise as a motor for growth and prosperity and started a shift of young professionals away from the public to the private sector.

These measures that the government took were also aimed at bringing the Spanish economy in line with the other Western European countries in the EC. By 1985 the economic indicators had begun to show a recovery but it was Spain's accession to the EC in 1986 which was the primary impulse for change. Membership of the EC was widely seen as a positive move, which would lead to a process of modernisation and to Spain gaining her rightful place in the Western world. However, there were problems. Membership subjected Spanish companies and industries to a level and intensity of competition that was unheard of, and these changes in the external environment forced organisations in Spain to review the technological, structural, personnel and management systems with which they worked. Some feared that Spain's accession to the EC and the corresponding loss of the protection of tariff barriers would lead to Spain's industries being overwhelmed, while others accepted that the internationalisation of the Spanish economy would provide the stimulus that businessmen and women needed to change attitudes, renovate the industrial base and learn to compete in foreign markets. Initially, during the difficult period of adjustment, many companies were forced to close in the face of foreign competition, but the last half of the 1980s saw Spanish growth rates surpass other EC member states, averaging almost 5 per cent between 1987 and 1990.

Although the economy slumped at the beginning of the 1990s, competition and government policy have gone some way towards modernising the organisational structures. The government has carried out a policy of privatisation, creating a new holding for profitable state industries and a semi-privatised banking group for the different state banks. Private banks have not been slow to adopt practices that have been introduced by foreign banks such as Barclays and NatWest, offering a wider range of services and changing the industry from one based on the bank–client relationship to that of 'an industry based on competition, price and service' (Canals 1994). The liberalisation of the banking sector has led to mergers between and greater competition from savings banks, and banks are at the forefront of new technology in Spain.

The attitudes and skills of the personnel in organisations in Spain is still anchored in the past. 'It would appear that conservatism and paternalistic employment relations remain the dominant characteristics of small-scale capital in Spain' (Ferner and Hyman 1994). The individualism which militates against group work, the acceptance of authority and the mistrust of new ideas are attitudes which need to be overcome if Spanish work organisations are to become more competitive. Another of the serious problems is the quality of education and training in Spain. Only 17 per cent of the working population in Spain between the ages of sixteen and sixty-five have the qualifications that employees are looking for. The demand for university graduates and qualified postgraduates in business outstrips the supply by three to one, and there is a proliferation of MBA courses on offer in the main urban centres.

Given the short supply of skilled manpower, one would expect that the commitment to in-house training in Spanish firms would be high. However, training is not a priority in Spanish firms, coming sixth on the list of priorities. The proportion of overall labour costs in companies dedicated to education and training is 0.2 per cent, compared to an average of 1.5 per cent in other EC countries. Training is often given on an *ad hoc* basis as a 'reward', and not included in the overall corporate strategy of companies, indicating that Spanish companies still have a long way to go in developing the skills that are required to be competitive. New managers are coming out of Spanish Business Schools at a rate of some 11,000 a year, however, with an international outlook and speaking one or two foreign languages. They are learning to be more flexible in the organisational environment and to work outside a narrow, precise sphere of responsibility.

Fears have been expressed that foreign investment and the sale of Spanish companies to foreign firms is leaving the Spanish economy dangerously dependent on the decisions taken abroad. The introduction of foreign capital has, though, meant a change in management structures in Spain, while direct foreign investment has brought with it new working practices and new organisational structures. In Spain there are still organisations with fourteen to sixteen different organisational levels which slows down internal communication and promotes inflexibility, but multinationals such as General Electric have initiated plans to reduce these to four levels in Spain. Decentralisation is also a strategy that the more forward-looking companies are adopting. This, given the authoritarian and hierarchical structure of organisations to date, has often met with opposition from regional managers who are not accustomed to taking important decisions without approval from head office.

The level of technological innovation in an organisation is another of the subsystems that can be used to analyse the competitiveness of a work organisation. Traditionally in Spain low labour costs have been the cornerstone of the competitive advantage of firms. Now, with the widespread application of technology and with spending on research and development programmes, low labour costs have become less of a competitive advantage. Again Spain still spends less than 1.0 per cent of her gross domestic product on research and development, compared to an average of 2.33 per cent in the four leading countries in the European Union – France, Great Britain, Germany and Italy. EC membership has thus had a positive impact, prompting greater official recognition of the need for research and development, but too much is still spent on importing foreign technology.

These are just some of the internal and external environmental influences that are affecting Spanish organisations. The pace of change in the past twenty years has been dramatic, and public and private organisations are struggling to adapt. In many respects Spain is still ten to fifteen years behind the leading member states of Europe, but the commitment to organisational change is coming from local, regional and national government bodies, the education system, and from large and small Spanish and foreign businesses.

 ## Activity brief

1 Prepare an environmental audit of the political, economic, social and technological factors which have most affected organisations in your country or region.

2 Discuss how the management functions in your country, region or immediate organisation differ from those outlined above.

3 Suggest how cultural forces accelerate or slow down changes in organisations in your own country or another country with which you are familiar.

Further reading

Almarcha Barbado, A. (1993), *Spain and EC Membership Evaluated*, Pinter.

Canals, J. (1994), *Competitive Strategies in European Banking*, Clarendon Press.

Ferner, A. and Hyman, R. (1994), *Industrial Relations in the New Europe*, Blackwell.

Randlesome, C. (1993), *Business Cultures in Europe*, Butterworth-Heinemann.

Shubert, A (1990), *A Social History of Modern Spain*, Unwin Hyman.

Case study provided by Bob Gould, University of Portsmouth.

 ## Square Deal plc

See Mullins, pp. 298–9.

 ## Activity one

1 Make a list, either individually or with others, of as many organisations you can think of not specifically mentioned in chapter 3 of Mullins (for example, a tennis club, an art gallery, an amateur theatre society, a children's play group, an orchestra, a farm, a public house darts league, a natural childbirth association, etc).

2 Test this list against the criteria established in Mullins (ch. 3) for identifying an organisation. For example: do they share the 'common factors' (p. 66); or the 'basic components' (p. 70); can they be classified according to one of the theories presented (pp. 73–8); may we think of them as 'open systems'?

3 Look back to the six characteristics that constitute a group (Mullins, ch. 6, p. 168) and consider whether they would be better classified as groups rather than organisations.

This activity should help you revise chapter 3 in Mullins and sharpen your understanding of the concept of the organisation by means of contrast (compare Mullins (p. 135) on external factors that increase attention).

 ## Activity two

1 Select three organisations with which you are familiar, trying none the less to get a good range of types (school, bank, toiletries factory, ferry port, employment agency, town council, etc.).

2 Using the diagram in Mullins (p. 80) as a prompt, establish which elements in the environment of your three organisations have most influenced their behaviour. This could be information technology at the bank leading to unemployment, customer self-service, extended range of products on offer, such as financial advice at the counter, and so on. In a school the environment might include government policy over the last decade or so in Britain: local management of schools, national curriculum, profiling, national testing, examination league tables, parents' charter, and so on. Notice though, that Mullins (p. 353) draws a distinction between 'impersonal' contingencies which the theorists have concentrated on and others such as cultural ones and, in this case, those resulting from 'power factors' (pp. 353, vi).

3 Invent a diagram to show how the behaviour of just *one* of your three organisations is contingent on those environmental factors. There are many kinds of diagram (Venn, flow charts, systems maps, rich pictures, matrices, company charts, etc.) a number of which are used in Mullins (e.g. pp. 5, 116, 121, 217 and 472).

4 Make a list of other variables that may have impinged upon the behaviour which your diagram has suggested is contingent on environmental factors. Remember, simple causal relationships between structure and performance have been queried (Mullins, pp. 352, i) and may indeed be 'casual' [*sic*].

 ## Activity three

See Mullins, p. 62.

 ## Activity four

See Mullins, p. 298.

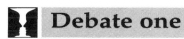

Debate one

'The study of the development of organisation theory has no practical relevance for today's managers.'

Starting points

For

- It provides frameworks and models for managers to measure and assess performance. The 'best' or most suitable aspects from the approaches can be taken and applied to specific organisational issues.

- It is only by looking to the past that we can set the present in its correct context and attempt to predict the future.

Against

- Many of the approaches are now outdated and do not apply to the 'modern' organisation. For example, scientific management is synonymous with 'work study' rather than with current TQM thinking.

- There are too many models and they are too confusingly interrelated to provide a coherent approach to practical application.

Further reading

Etzioni, A. (1986), *Modern Organisations*, Prentice Hall.

Perrow, C. (1986), *Complex Organisations: A Critical Essay,* Random House.

Stewart, R. (1986), *The Reality of Management*, Pan Books.

Debate two

'Profit maximisation is the only criterion by which organisational effectiveness can be judged.'

Starting points

For

- It is the only criterion which can be applied to any organisation and which, therefore, can allow for direct comparison.

- At the end of the day, profit must be any organisation's guiding principle. Without it, there would be neither organisation nor any of the so-called 'soft' objectives.

Against

- Whilst all organisations need to make a profit in order to survive, there is a difference between this and 'maximisation'. The statement implies that this should take precedence over any other issues such as people development, social responsibility, and so forth.

● The statement implies a return to Taylorism. Profit is not the *only* criteria on which effectiveness can be judged and should be considered alongside other, more qualitative measures as well.

Further reading

Drucker, P. F. (1989), *The Practice of Management*, Heinemann.

Roddick, A. (1989), *Body and Soul*, Ebury Press.

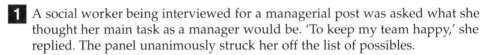

✓ Look, it really works!

 A social worker being interviewed for a managerial post was asked what she thought her main task as a manager would be. 'To keep my team happy,' she replied. The panel unanimously struck her off the list of possibles.

But was she so far from the truth?

Librarians may be heard complaining that people disturb the books on the shelves, university lecturers say how nice it is in the vacation when the students are not in college, and in Britain it has been rumoured that hospitals have been turning away patients who are too sick. These reactions are not surprising if quality (and therefore remuneration and advancement) in these professions is to be measured in terms of short waiting lists, research output and – who knows, one day – clean books? If a charity for the blind specialises in training clients to be more independent, it would be natural enough to select people who are not so very blind, for they would produce better outcome statistics.

Who, then, are the true clients of the organisation?

In a university is it the students, or the agencies that pay their fees, their grant authorities, their parents? Or is it the omnipresent tax payer? Or the government, or the research councils, or the loans agencies and banks that lure needy students, their affluent customers of the future, with free offers? Or is it the lecturers with their interesting, reasonably paid, secure jobs? Are they the 'prime beneficiaries'? (Mullins, p. 75).

Managers need to know not only *what* an organisation is for (to produce bicycles or trained nurses, etc.) but also *who* it is for. The organisation is not only an open system sending useful outputs into the environment, but also a homeostatic one concerned for its own survival. The two should ideally be complementary, but sometimes they get out of kilter, and then librarians, lecturers, charity workers and the like seem to put the customer far from first.

'Organisations exist in order to achieve objectives and to provide satisfaction for their members' (Mullins, p. 63). That social worker was at least half right.

2 You can still find pockets of English people (in bowling clubs and other such bastions of tradition) who think that French plumbing stinks, metaphorically and literally. But the *pissoir*, the male urinal open to public gaze and sniff, gave way long ago to the high-tech loo. And its inventor, that backward nation France, soon began exporting this sweet-smelling, self-disinfecting, musical lavatory to as many countries as could afford such luxurious latrines. France also exports its space rockets, air traffic control and field communication systems, Exocets, nuclear-produced electricity, digital telephones, fibre optics, and the fastest train in the world.

One of the most remarkable of this stream of technological successes appeared in the 1980s when the state postal and telephone company distributed free, in place of the phone directory, millions of dedicated computer terminals, *minitels*, connected to the nation's telephone network. This telematic system provides the whole country with access to data banks (including a nationwide telephone directory), interpersonal communication by electronic mail and notice boards, and commercial transactional facilities. Businesses rushed to avail themselves of this immediate and interactive access to a vast network of potential customers, and services available include: teleshopping, telebanking, educational back-up for pupils revising for exams, research and reservation facilities in libraries, booking restaurants, trains, theatre tickets, buying and selling wares such as shares, placing bets, and so on. There is notably the *minitel rose* where lonely hearts, singles, plea-sure-seekers and the like are served by all manner of ingenious agencies.

No French organisation can afford to neglect the opportunities offered by this remarkable technological system, which far from having detrimental consequences such as unemployment (Mullins, p. 89), actually provides new work for hardware manufacturers, maintenance technicians, data input typists, games inventors and manufacturers, graphics designers, and so on and so on. Very much, then, the breakthrough technology Drucker identified (Mullins, p. 289).

 ## Assignment one

In order to complete this assignment you will need to finish 'Activity one' first. Choose one organisation from the list you made in 'Activity one' and, using techniques such as reading publicity material, interviewing, work shadowing and so on, investigate an example of one of them in your area (a local museum, a community care unit, a pub quiz league, a live music club, etc.).

In 1,000–1,200 words, write up your findings in the form of a case study to support either chapter 3 or chapter 9 of Mullins. To do this successfully you will need to emphasise those aspects of your chosen organisation which illustrate analyses in the selected chapter. It is unlikely, however, that you will be able to 'cover' all aspects of the chapter.

Now complete your case study by designing three questions or activities which would help a student get the most out of studying it.

Assignment two

Consider the introduction of a new technology you have experienced or witnessed in an organisation. Typical examples might include:

- A network of computer terminals providing electronic mail and notice boards.
- Company bicycles for travelling round a large industrial plant (e.g. an oil refinery).
- Electronic databases replacing card filing systems in a library or hospital.
- Student study packs (audio- and videotapes, manuals, etc.) for open or distance learning.
- Mobile phones or pagers for employees in a construction firm or university.
- Drop-in computer-based training stations in the workplace.
- Video- or conference-phones to reduce travelling to meetings in an aviation engineering firm.
- Telesales (i.e. selling by telephone and/or television).
- Laptop computers issued to sales staff, maintenance workers or consultant accountants.
- Home-based electronic offices to enable commuting staff to 'telework' part of the week.

Focusing on one such change write a 1,500 word essay that assesses the extent to which working practices will be, or have been, altered by it, and evaluate its impact on efficiency and job satisfaction (see Mullins, pp. 86–9).

Key issues that might impinge upon your evaluation could include: access, control, reliability, safety, cost, training, pace of change, consultation, privacy, health, and law.

 # Assignment three

See Mullins, p. 93.

 # Assignment four

See Mullins, pp. 91–2.

! Pause for thought

1 Much has been written over the years about how an organisation should treat its employees. The Quaker factory owners of the nineteenth century built housing for their employees, American and Japanese corporations in the twentieth century provide crèches for employees' children and expensive work-out areas to alleviate executive stress. As we approach the millennium, companies are urged to be more caring both towards their staff and the environment: 'printed on recycled paper' and 'not tested on animals' have become *de rigueur*. Indeed, Body Shop founder, Anita Roddick, when announcing plans recently to open an 'alternative business school' for the twenty-first century said, 'All that . . . stuff about the only responsibility of business being to the shareholder's pocket can be dumped' – *her* school will challenge traditional theories and get students to look beyond shareholders at issues of animal, human and environmental rights. We have seen the paternalism of the human relations school not only going full circle but off at a tangent.

However, an interesting comment on paternalism as the perceived 'duty' of the employer is given by Ricardo Semler in his book, *Maverick!* (1993). Semler took over the family business, Semco – Brazil's largest marine and food-processing machinery manufacturer – in 1981 and since then has adopted such an unorthodox approach to management that not only is his company the fastest growing in Latin America but he is also much in demand as a public speaker and organisational 'guru'. Semler says that paternalism is 'a dirty word at Semco. We don't want to be a big, happy family. We want to be a successful business. We're only concerned with our employees' performance on the job not their personal lives. You won't find a running track, swimming pool, or gym at Semco. If our people want to join a health club, that's their business. We do offer health insurance and other benefits, but we ask employees to help manage them. Occasionally, Semco will lend employees money, but only for unpredictable emergencies. Instead of treating employees as children who need looking after, we treat them as adults who are capable of making decisions on the job.'

2 The word 'bureaucracy' has come a long way since it was originally coined by Weber who used the term to describe a structure which he saw as bringing order and rationality to our lives. Today the word has come to be synonymous with, and used to express our exasperation over, red tape, officialdom and excessive rules and procedures – exemplified, perhaps, in the person we love to hate, the traffic warden.

Bureaucrats, like garden weeds, are not only always with us, popping up when you thought you'd finally conquered them but, in these days when 'downsizing' and 'delayering' are trendy buzzwords, actually seem to be increasing. Where are they all coming from? It can't, surely, be from local authorities who, in preparation for their new structures, are trying to lose people? No, this new breed of bureaucrat is coming from further afield – all the way from Brussels, in fact. The last few years have seen a veritable plethora of regulations and directives all apparently aimed at curbing our freedom. At first these were met with exasperated amusement (remember the 'leave the British sausage alone' campaign?)* but then amusement was replaced by howls of frustration (except in 'The Archers' where Brian seems to be doing quite well out of subsidies . . .)

---

*As we go to press, the latest EC ruling has halted Mr Spock in his efforts 'to boldly go'. Toys made in China can only be imported if they are 'human-like': Christopher Robin is in, Pooh Bear is out; Postman Pat is OK, his cat isn't; Batman gets the elbow but sidekick Robin is acceptable; and no doubt a subcommittee will be formed to decide if Big Ears is human . . .

However, whilst the British rail against such an apparent straitjacket, muttering 'I knew this would happen if we went in to the EEC' under their collective breath, they attempt to use the rules to win their case: they do what they are told – follow the appeals procedure all the way to Brussels or Strasbourg, wait for two years and are then turned down. Why is it that in the UK we seem to be strangling ourselves in a tangle of regulations when the rest of Europe seems to carry on in spite of, rather than because of? The answer lies in the fact that while Fred in London pours laboriously over his forms, the French, Italians and Dutch all 'know a man who can' – be it a Pierre, a Marco or a Hans. This is not to suggest that a well-greased palm is the key, simply that these countries have become so over-regulated that nobody follows the rules any longer and the resulting lack of recrimination has brought about a freedom of its own.

What happened to Weber's idea of 'technical superiority'? Given that, in some form or another, we *need* bureaucracies, should we work through them (as we do currently) or should we work around them (as everyone else does)? As the French might say: '*C'est la vie*'.

? Still not convinced?

1 'In 1987 people began to flee to Malawi . . . we fled to Mozambique because Renamo and Frelimo were shooting against each other . . . they would shoot people who even looked at them who were only children and women . . . armed bandits arrived one Sunday morning . . . they burned all the houses and killed every family in our area . . . my brothers and my sister were all killed . . . we walked for three days in the shrub . . .

- "Where are you going?"
- "To the Changlambica camp . . ."
- "You are armed bandits."
- "No, here are our documents, rosaries, crucifix . . ."

We were imprisoned for three days . . . but in Malawi the government began to distribute flour, beans, salt, sugar, clothes and soap . . . they built a hospital, a school, a store and wells . . . in that same year I began to study in the first form and now in 1994 I am in the sixth form . . . in the first lesson we received an exercise book and a biro . . . I am very happy to hear the war in Mozambique has ended . . . I would like to be there in my country . . .'

After independence in 1975, Right-wing guerillas began undermining the pro-Soviet government in Mozambique. The resultant civil war saw hundreds of thousands killed. Over a million took refuge in Malawi, and many more in other neighbouring states.

Compositions like the ones the above extracts – from Changlambica camp – are taken from are being collected from all over the world by Martin Smalley at The Body Shop with a view to publishing them to sell for charity. Save The Children are closely associated with this venture. The idea was conceived under the scheme that organisation operates whereby employees may use company time to work on projects of social worth.

'Some organisations extend the range of social responsibilities . . . to the needs of developing countries' (Mullins, p. 295).

As we write news has come in from Zaire that a hundred Rwandans have been killed by a mortar bomb attack emanating from the country they had fled. The world needs as many socially responsible organisations as it can get.

2 A look at the future . . .*

The following is an extract from an Information Services Strategy Document for a university.

'Telecommunications, broadcasting and publishing technologies are converging. The implications of the convergence for education and entertainment are most significant. As legislation lifts the constraints, the impact of developments in consumer electronics will be immense and is largely unpredictable. However, the convergence will have tremendous implications for the future operation of our higher educational establishments. Any university which fails to take a positive and proactive approach to the new technologies will rapidly become disadvantaged in the marketplace and reside in the second division or even risk becoming absorbed by a more aware institution.

In the effective university there will be a comprehensive communications network spanning the entire university, and available to every member of staff and every student. On the desk of each member of academic staff will be a personal computer (PC) linked to the network, or at very least an access point for the connection of a portable PC. A similar facility will be available to the great majority of support staff. In general the computer will become "an information access device" first, and a "computer" as a secondary role.

Students should have their own-low cost portable PCs and have access to the network at a variety of points (e.g. the library, seminar rooms, laboratories, halls of residence and even in the "bed sits" in the town).

The network will provide a range of information and communication services, available to a common standard at every access point. These will include: electronic mail; a standardised "bulletin board" providing administrative information; commonly available teaching and learning materials; library services; and access to off-campus networked materials and services. The network will also offer the opportunity to interwork nationally and globally with industry and commerce, which in turn could generate new commercial revenue streams to augment university funds.

For a university whose buildings are dispersed the consequent changes in working practice would be massive and beneficial. The IT revolution, long heralded, is available at last at reasonable cost to transform the working practices of the University. A sound Information Services Strategy, properly implemented with strong corporate leadership and coordination would usher this university into a position of institutional leadership within the UK and Europe.'

---

*With thanks to Jim Brookes, University of Portsmouth.

10 Organisation structure

Midshires Housing Association – coping with success?

Background

Housing associations are non-profit-making bodies, run by voluntary committees, providing housing, including hostels and associated amenities. They may be bodies registered with the Registrar of Friendly Societies, trusts registered with the Charity Commissioners or companies which are also registered as charities. However, in order to receive public funds for the provision of housing they must register with the Housing Corporation, which acts as the regulatory agent for central government.

The origins of the movement date back to the twelfth-century almshouses but it was during the nineteenth century that the movement developed. However, the spur to creating the movement as it now is came in the late 1960s and early 1970s – the time of *Cathy Come Home* and the reawakening of public awareness of the housing problems facing many people.

The 1974 Housing Act enabled the movement to receive considerable public funds with which to build new homes for rent at a level that those in housing need could afford. New associations were formed at this time either as a consequence of pressing local needs that local authorities were perceived not to be meeting, or as a reaction against the policies of redevelopment of areas through demolition rather than refurbishment. In 1974 the movement provided some 200,000 homes and by the late 1980s this had risen to over 600,000 involving some 26,000 voluntary committee members and a similar number of staff.

The change of government in 1979 heralded changes for housing associations. Whilst the 'right to buy' policy did not apply to charitable housing associations, the 1980 Housing Act provided the opportunity for new associations to be set up, specialising in initiatives that enabled people on low incomes to buy their own homes on what is described as a 'shared ownership basis': that is, to buy part and rent the remaining part of the equity until such time as the remainder could be afforded.

The 1980s were also a time when the responsibility for providing homes began to shift away from local authorities to housing associations and the idea of wholesale transfer of local authority housing to new or existing associations took hold. Now, in the mid-1990s, housing associations are perceived as the main providers of new social housing.

However, at the same time, public expenditure came under greater scrutiny and the Housing Act of 1988 introduced an important change in the way that the development work of housing associations was funded. From a position of having the total costs of a scheme met by grants from the Housing Corporation, now only a proportion of those costs are met, the remainder have to be found by borrowing from funding institutions such as banks and building societies. Any overspend has to be met from the association's own resources. Additionally, they have to set their own rents rather than relying on 'fair rents' being set independently. 'Risk management' is the phrase bandied around at management committee meetings now.

As the focus has shifted from local authorities to housing associations, so questions have been raised about who the voluntary members are that sit on the management committees. These are unpaid people who have the ultimate responsibility for the work of the association; they are not appointed by local authorities or, indeed, the government, but rely on being voted into office from the voluntary membership of the organisation. More often than not there is no necessity for an election since these people often stand unopposed. The issue of governance has come to the fore where phrases such as 'Are the days of the amateur now over?' are often heard.

The tensions within the movement are increasing, partly as a consequence of the increased focus being placed on them from external sources, but also from within, given the diverse nature of the organisations themselves. The movement includes associations which are very small (so small, in fact, that the committee does the work and no staff are employed) to national organisations who are responsible for thousands of properties, operating on a regional level with staff resources to match. These larger organisations are the ones that have thrived in the current climate.

The pressures for change and the dilemma facing many people in the movement are such that for those involved in still locally based associations, working within a couple of local authority areas, the words of Michael Simmons ring true: 'It is all a far cry from small knots of people crowding into tiny, improvised committee rooms agonising over how to provide decent accommodation for people in need. These same small knots of people, in many instances, are still meeting, trying to hold things together. But in many instances they are wringing their hands and wondering why they bother' (the *Guardian*, June 1994).

Midshires Housing Association

In the late 1960s and early 1970s the city of Midtown was pursuing a policy whereby large areas of terraced homes were demolished rather than being refurbished and let. This, coupled with increasing problems of homelessness, created an environment where local people came together to find ways to help meet these needs in a manner more sympathetic than that expressed by the local authority.

In 1973 Midshires Housing Association was formed from a local Shelter group. It had no staff, no office premises and was run on a voluntary basis by the founding members. In 1975 the first house was completed ready for occupation and by the end of 1976 there were two members of staff. Once the group were able to demonstrate their ability to deliver their promises they were able to work with Midtown City Council whose support enabled them to receive significant funding from the Housing Corporation. On the back of the Housing Act 1980, a new association was formed to provide homes for sale on a shared ownership and low-cost basis. Soon, the association, whilst maintaining its roots and focus of activity within the local area, acquired a reputation for innovation and willingness to provide a broad range of housing serving different needs. This innovative approach even extended to the creation of an organisation that provided employment opportunities under the government-funded Community Programme. The table of stock shown in Figure 10.1 illustrates the growth experienced by the association.

Fig. 10.1 Midshires Housing Association: stock in management

Year	Rent	Special needs	Shared ownership*	Other
1976	1	–	–	–
1977	8	–	–	–
1978	66	4	–	–
1979	194	6	–	–
1980	286	55	–	–
1981	355	55	–	–
1982	383	91	–	–
1983	422	91	5	5
1984	538	106	103	22
1985	605	121	146	29
1986	657	121	162	36
1987	696	157	176	37
1988	775	160	259	39
1989	820	198	296	40
1990	876	198	341	40
1991	994	231	396	95
1992	1,142	272	466	96
1993	1,338	273	465	123

*Once a property has been bought outright, it falls from the table.

Therefore, within twenty years the Association grew from having no housing stock to managing over 2,000 units – still a small to medium-sized association in national terms but nevertheless one with a sound reputation, both locally as well as with the Housing Corporation.

However, there was a recognition within Midshires that, if the problems associated with homelessness were to be combated, simply providing housing was not enough. To enable new activities to be pursued, a trust was formed in 1985 from which grew a network of day centres for those in bed and breakfast accommodation and the task of fund-raising from non-government sources began.

Staff numbers have grown from a zero base in 1973 to two in 1976, eleven in 1979, seventy in 1989 and some 130 in 1992. The first offices were situated in a church which gave part of its premises to community use, but since then space demands have meant two moves, in 1982 and in 1987 to its present offices.

Once staff were employed the involvement of the voluntary members in day-to-day work gradually changed. From one committee of some seven people at the beginning, the organisation soon spawned subcommittees and other committees so that the number of voluntary members grew to fourteen, with fifteen co-opted members, in 1982 and by 1989 to twenty-five members, twenty-three co-optees and eight committees. By 1992 there were twenty-eight members and twenty-three co-optees for nine committees. In 1994 arrangements for a group structure were put in place that incorporated three small local associations, adding to the number of members involved with the organisation.

By 1989 the last of the founder members had left the main management committee. Although there still remained a number of members with experience going back to the early 1980s, it was the chief executive who became the main focus for the link with the past. He had joined Midshires in a voluntary capacity in 1977 but by 1979 was an employee and, in 1981, its chief executive. With the original band of founder members, who pushed to find new ways of helping those in need, he has been the driving force behind the investigation of new initiatives.

The chair's statement in the annual report of 1986 set the tone for the mid-1980s: 'There are two things that worry me greatly. One is that Midshires Housing Association faces the problem common to almost every organisation that grows – it is in danger of becoming too bureaucratic, losing touch with its roots and thus pulling its punches with the Establishment, to the possible detriment of those it most needs to help. The other is more serious in that while all those working in public sector housing report a growing need, resources from central government are reduced.'

 ## Activity brief

1 Assuming the role of an outside consultant, consider Midshires Housing Association, describing those internal management issues which would need to have been addressed as the organisation grew, indicating what steps you would have expected to have been taken to resolve them. Looking to the future, assuming a constant

growth projection, how should the interests of the voluntary committee members and the full-time staff be addressed in order to achieve an agreed way forward? In particular, how should the management style of the chief executive have changed up to now and in the future?

2 We have already seen that Midshires is becoming more bureaucratic in its structure and is actively seeking policies of innovation and competitive advantage. Given that salaries, although competitive in the voluntary field, are probably lower than in industry, how would you gain and maintain commitment and motivation levels of employees?

Further reading

Handy, C. B. (1988), *Understanding Voluntary Organisations*, 4th edn, Penguin.

Case study provided by Chris Jenkins.

 # The Jeyes Group

Introduction

The Jeyes name is more than a century old; the company began business in 1887 and bult up a powerful brand identity making domestic cleaning products which included names such as Pinefresh, Jeyes Fluid and Sanilav. Cadbury Schweppes bought it in 1972 and finally sold the Group in 1986 to the incumbent management team by way of a management buy-out (MBO). Two and a half years after the MBO, Jeyes was floated on the unlisted securities market (USM) with a valuation of £15 million.

In the 1984 annual report, Cadbury Schweppes redefined their business objectives. One objective was, 'to concentrate on its principal business areas of confectionery, soft drinks, beverages and food products. Our objective is to maximise the use of existing assets rather than diversify into unrelated areas': a pointed lack of reference to the Health and Hygiene Division (i.e. Jeyes). It was, therefore, no real surprise that during 1985 Cadbury Schweppes announced its intention to sell this particular division. The sale was in line with the company's objective of concentrating on their core international businesses.

During its final year under Cadbury Schweppes' control, the Health and Hygiene Division was separated into three businesses: consumer products, industrial cleaning, and aerosols. The sale of the three businesses for £19.2 million, to three separate management teams, represented a premium over their asset value to the company.

Undoubtedly at the time of their purchase of Jeyes, Cadbury Schweppes believed that there was considerable synergy between the two companies, particularly in the sales and marketing areas. After all, weren't they both selling into the same retail outlets? In fact, there was really little synergy. Cadbury Schweppes was a large international company with big formal marketing concepts supported by massive advertising using up large budgets. The Jeyes culture was totally different: they were a 'me too' company who copied the market leaders; they had low overheads, surviving by their wits and taking quick advantage of opportunities as they arose. The high corporate costs in centralised human resource management, computer services, industrial engineering, and so on, could not be swallowed by the slender margins which Jeyes were making.

Why a management buyout?

In 1984, Cadbury Schweppes had head-hunted James Moir from paints and aerosols maker, Tetrosyl, and appointed him sales and marketing manager of the Jeyes Group. Moir spent two years putting together a business plan to reverse the losses which he found in the consumer products company. At the end of 1985, the management team at Jeyes found that Cadbury Schweppes had been talking to four potential buyers of their division. However, because the consumer business had been in such trouble, the amounts that potential buyers were offering were quite low. It was at this point that Moir and his team approached Cadbury Schweppes and found that their parent was willing to consider an MBO, telling Moir that he had three months to put together the finance and business plan. Although, privately, they doubted if the money could be raised by Moir and his team, in fact the latter found venture capital firms eager to support him and the £5 million was quickly raised with 25 per cent of the funds being equity and the remainder, debt raised with Standard Chartered Bank. Moir himself raised £60,000 of the management's £312,000 of equity by remortgaging his house.

The mechanism for the MBO was an initial purchase of an 'off the shelf' company, Dickappa (No. 375) Ltd, incorporated on 16 December 1985 with its name being changed to Jeyes Holdings Ltd on 18 February 1986. The company was set up by Moir and team in order to purchase the Jeyes consumer products business from the parent company. On 7 March 1986, Jeyes Holdings Ltd issued shares at par to raise cash of £749,988 which was then used to buy the share capital of Jeyes Group Ltd and its subsidiaries, Jeyes Ltd and Jeyes Overseas Ltd. On the same day Jeyes Ltd sold its Hygiene Division to a company set up by the management of that division and its financial backers. Jeyes Holdings Ltd changed its name to Jeyes Group Ltd by a special resolution passed on 9 June 1988 and on 6 October 1988 reregistered it as a public limited company, Jeyes Group plc.

What happened to Jeyes Group plc after the MBO?

The 1986 annual report announced that 'everyone, everywhere, needs cleaning products' and at the time of the MBO Jeyes believed that their chief role was to satisfy this demand, particularly in domestic cleaning tasks where hygiene is considered to be of particular importance. Jeyes divided their product range into four main areas: bleaches; disinfectants and antiseptics; toilet cleaners and flush colourants; and toilet paper. The products were sold in both branded and 'own label' form.

Employing 650 people, the company was international, operating in twenty-five countries around the world, principally through licence and royalty arrangements. Manufacturing processes and research and development activities were based in three factories, Thetford (Norfolk), Cheltenham (Gloucestershire) and East Kilbride in Scotland.

Immediately following the MBO, Jeyes senior management reported a significant change in morale amongst the workforce with improvements in efficiency and a decline in absenteeism and, following the introduction of monthly team meetings designed to increase employee involvement in decision-making, there was also a feeling that an improvement in industrial relations had been achieved. From the beginning, profits were distributed to all employees, £57,000 in the first year rising to £120,000 by 1990. Other changes were also taking place within the company; for example, Moir changed his Jaguar XJ6 for a more modest car, did away with designated car-parking spaces and introduced single-status canteens.

The board of Jeyes had made it clear that part of their strategy was to grow by selective acquisition. The year 1986 saw the first of these with the purchase of the Izal range of consumer products from Sterling Winthrop. On the other hand, early in 1987, contracts were exchanged for the sale of their 50 per cent shareholding in Scrubbs SA (Proprietary) Ltd, a South African marketing company.

Also in 1987 Jeyes bought the liquid-filling business of Fort Sterling. Much of this company's business was in retailers' own brands which fitted extremely well with Jeyes' strategy of expansion by acquisition which would strengthen their core product area. At the same time Jeyes continued their strategy of innovation and improvement through the development both of existing products and products allied to their current range. This latter aspect was underlined in 1987 when Jeyes also bought a small branded air freshener business.

The year 1987 also saw the introduction of range extensions of their Ibcol disinfectant and Sanilav toilet cleaners as well as new lines and formulations for retailers' own label products. Jeyes felt that much of their competitive advantage came from developing brands and own-label products, utilising their extensive consumer market research knowledge and their strong technical resources.

Jeyes have also been aware that price competition is one of their main threats. The UK market is the most price-competitive in Europe and price wars are seen as an unavoidable part of the British scene in slow growth markets. The Jeyes response was, in 1989, to direct their efforts towards improving operating margins by putting particular emphasis on their purchasing and materials management systems together with further computerisation.

Moir established his own board at Jeyes with the following personnel:

Chairman (non-executive)	M. P. Moseley
Managing director	J. C. Moir
Marketing director	A. R. Blackburn
Sales director	M. T. Bromley
Finance director and company secretary	D. W. Deeks

Operations director	P. H. H. Symonds
Non-executive director	P. J. Welch

Moir already knew the chairman, having worked with him previously at Proctor & Gamble. Welch was appointed by County NatWest as a nominee director to look after their interests.

The current management structure of Jeyes takes a matrix form: each of the major selling activities is headed by a general manager – UK Consumer Products, UK Away From Home Products, and Industrial Products. However, in addition to these responsibilities, the general managers also have cross-market responsibilities for product types, that is, bleach, automatics and wipes. They are supported by a small corporate centre and three functional arms: finance and administration, operations, and purchasing.

Jeyes believe that this matrix structure enables them to place a strong focus on their product strategy which is complementary to their market strategy. This structure also enables the company to develop its own idiosyncratic strategies towards human resource management – for example, its 'best way' communication system for involving all employees in the drive towards higher productivity and quality. Similarly, many of the personnel policies in place could be considered to be equally idiosyncratic: Jeyes operate a very flexible car policy and salaries are flexible with no grading system – payment being strictly by results. Their policy is to recruit high-quality people, put them in the centre of the organisation and give them a high level of involvement.

Despite these initiatives and the employee profit-sharing scheme, industrial relations in the plants were, until recently, regarded as an area of concern by management. For this reason, developments such as TQM programmes have not been introduced by the company.

In the second half of 1990, short- and long-term substantial cost reduction exercises were undertaken; redundancies were announced and the materials management function was, once again, the centre of much focused activity in a bid to improve Jeyes' supply costs. The Overseas Sales Division was restructured with an enlarged resource to support their market management team and with separately dedicated finance, technical and marketing functions.

At the time of the MBO Jeyes employed 600 people; they now employ over 800 – 75 per cent of them in manufacturing. Most of the new staff have come from the business which Jeyes has bought since the MBO.

Jeyes' initial plan of flotation in three to five years has been partly achieved by joining the USM and only the high costs associated with a full listing have prevented them from totally achieving this plan, although this is likely to come with the next big acquisition.

According to Moir, 'the prospects for growth remain strong. One of the odd things about hygiene is that the more of it people have, the more they want. People never think they can't get cleaner!' (*Business*, October 1990).

Activity brief

1   Critically evaluate the organisation design and culture characteristics of Jeyes and examine their implications for personnel policies and practices. Produce a report for the management board of the Jeyes Group, outlining your recommendations for future actions.

2   By examining the political, legal, economic and social implications which might impact on Jeyes Group business environment, what operational management issues should the board review in order to improve their business performance?

3   How could the application of traditional management science techniques assist managers at the Jeyes Group? What do you consider to be the practical benefits which they could achieve from this managerial discipline?

Case provided by Michael Townsend, University of Portsmouth.

 Case study

See Mullins, pp. 334–5.

 Activity one

For this activity you can work either individually or in small groups.

Using the pictorial example given in Mullins (p. 331), refer to an organisation with which you are familiar (this can be either a traditional 'work' organisation or a voluntary organisation) and draw the formal organisation chart. Identify key people in the organisation and interview them informally. From your discussions with them draw the 'alternative' organisation chart.

In a presentation to the rest of the class, attempt to answer the following questions:

● Is there a difference between the two? Why or why not?

● What are the significant variables impacting on the 'alternative' chart?

● Which of the two should the organisation retain? Why? What difficulties do you foresee?

 Activity two

Make a diagrammatic representation of *one* of the following organisations:

● a power station

● a dairy farm

- a subsidised theatre
- an army
- a car factory.

Aim to illustrate:

1 The variety of inputs (staff, capital, energy, etc).

2 The ways goals and feedback influence those inputs (e.g. union policy affecting recruitment practices or European Community directives determining stock size).

3 The ways outputs might be made to fulfil social responsibilities in some measure (e.g. actors running morning workshops in day centres for the disabled, or water, warmed from being used as a coolant, being piped to a local shellfish farm).

If you decide to use the input/output systems model (Mullins, pp. 79 and 280), try adding a new box through which both goals and feedback pass to be processed together before being passed on to influence inputs. The box could be called 'strategic planning' (Mullins, p. 285). Thus the difficulties overly institutionalised soldiers can experience when seeking employment in 'civvy street' could influence the kind of training programmes the army might purchase or design, or the assessment tests used for selecting recruits to the force.

 ## Activity three

See Mullins, p. 30.

 ## Debate one

'All organisations of a certain size must have a bureaucratic orientation.'

Starting points

For

- Bureaucracy, in the Weberian sense of the word, ensures rationality; coordination and standardisation are products stemming from this which are a vital survival mechanism for any large scale organisation.

- Bureaucracy allows us a high degree of predictability about human behaviour in a large and complex organisation.

Against

- Whilst it might have been a suitable organisational model for the first sixty years of this century, it is now becoming outdated, particularly so given the need for diversity in an unstable and changing environment.

- Managerial behaviour has changed to the extent that we have a greater understanding of human needs. This replaces the bureaucratic concept of coercive power and mechanistic, depersonalised values.

Further reading

Blau, P. M. and Meyer, M. W. (1987), *Bureaucracy in Modern Society*, Random House.

Mieward, R. D. 'The Greatly Exaggerated Death of Bureaucracy', *California Management Review*, **13** (2), 65–9.

Perrow, C. (1986), *Complex Organizations: A Critical Essay*, Random House.

 # Debate two

'The structure of an organisation is unimportant. What matters is whether individuals do their job or not.'

Starting points

For

- Work is done by people, not concepts like 'group' or 'organisation'. As Mullins puts it 'Strictly, organisations have no goals, only people do' (p. 273).

- Individuals work hard because they are motivated (they need the money or find the work compelling), not because they know they are in a 'tall' or 'flat' structure, in a wide span of control, or on a scalar chain.

Against

- An individual can be as motivated as possible, but if another individual is pursuing different goals, pulling in another direction, there will have to be some organising done to avoid inertia. Look how frustrating a bureaucrat's rules can be to a would-be innovator; lateral communication channels on a scalar chain can avoid problems of that type.

- 'Organisation' may be an abstract term, but so are 'love', 'home' and 'justice'. People have very strong attachments to such concepts, and very vivid images of them – and not just organisational charts either.

Further reading

Argyris, C., and Schön, D. (1980), 'What is an Organisation that it may Learn?', in M. Locket and R. Spear (eds), *Organisations as Systems*, Open University Press.

Goss, D. (1994), 'Investing in People: Human Resource Development and Organisational Change', in D. Adam-Smith, and A. Peacock) (eds), *Cases in Organisational Behaviour*, Pitman.

Morgan, G. (1986), *Images of Organisation*, Sage Publications.

Morgan, G. (1989), *Creative Organisation Theory*, Sage Publications.

✓ Look, it really works!

1 Gillian, one of our part-time management students is a freelance management trainer. As part of an assignment for us, she produced the following story.

Phillippa MacIntyre Associates is a management consultancy whose main area of activity is in interpersonal skills training. Before becoming self-employed, Phillippa was training manager for a leading chain of high street fashion stores who not only had their own shops but also operated a shop-in-shop concept in large department stores.

The recent economic recession caused the company to think long and hard about its overhead costs and, as is usual, training was the first thing to come under the corporate axe. However, the company was rather more proactive than its rivals and rather than axing training all together, they offered generous redundancy packages to their training staff and then bought back their services on a consultancy basis. It was a solution which suited both parties: overhead costs were reduced and Phillippa and her colleagues had the opportunity to become self-employed but at less risk than would normally be the case. Thus Phillippa MacIntyre Associates (PMA) was born. PMA consisted of just Phillippa and an administration assistant – the other associates, some ten in total, whilst working primarily for PMA, were self-employed and free to pursue their own sales leads as they wished, a point which Phillippa continually stressed.

PMA went from strength to strength, largely due to Phillippa's dynamic personality. She believed wholeheartedly in her company and her drive and enthusiasm brought in a steady stream of work which kept most of her associates busy, working solely for her. As the economy began to pick up and Phillippa was offered a huge contract from a rival fashion chain which amounted to 1,000 days of consultancy. Clearly the existing ten associates were not going to be able to cope with this massive influx of work and so she advertised for other freelance trainers to join PMA on a subcontract basis so that the total complement would number fifty. The response to the advertisement was considerable and Phillippa spent a long time interviewing candidates to ensure that not only were they competent to do the job but also that they had the right attitude and personality to be able to fit in to her culture. Successful candidates were invited to an induction day to ensure that not only were they *au fait* with the training programme but were also inculcated into the PMA culture. Our student, one of the freelance trainers, did not go away empty-handed . . . on the contrary she left the meeting with three lever-arch 'bibles' containing background information and paperwork including all the returns she would need to make to PMA after each training visit (six in total plus two invoices).

When we asked her how she was getting on, she replied, 'Well, I thought it was going to be the perfect subcontract: some guaranteed days work and no ties to PMA. Unfortunately that isn't proving to be the case; Phillippa gets really upset if you can't make meetings because you have other work not generated by her and the operations manual keeps changing – I've got enough paper to make a rain forest. I'm thinking of giving it up.'

Chandler suggests that structure should follow strategy. If the structure becomes outdated, people are added on with little thought resulting in a loss of control. Can you see where PMA didn't take an open systems approach and didn't consider the inputs, outputs and the effect of the environment?

Also, taking the contingency factors into consideration, the increasing size would indicate that she needs to be more mechanistic in her approach and although she is trying to do this in terms of paperwork, she is operating an essentially organic organisation.

2 For this one we'll need to go back to Midshires University (the case from Chapter 6). The Law Department is in the faculty of Humanities but actually only has one pure law degree. The rest of the teaching is 'serviced out' to other departments. This is by no means a rare occurrence in colleges and it happens when other degree courses have a specialised unit of some sort, no expertise in their own department to teach it, and the demand is such that it would be uneconomic to employ a lecturer specifically to teach it.

Thus law lecturers may find themselves with the timetabled courses set out in Figure 10.2. The timetable for this particular lecturer means that they don't actually teach in their own department nor, since Midshires has a campus which is spread over quite a wide geographical area, even on their own site. Whilst they are ultimately responsible to their own head of department, they also have a reporting responsibility to the course manager in whose department the particular course is located.

Fig 10.2

Course	Department
BSc Engineering	Mechanical Engineering
BA Architecture	School of Architecture
MA Human Resource Management	Business School
Employment Law Short Course	Management Centre
BA Hotel and Catering Management	Business School

Prior to incorporation, this arrangement worked well, probably because it was informal in nature and relied on personal contacts and unofficial reciprocal trading. However, after incorporation, the culture of the 'new' university changed subtly and an 'official' matrix structure was brought in. We can see from the case in Chapter 6 that there was greater pressure to 'perform and deliver' both teaching and research. Demands on lecturers now became formalised and much of the earlier goodwill began to dissipate.

A fly on the wall in the staff coffee room overheard the following comments:

- *'I didn't mind going to Boards of Studies and Boards of Examiners before, but I object to being notified formally of my requirement to do so – especially having to complete the tear-off slip with the reasons **why** I can't attend: it's like being back in school.'*

- *'I don't teach one single course in this faculty and yet my head of department is supposed to be doing my appraisal under this new scheme they've brought in. How can he when he doesn't really know what I'm doing?'*

- *'I'm supposed to be schools liaison officer – how can I find the time to do it when I'm never on site and I'm supposed to be on the committee for a new exam in the Engineering Department?'*

Here we can see that prior to incorporation, the 'unofficial' matrix structure worked because the culture of the organisation and the attitudes and behaviour of the members made it work. However, once the matrix was made 'official' throughout the university, the structure became too complex and the attendant problems associated with this form became all too apparent (see Mullins, p. 328).

 ## Assignment one

An article has recently appeared in *Management Issues*, a journal aimed at both academics and managers, with the following synopsis: '*It is predicted that by the turn of the century at least half of the British workforce could be working at least part of the week from home. This idea of "teleworking" will have far-reaching implications for organisation design.*'

In *not more* than 2,000 words, complete the article as if you were submitting it for publication. You should bear in mind the following:

1 Your target audience will be both academics who know the theories of organisation design in detail and practitioners who probably won't have the same understanding but will have a basic knowledge (in other words, you don't need to draw lots of diagrams depicting a functional structure, a matrix structure, etc.). The non-academics who read your article will be practising mangers and you will therefore need to relate your theoretical arguments to the workplace.

2 As with all academic journals, your article will be sent to at least two people with a knowledge of the area in order to obtain their views prior to it being accepted for publication. Your arguments, therefore, must be clear, logical and lead the reader to an obvious conclusion (a one sentence statement beginning 'Thus it can be seen . . .' will not only be an unacceptable cop-out but will also show that you haven't done 'Assignment two' in Chapter 6).

3 Your work must be referenced (for an example of referencing using footnotes, see the final pages of any chapter in Mullins). There is nothing wrong in quoting other authors' views or opinions, but at least give them the credit for having stated the point before you did!

✎ Assignment two

'There is the risk that the creation of unitary councils in some areas may remove economies of scale, duplicate bureaucracies and increase local taxes' (*The Times*, 25 January 1994).

The 1992 Local Government Act required a Local Government Commission to consider whether so-called unitary councils would give more effective local government than the prevailing two-tier system (county and district councils). In Hampshire, for example, the arrangement whereby the county council manages services such as education, libraries and social welfare while the district councils manage housing, refuse collection and so on, could change to one where seven unitary councils manage all such services for their own district, or, alternatively, where the two cities of Southampton and Portsmouth become unitary councils while the two-tier system remains in place for the rest of the county.

Task

With reference to Chapter 3 in Mullins, write a 1,500 word essay assessing the merits and demerits of changes such as these in the structure of local government.

Tips

- Your local authority offices and libraries should hold leaflets presenting the case for one or other of these choices.

- Diagrams can often save a lot of words when expressing notions about organisational structure.

- Remember that many councils have already contracted out or privatised many of the services traditionally provided by them including refuse collection, school meals, and communal transport, a trend which, if continued, could impact on this question of structure (see Mullins, pp. 286, 304–5, 378).

❗ Pause for thought

1 We hear much these days about 'delayering', downsizing', 'business re-engineering' and the like. We are exhorted to be 'leaner and fitter' to 'think globally and act locally' (the latter slogan appearing everywhere from the lips of the management gurus to local authority bottle banks). It seems that senior management are taking an organisational machete to hack out layers of management, seemingly, sometimes, without much thought to the consequences (we suggest they read Mullins, pp. 328–30 for a synopsis of the consequences of a badly designed structure).

We are bombarded with articles and case studies about companies who have 'flattened their pyramid' and even, on occasion, turned it upside down. Ricardo Semler, however, has gone one further and 'rounded it out' (Semler 1993). Claiming that the traditional pyramid is dysfunctional not only for efficiency and effectiveness but also for personal growth and development, he has replaced it with a series of concentric circles, the smallest forming the core of senior, strategic managers (renamed 'counsellors'). The next circle out from the core encloses seven to ten business unit leaders (now renamed 'partners'), and the final circle would comprise everyone else in the organisation who would be renamed 'associates'. 'Floating' outside the circles are six to twelve triangles, each composed of one person (a 'coordinator'), who would, in the old system, be the first level of management but who, in the circular system, coordinate such activities as marketing, sales and production.

Semler claims that although this new design took a while to be accepted it is now working successfully. Movement around the organisation is as easy and as quick as individuals want (or don't want) and decision-making has both speeded up and improved through a weekly team briefing and a further meeting of the counsellors and a representative from each unit. In Semler's words: 'Just three circles, four job categories, and two meetings. That's it.'

But is it? Semler is accepted as an entrepreneurial leader, a maverick (indeed, it is the title of his book). This, together with his charismatic personality and lateral-thinking approach, has clearly worked for Semco. Would it work for, say, a local authority Trading Standards Department or a university? Has the time come to call a halt to these 'me too' approaches to organisation design and, instead, consider incremental changes over a much longer period of time when their long-term effects on structure, performance and people can be assessed?

2 In 1992, led by chief executive Greg Hutchings, the Tompkins Group bought Rank Hovis MacDougall for £1 billion against speculation from the City that it would be a major disaster. Despite giving the lie to this speculation in July 1994 by declaring annual profits of £257 million – a rise of 50 per cent – the market remained unimpressed with shares rising by only 6p over the following week.

What has happened? The Tompkins Group business (described somewhat disparagingly by one analyst as 'the guns to buns company') ranges from Smith and Wesson firearms, through Hayter lawnmowers to RHM and it is this diversity that is apparently the cause of the problem. Hutchings' vision is of 'building a true conglomerate, bringing together a wide range of different businesses'; he is quoted as saying that he believes that there is no difference between food and lawnmowers. However, fund managers are becoming increasingly disillusioned with the notion of conglomerates, dismissing them as 'a 1980s idea that has drifted into the 1990s' and preferring a more focused approach (*Sunday Times*, 17 July 1994).

Does this sound the death knell for the divisional structure? On paper, Tompkins appear to be doing well; is it, therefore, for genuine reasons that fund managers have sounded the death knell or because another 'fad' has come along?

? Still not convinced?

This one* either needs a long memory or satellite television.

A helicopter hovers overhead, the camera pans over a range of ramshackle tents and the tannoy squawks, 'Casualties coming in'. Yes, dear reader, we are on the set of 'MASH'.

Now the 4077th Squadron vs The Army is a classic example of Burns and Stalker's Mechanistic and Organic Model of Organisations. The MASH Unit is trying to function effectively in a (literally and metaphorically) turbulent environment; it needs to be able to respond rapidly to changing circumstances, frequently 'bending the rules' in order to do so. The Army itself, back in the relatively safe environment of Washington, can afford to be mechanistic and it can't understand any other way. Thus you have Radar O'Reilly taking on a *boundary spanning* role, trying to keep both parts happy and working on the principle of 'ignorance is bliss'.

Too often the Burns and Stalker model is seen as bi-polar/one or the other/good or bad. 'MASH' is a good example of how it is sometimes necessary to have *both* structures in an organisation. (Look at characters like Colonel Potter and Hotlips Houlihan and ask yourself in which organisational form are they likely to function best?)

Note: Having used this example recently with a group of first-year undergraduates, they had assumed that the MASH Unit was operating in Vietnam rather than Korea. What does this tell you about perceptual processes?

With thanks to Laurie Mullins for supplying the original idea.

11 Organisational culture

Every dog has his day

Michael Watson paused outside the imposing front entrance of Simkins & Co., the international firm of chartered accountants and management consultants. He nervously adjusted his new suit and walked in. Six months previously Michael had approached a recruitment agency to seek a new job. He had been a university lecturer for fourteen years, rising up the career ladder to become a professor of systems engineering and head of a university department at the age of thirty-five. It was time for a change, if only for two or three years.

The recruitment agency had been very efficient and, much to Michael's surprise, had arranged an interview with a partner in the engineering section of the management consultancy wing of Simkins & Co. Simkins had been established in 1892 and in 1956 the firm started a management consultancy firm which grew out of referrals from audit and taxation work. Over the years, and especially since 1986, this diversification activity had developed into a consultancy business employing 600 people in the UK out of a worldwide empire of 60,000 employees. There was an office in most countries of the world.

At his initial interview, it was explained to Michael that the management consultancy firm had six divisions in the UK covering systems engineering, softwear engineering, leisure, public sector, financial services and education. If successful, Michael would join the systems engineering division, which had been a separate company until 1988. The systems engineering division consisted of three partners (Heinrich Spiegel, Donald Roper and Robin Elcock), four associates, four managing consultants, four senor consultants, twelve consultants, two analysts, two technical assistants, three secretaries and one librarian/researcher. Robin Elcock, the interviewing partner, explained that Simkins was not a hierarchical firm and although there were different grades, everyone was valued for the contribution they made to solving client problems.

Michael was even more surprised to be called back for a second interview which would be preceded by arithmetic, writing and psychological tests. The tests went well and in his short interview with Donald Roper, the senior partner of the systems engineering division, Michael felt that the interview had also gone well.

'What an enlightened firm,' thought Michael as he left. No hierarchies, no bureaucracy, good promotion prospects, a company car, BUPA and a decent salary some 20 per cent higher than his current salary. When Robin Elcock phoned him that evening Michael asked for time to consider the job offer. It was not quite what he had expected – the job offered was at senior consultant, not managing consultant, grade, although Robin explained that this would surely be a temporary stage prior to a move up the career ladder. Two days later, Michael took the plunge. This was a gamble – he was thirty-nine, married with three children and moderately successful in the academic world. Could he make the transition to commercial consultancy work? Would he like the work and, above all, would he be accepted by his new colleagues? Would he be seen as an unworldly academic?

Day One of the new job involved a quick chat with the management consultancy associate who controlled assignment scheduling. It was not a good start, neither was the tedium of being photographed for the security pass nor the folder of rules, forms and sundry regulations. Michael scanned the other new recruits. Each one was younger than he was, in fact some ten years younger – all fresh faced and bristling with ambition. He shuddered. He seemed to have so little in common with them, indeed most of them he would not cross the street to say hello to under normal circumstances.

The visit to the systems engineering division was also rather an eye opener – a huge open plan office housed on one floor of the building containing all 600 people involved in management consultancy plus support staff such as accounts, marketing and personnel. Each consultant was assigned to a desk but each desk provided accommodation for at least two consultants, so that possession was a case of 'first come, first served' (that is, first in the office). Michael was introduced to those consultants working that day in the systems engineering part of the office. The thought struck him that he had actually taught five of the colleagues he would now be working with. Would they accept him as an equal or would they play games?

Michael was also introduced to the computerised staff locations system which recorded contact telephone numbers and location of each person for each hour of the working day. There was plenty of food for thought. Heinrich Spiegel, one of the three partners in the division, outlined his first assignment – a desk research job involving the collection of data, required by Robert Goldschmit, one of the four associates in his division. Spiegel was an aloof character, proud of being a partner in an international firm, cunning and shrewd but not overly blessed with intelligence. Michael was to realise in the months ahead that intelligence was not necessarily an admired quality in a consultant; having been a university professor Michael was already regarded with suspicion by almost everyone in the division, not least by Robert Goldschmit, who saw in Michael a possible rival and one who needed to be kept in check. On the train home from his first day in the Simkins office, Michael ruefully reflected on the sheer boredom of the day and indulged for a while in nostalgic thoughts of his former working life. No longer was it the lecture room and leisurely chats over coffee in the staff common room – it was now 'grey suit' time, commuting into London, hoping to secure his desk and 'watch your back' time. He now needed to conform to the corporate culture – seen to be working long hours in the office at his desk, to be working in the office on a Sunday, being seen to be eager to please partners and associates, filling out fortnightly time sheets and meeting impossible deadlines imposed by the rigours of the company underbidding to secure assignments. And, heaven forbid – he now needed to wear a suit each day with sensible city shoes (not the scuffed loafers he always wore).

As the weeks went by so came the opportunity to leave the office from time to time and work at client premises. This was interesting and all added to his experience. He quickly found, however, that his ex-students were extremely wary of him. They were not openly hostile but he had a vague feeling that they were running to the partners with little tales.

'I was looking for you,' said young Jennifer Coombes, one morning when Michael arrived at 8.30 a.m. Michael smiled wryly. So this was the game – pop in and see one of the partners (usually Robin Elcock who was always at his desk by 7.00 a.m.) and casually mention that you had an urgent task but you couldn't find Michael Watson. The 'drip drip' approach of planting doubt and suspicion about a colleague was a well-practised art but Michael was new to this consultancy game and rather naïve. To some extent, you could see Jennifer Coombes coming. She was a fully paid up member of the 'blue stocking young fogey' set. Fiercely ambitious, she was flattering her way to the top with a hint of additional favours. Michael had once observed her looking adoringly at Robin Elcock across the meeting room table. She had what, under normal conditions, would be regarded as a crushing disadvantage – she was not good at finishing consultancy assignments but there were always naïve, unsuspecting colleagues like Michael Watson who could take the blame.

Working with Coombes became a trial. She alternated between petulance, bossiness and rudeness. Michael found this difficult to handle, indeed he found it profoundly disturbing. He began to avoid her if he could and sought the company of other disaffected consultants. Three of these became good friends, and when all three were in the office they would go out for a drink at lunch times. Alcohol was a good way of getting through the afternoon, it eased the pain, although there were occasions when Michael overdid the medicine.

Unknown to Michael, two of the associates in his division (Robert Goldschmit and Richard Vine) had formed an unholy alliance – Michael Watson was a 'smart ass' who needed to be taught a lesson. He had never fitted in, he had refused to conform – he was never in the office before 8.30 a.m., never in on a Sunday and he continued to wear those awful shoes despite the recommendations of the company image consultant to 'ditch those "Saturday" shoes'; he was a 'Prof' and too smart for his own good. He would have to go.

Michael knew that the noose was tightening around his neck but so long as he worked on assignments away from the office (and there were plenty of opportunities, where engineering businesses needed managing under receivership conditions) he felt happier.

Three months before his third anniversary with Simkins, Michael decided that enough was enough. He quietly made contact through his academic networks, in the slow but steady pursuit of a new job back in academe. The writing was on the wall – he needed to 'jump ship' at the first opportunity. However, events moved quicker than even Michael had anticipated. 'I need to see you,' Donald Roper had said on the telephone one afternoon. 'Michael, business is very low in systems engineering at the moment; if things don't pick up in the next week we will have to make you redundant.' A week went by and no word was heard from Donald Roper. It was to be nearly three agonising weeks before Michael was finally called in to see Donald Roper. Michael was to be made redundant at the end of the month.

What hurt was not the redundancy itself (Michael felt sure that he could get another job even though he was forty-two), it was the release of this information to the other consultants before he had been told himself which hurt.

The other consultants reacted with a mixture of smugness and pity, thankful it was not them. Michael quickly became a pariah, a person to be avoided at all costs. Keeping a brave face on things Michael determined to face this hostile crowd out. He went to the office with heavy heart but once in the office he laughed and joked with colleagues. Michael was determined that these people would not see him in distress. The divisional partners found this disturbing – this was not part of the script. This was not expected.

Just two months later, on the third anniversary of stepping through the front door of Simkins & Co., Michael was greeted with the words 'Welcome Professor Watson' as the vice-chancellor introduced him to senior management on the first day at his new university.

'Phew that was a close shave,' thought Michael as he contemplated the duties of his new job. Anyway, three years in management consultancy will look good on the cv, and how many academics had recent industrial experience, let alone had managed a company? 'Screw Simkins' he thought, and he smiled as he remembered the fat redundancy cheque – a nice bonus, that, seeing as he would have left anyway. 'They'll have to get up earlier in the morning to catch Michael Watson,' he said to himself!

Activity brief

1 Michael Watson found it difficult to be accepted into the working group he joined. Why was this and was there anything he could have done to prevent or alleviate the difficulties in which he progressively found himself?

2 Consider how the management of Simkins & Co. (that is, the partners) can reward conformity with organisational requirements, and how deviant behaviour can be punished.

Further reading

Huczynski, A. and Buchanan, D. (1991), *Organizational Behaviour*, 2nd edn, Prentice Hall (Chapter 9, 'Social Control Through Groups' and Chapter 10, 'Group Effectiveness').

Mullins, L. J. (1993), *Management and Organisational Behaviour*, 3rd edn, Pitman (Chapter 17, 'The Nature of Management Control').

Sveiby, K. E. and Lloyd, T. (1987), *Managing Knowhow, Add Value by Valuing Creativity*, Bloomsbury.

Case study provided by Professor Gary Akehurst, Southampton Institute of Higher Education.

Corporate culture at Garden Festival Wales – grown from seed or grafted on?

Introduction

Traditional approaches to the development of culture suggest that there are a number of key influences (for example, history, primary function, size and objectives (Handy 1993)) which play a major role in its formation. A further influence put forward (Mullins, Meudell and Scott 1993) is the extent of the match between culture and employee perceptions of the psychological contract.

These approaches suggest that the development of organizational culture is an incremental process, evolving gradually over time. However, this is not an appropriate strategy when considering those organisations which are established for a specific purpose and are of a specific duration: the short-life organisation. It is this specificity of purpose and short duration which renders traditional approaches to cultural development inappropriate: there are, for example, no existing rites, rituals, myths, stories and organisational history on which to draw in order to ensure cultural survival through the inculcation of new members and no time for these to form.

It is perhaps appropriate at this juncture to discuss the difference between culture and climate, a difference that is often overlooked. Climate, probably because it is less obviously manifested, has become to a large extent subsumed within the topic as a whole, probably as a result of the increase in popularity of the subject which stresses the correlation between strong 'cultures' and organisational excellence (Peters and Waterman 1982). However, it is important to appreciate the often subtle difference: whilst culture describes how the organisation is depicted and what it is about, climate, to a much greater degree focuses on employees' *perceptions* of what the organisation is about (Taguiri and Litwin 1968) and will subsequently affect morale and attitudes. This is a particularly important distinction in services industries, not only from the point of view of guest perception of staff but also from the point of view of teamworking: the culture may, for example, encourage a hotel-wide quality circle but it is only a suitable climate which will prevent verbal and, possibly, physical violence when a laundry worker suggests changes in procedures for issuing kitchen whites which could improve efficiency!

The research study

Work was undertaken by the Employment Relations Research Group at the University of Portsmouth between May 1992 and December 1993 into the study of organisational culture as an underlying basis for successful performance. Specifically this focused on the development of culture in short-life organisations, in particular, the National Garden Festival Wales which ran from May to October 1992.

The specific focus for the research sought to establish two main themes:

1 How culture develops in an organisation with little or no history and a short-term horizon for the accomplishment of goals and objectives.

2 Given the limited time for managers to exercise any influence over culture, how may performance be maximised?

Garden Festival Wales

Representing the last of the National Garden Festivals initiated by the government following the Toxteth Riots and with the policy of reclamation, recreation and regeneration, a deliberate attempt was made by the senior management team to define and create a specific culture. The overarching themes were, 'Excellence is exceeding visitor expectations – I *can* do it' and 'The spirit of hospitality'. The operations mission of the Festival was identified as: '*To provide the safest, friendliest, cleanest and most efficient family fun day out in 1992.*'

Despite claims to the contrary, it would seem that a pre-opening fact-finding visit to Disneyland influenced both the physical layout and attempts to inculcate the chosen culture. Parallels can be drawn with induction procedures at EuroDisney (Bengtsson 1993):

1 A deliberate attempt was made to create relevant terminology: visitors were to be treated as 'guests', staff, therefore, became 'hosts' and uniforms were referred to as 'wardrobe'.

2 A three-stage training programme was devised and implemented. Titled Gryff's Academy (after the Festival mascot who was rather more gnome-like than mouse-like), it was intended to transmit the operations mission in three phases:

  (a) Phase One   *Achieving excellence*: I can do it.
  (b) Phase Two   *Maintaining excellence*: I am doing it.
  (c) Phase Three *Excellence elsewhere* (an outplacement programme).

Employees were exhorted to: 'Be proud of it – dress it – look after it – excel at it – enjoy it – live it!'

3 An emphasis on the importance of role rather than job title – indeed, the Host Handbook suggested that staff complete the page entitled 'My role' in pencil to allow for probable changes. This was particularly apparent when emphasising the importance of cleanliness and safety. On numerous occasions the researchers were told: 'It's everyone's job to pick up litter.'

4 An emphasis on family togetherness and having fun with feedback from visitors in the form of 'Gryff-a-Grams' where Gryff was depicted as either smiling or frowning.

Research methodology

The research methodology was based on the work of Peters and Waterman and their premise that a characteristic of excellent organisations was the possession of a specific set of beliefs or values, understood and shared by all organisational members. An organisational beliefs questionnaire (OBQ) was developed by

Sashkin (1991) to measure the overall 'excellent' culture of an organisation. To Peters and Waterman's seven basic beliefs were added a further three and these were organised into ten 'pillars of excellence', each of which can be measured separately and analysed using a construction analogy (see Figures 11.1 and 11.2).

Fig. 11.1 The ten 'pillars of excellence'
(Source: Sashkin (1991))

Pillar	Basic belief
1	Work should be fun
2	Being the best
3	Taking (thoughtful) risks
4	Attention to detail
5	The worth and value of people
6	Quality
7	Communicating to get the job done
8	Growth, profit and other indicators of success
9	Hands-on management
10	The importance of a shared philosophy

Fig. 11.2 Analysis of organisational excellence using construction analogy
(Source: Sashkin (1991))

Grand total score range	Level of organisational excellence	Percentage of organisations in each category
211 – 250	Roof's up (excellent organisations)	About 5%
186 – 210	Pillars in place	Less than 20%
156 – 185	Foundation laid	More than 50%
131 – 155	Site cleared	Less than 20%
Below 130	Planning stage	About 5%

Initial evaluation

Our initial findings indicated that the 113 staff who completed the questionnaire felt that the level of organisational effectiveness had reached the upper stages of 'Foundation laid': an achievement in six months of a level similar to 50 per cent of all companies initially surveyed by Sashkin.

A statistical correlation (Meudell and Gadd 1994) was carried out to determine relationships, if any, between age, sex, length of previous unemployment, length of Festival service, job category, previous job and scores obtained on each of the ten pillars with jobs being categorised into visitor services (i.e. those with direct visitor contact) and support services. Figure 11.3 shows the pillars which proved to be significant:

Fig. 11.3 The most significant of the 'pillars of excellence'

Pillar	Support functions: emphasis on	Visitor functions: emphasis on
2 (Belief in being the best)	Managers	
5 (Belief in the worth and value of people)	Hosts	Managers
6 (Belief in quality)		Managers
10 (Belief in the importance of a shared philosophy)	Managers	Hosts

Some individual comments reported to the researchers included:

- 'They (the management) want the most and offer the least.'
- 'It would seem that the organisation only wants me to carry out the work required and not to put forward my own ideas on making events better or more enjoyable.'
- 'Although GFW management have set out certain guidelines, mission statements and objectives to encourage the staff . . . the majority . . . feel that money is more important . . . the guidelines set out by management have not actually been encouraged (by them) during the working day.'

 Activity brief

1 How successful have Garden Festival Wales been at attempting to inculcate their predetermined culture?

2 Has the culture identified occurred 'in spite of' rather than 'because of' Festival management?

3 Can any difference be identified between the inculcation of culture and that of climate at the Garden Festival?

 ## Activity one

The following is an extract from *Doing the Business in Europe: A Guide to Chinese Exporters* written by Hay-lo and S. F. Profesee, published by Shi-Ster Press in the year 2003.

BEHAVIOURAL CHARACTERISTICS

Always remember that the European nations exhibit quite distinct patterns of behaviour among their citizens. *These can be both positive and negative!* The following provides a summary of some of the key points about the people you will meet.

Germans

For

Always punctual and hospitable. Disciplined. Flair for production. Don't allow women in the board-room. Don't joke at work. The only nation unaffected by BSE (mad cow disease).

Against

Little imagination or humour. Regimental. No flair for marketing. Don't allow women in the board-room. Consider they are the best business nation in the world. Worriers (e.g. about BSE (mad cow disease)).

English

For

Fair-minded and courteous. Entrepreneurial. Low staffing costs. Not given to emotional outbursts. Unique sense of humour. Sang-froid, (e.g. over BSE (mad cow disease)).

Against

Xenophobic. Rude public service workers. Repressed soccer hooligans. High strike rate. No dress sense. Consider they are the best business nation in the world. Largely wiped out by BSE (mad cow disease).

Draw up a similar list of plus and minus characteristics for any two of the following nationalities:

French	Italian	Swedish
Japanese	American	Greek

Compare your list with those of other people in your group and then discuss the following questions:

- What logic do we follow when we culturally stereotype people in this way?
- What are the dangers from both a psychological and business point of view of stereotyping others?
- Why should individuals be regarded as unique?

Activity provided by Dr Ray French, University of Portsmouth.

 # Activity two

Annually, the town of Midshires hosts a month-long cultural festival which includes plays, music (both popular and classical), poetry readings, comedians and various exhibitions.

The managing board of the Midshires Festival has commissioned you to prepare a report on how they can enhance profitability by ensuring that their corporate culture is both strong and appropriate. Using the case 'Corporate culture at Garden Festival Wales' as your starting point and working in small groups, prepare and present your report.

 # Debate one

'The socialisation of new members into an organisation's culture is no more or less the manipulation of the individual and is therefore unethical and should be condemned.'

Starting points

For

- The inculcation into a culture serves only the organisation's goals and to produce compliant employees to continue the culture. Any satisfaction gained by the employee is a spurious one gained from conforming to the organisation's wishes.

- Not only is it unethical but in the long term could prove detrimental to the organisation. Overly compliant employees are less likely to be creative and innovative.

Against

- In order to survive, an organisation needs members who are all pulling in the same direction – otherwise divisiveness will lead, ultimately, to the downfall of the organisation.

- Studies have shown that there are clear links between culture and satisfaction (Hellriegel and Slocum 1974); socialisation is therefore an important and necessary mechanism.

Further reading

Feldman, D. C. (1981), 'The Multiple Socialization of Organization Members', *Academy of Management Review*, April.

Hellriegel, D. and Slocum, J. W. Jr. (1974), 'Organizational Climate: Measures, Research, and Contingencies', *Academy of Management Journal*, June, 225–80.

Van Maanen, J. and Schein, E. H. (1977), 'Career Development', in J. R. Hackman and J. L. Suttle (eds), *Improving Life at Work*, Goodyear.

 # Debate two

'Culture is such a deep-seated phenomenon that it is impossible to change successfully.'

Starting points

For

● Culture develops over years and is therefore deep-rooted with strongly held core values. Rituals, stories and management style serve to sustain this culture in a way which is too difficult to change.

● The culture of an organisation is self-perpetuating through its selection and socialization procedures; these alone probably guarantee that culture cannot be changed.

Against

● Culture *can* be changed, although it is an extended process involving changing both attitudes and behaviour.

● Culture *is* a deep-seated phenomenon but it can be changed by changing the determinants of culture – the rituals, selection process, and so on – which will therefore change the core values.

Further reading

Anthony, P. (1993), *Managing Culture*, Open University Press.

Gagliardi, P. (1977), 'The Creation and Change of Organizational Cultures: A Conceptual Framework', *Organization Studies*, **7**, (2), 117–34.

Kilman, R. H., Saxton, M. J. and Serpa, R. (1985), *Gaining Control of the Corporate Culture*, Jossey-Bass.

 # Look, it really works!

1 One of our summer school students was an overseas student who joined our programme having completed his compulsory military service. Over coffee at the start of the programme he told us about it:

'First you have your hair cut, even though it might already be short enough, and then you get issued with your kit which you have to put on immediately. You catch sight of yourself in the mirror and you *know* you're in the Army – all your individuality has gone and you look just like everybody else. You get given a bunk with army-issue bedding and a cupboard which looks like all the rest – you can't even fill it up as you want, there's an order for how you put your gear in it. You sit on your hard bed and look around at all the others – the people you'll be spending at least the next six months with, whether you like it or not. Their expression mirrors yours: "We knew we'd have to do it sometime, we just have to get through it with as little hassle as possible."

'The next few weeks merge into a blur of following often apparently illogical orders. Your life becomes dominated by Senior NCOs shouting at you, bells and klaxons ruling your every move from when you get up to the time you have to go to bed. You have to change uniforms at the drop of a hat for no reason and go through mindless drills and marching at all hours of the day and night. If you dare to question anything you end up peeling potatoes, cleaning out baking tins or painting the stones around the parade ground. You even get used to the terrible food. Throughout it all, you have to wear your uniform and stay on the base, you get a pass-out only when you've finished basic training.

'Eventually that day arrives and you get your next set of orders. Even then you probably won't get what you asked for. I'm a computer programmer so for my first posting I was put in the kitchen. As you march out of training camp for the last time you notice the next batch arriving. You look them over and catch yourself saying, "look at that lot – he'll have to get his hair cut, that one will have to stand up straighter, *he's* going to get a rude awakening . . . what a shower!" You pull yourself up short and suddenly you realise you *are* the Army – it's crept up on you . . .'

Can you see where the role of socialisation fits in here? Using a variation of the socialisation model suggested by Feldman (1981) we can see the *encounter stage*, in which the new employee sees what the organisation is *really* like and faces up to the fact that expectations and reality might differ. The second stage is *metamorphosis* where the new employee adjusts to their workgroup's values and norms. These two stages result in outcomes of productivity, commitment and turnover, although presumably in the case of military service the latter is not acceptable.

(For those of you old enough to remember UK National Service, this may bring back some memories. For those of you too young to remember, perhaps you should be grateful.)

2 Gerry is currently employed by Solent Marine as a ship's laminator. Solent Marine is a boat-building company which specialises in the construction and refitting of yachts and although Gerry is principally employed on GRP laminating of hulls, decks, and so forth, his job description also requires him to turn his hand to whatever needs doing (this bit of the job description is often called 'the slave clause' and usually begins with 'any other reasonable duties which may, from time to time . . .')

On this particular day, Gerry was painting something on the deck. He did the classic thing: stepped back to admire his handiwork and promptly fell through the forward hatch and into the cabin space below: a descent of about fourteen feet. On climbing back up he realised that he'd bruised his back muscles where they'd caught the edge of the hatch and was in considerable pain. He reported sick to his chargehand who said, 'You'd better drive yourself to hospital, then, and get it checked!' As Gerry limped off the chargehand shouted after him, 'Can you drop Mr Durrant at his house on the way to hospital?' Gerry said afterwards, 'Not only did I have to drive myself twenty miles to hospital when I was in so much pain that I couldn't put the clutch in, but I also had to drive up this pot-holed lane to give a customer a lift home. To cap it all I've got a trapped nerve and a cracked rib and I've found out that the company doesn't even pay sick pay . . .'

What does this tell you about the particular culture and likely levels of commitment engendered by this company? Would *you* work for them?

Note: When one of the authors told Gerry that his example would be included in this book but he was not to worry because the example would be presented as fictitious, his reply was, 'The whole **** company ought to be fictitious if you ask me!')

 ## Assignment one

Using either your work organisation or your college, critically analyse the contents of notices (e.g. in car parks, on boards, etc.) as evidence of the manifestations of organisational culture. Some points you'll need to bear in mind include:

● Which definition of organisational culture you're going to use.

● How you anticipate the evidence of culture to be manifested.

Analyse and evaluate your findings. What do they tell you about perceptions and manifestations of organisational climate and culture?

 ## Assignment two

Take two contrasting types of organisation and using the Handy influences on the development of culture (Mullins, p. 649) as your model, compare and contrast your two organisations.

Your two different organisations could be:

● private and public sector;

● for profit and not for profit;

● service sector and manufacturing sector;

● production and academic.

In not more than 1,500 words critically analyse your findings, suggesting reasons for any differences.

How would you describe the current culture of the two organisations? Do you consider this to be a suitable culture for the environment of the organisations?

! Pause for thought

1 Almost forty years ago Whyte (1956) described 'organization man' as a person who not only worked for the organisation but also belonged to it. This was echoed by Lawrence (1958) two years later who wrote: 'ideally we would want one sentiment to be dominant in all employees from top to bottom, namely a complete loyalty to organisational purposes.'

Thirty years later this theme was still being hailed by leading management writers such as Peters and Waterman (1982) and Kanter (1983) who suggested that strong cultures which supported organisational objectives were vital prerequisites for success.

We have, then, an assumption that strong culture and high levels of commitment need to go hand in hand to ensure organisational success: we need a company peopled by 'organisation men'. However, what happens to creativity and innovation when this happens? It is interesting to note that some of the organisations identified by Peters and Waterman as 'excellent' have had serious declines in their financial performance (for example, Caterpillar Tractor and Schlumberger) – is this in spite of or because of their culture and levels of commitment?

What, then, is the answer? Do organisations deliberately employ people who are not 'organisation men' in order to foster a climate of creativity and innovation? If so, what is likely to be the commitment levels of these people and, therefore, the subsequent effect on organisational performance?

2 The last five years have seen a dramatic increase in organisations investing in customer care programmes. Larger companies have spent considerable sums of money not only in training their employees but also in telling the world at large about it – remember 'We're getting there' (British Rail) and 'Ask for Tom' (Texas Homecare)? For the most part, these programmes were introduced in order to give the organisation a competitive edge in the market place: 'We may not be cheaper than Company X but we care for you, the customer.'

However, after a while, the bandwagon became so popular that an in-house customer care programme became a necessity, a way of 'keeping up', rather than trying to gain or sustain competitive advantage. One of the authors was inundated with consultancy requests to 'change the attitudes of my shopfloor with a half-day customer care course', followed by 'No, the rest of us have got the right approach, it's just the shopfloor/front facing staff who've got the attitude problem'. What is actually needed here is a long-term programme of culture change rather than an ineffective quick-fix solution (as one employee said, 'Why should I care about the customer when the company doesn't care about me . . . ?').

All too often these programmes, including a recognition of the need to change the culture itself, are seen as quick-fix solutions and then the organisation wonders why it hasn't worked – except that it's all the fault of the staff, isn't it?

Customer care is now being replaced with 'empowerment' as the ultimate panacea for the organisation's ills. Will we be updating this 'Pause for thought' in a few years time by replacing the references to 'customer care' with references to 'empowerment' and adding in the latest fad at the end of the piece?

Still not convinced?

1 'A change is as good as a rest', they say, so you go abroad for a good holiday (even if you don't like the food), because foreigners are such a change. But *working* with them is another matter: there the difference can be stressful rather than restful.

Books and articles advising managers about cultural differences abound, especially since the Single Market pushed Europeans even closer together, causing a spate of mergers and takeovers.

The *Independent on Sunday* (3 July 1994) tells of the frustration of Japanese consultant Chihiro Nakao, for instance. He is used to gauging the commitment of managers by how much shoe leather they wear out 'walking the factory', but at Porsche he found that the Germans had their shoes resoled. To write *Riding the Waves of Culture* (Economist Books, 1993) Frans Trompenaars compiled a database of thirty companies in fifty countries, and recommends that managers stop seeing cultural problems as other people's stubbornness. The *Guardian* (16 March 1993) claims the French and Germans only get on in border firms in places like Strasbourg. Elsewhere it is Protestants against Rationalists throughout the working day in the 3,000 or so companies with Franco-German management. John Mole (1990) warned of culture clash in *Mind your Manners*: don't take your jacket off in Germany, avoid levity in the office in France, in Holland be blunt and direct, and make it a point of honour in Italy to get round regulations. His principal advice is 'learn the language'.

That is just what everyone is doing all the time in Midshire University's Department of Languages, where a curious cultural contamination rather than cultural clash may be witnessed taking place. The British lecturers appear to take on the cultural characteristics of the people whose language they specialise in. So the staff in the Spanish section do everything *mañana*, while in the French section negotiating in abstractions, like justice and equality, is normal, and the long-suffering students have to acquire a very un-British rational approach to every bit of work they do. The secretary in the Russian section says her lecturers are an Eastern European version of the Spanish, the head of Italian is renowned for working her way around the bureaucracy, and as for punctuality in the German section, well the hapless secretary arrives each morning to be met in the entrance by the otherwise thoroughly English head of section who has been pacing up and down for ten minutes waiting for her.

There is clearly not much hope of the global village occurring in *that* particular organisation.

2 For this one we're still at Midshires University. Anne (our candidate from Chapter 6) was, as expected, appointed to the post in the Engineering Department and on 1 September that year she duly reported for work. Having gone through the required two days' induction she then set about trying to settle in to the job. Six days later she'd finally got an office (but no computer or telephone as yet) and three weeks later (just as term was about to start) she'd finally been given her teaching schedule, although she hadn't been able to make contact with the relevant course managers because they were still on holiday. It was certainly a far cry from industry and she hadn't found people to be particularly helpful; it wasn't deliberate, she thought, but everyone seemed wrapped up in their own little worlds.

On the first day of term she donned a smart business suit from her industry days and went in to teach her first class. She was surprised to see that her colleagues were dressed in the same way as they had been in the summer except that the shorts had been replaced by a variety of jeans and cord trousers (invariably baggy) and that trainers or loafers had replaced sandals. Here and there a tie was in evidence but it was of the knitted variety last seen outside academia thirty years ago. As the first semester drew on, baggy corduroy jackets appeared against inclement weather. 'This lot are so scruffy,' Anne thought, 'I'm not going to let myself get like them – I think we've got a professional status to uphold and one of the ways to do it is to look smart.' She was determined to retain what she thought of as her image, even though she was aware of the nickname given to her by both students and colleagues – in fact she was quite flattered to be called Mrs Thatcher.

The first semester was drawing to an end and Anne found herself unconsciously replacing her jackets with comfortable sweaters. By the end of the second semester she was to be found in leggings and baggy T-shirts. At a meeting called to discuss a new degree she found herself sitting next to a man in a business suit and tie. 'You can tell he comes from the Business School,' she thought as she drove off in the second-hand Citroen 2CV which had recently replaced her BMW.

The main point to make here is the socialisation of new people into an organisation in order to inculcate them and get them to adopt cultural norms. Here we can see that the process was quite a long one and was accomplished almost unconsciously – quite a different approach from our Army example.

Afterthought

The difference between involvement and commitment has been described as being similar to a plate of eggs and bacon: the hen is involved but the pig is committed . . .

12 The nature of management

Effective management: hard news or soft sell?

In this case study you will be introduced to two managers, Harold Plumb and Ian McCullem, both of who work for the same small company, Timothy Willis Ltd. Having made their acquaintance you will be asked to make an assessment of their behaviour and effectiveness as managers; but first, let's tell you a little more about the company which employs them.

Timothy Willis Ltd

Founded in the last quarter of the nineteenth century, the company is a weekly newspaper publisher and 'jobbing' printer located in an essentially rural part of north-east Scotland. Family owned (by the Willises) since it was established, the current managing director is a member of the fifth generation to have a direct involvement in the running of the business, succeeding to the post upon her mother's retirement some five years ago. The family has a high profile in the community, supporting local causes and charities, and often using 'the power of the press' to publicise important issues.

The company was established by Timothy Willis to realise his dream of becoming a newspaper publisher. Although never becoming a 'media baron' he was successful in launching a weekly paper, the *North East News* or 'the *NEN*' as it is affectionately known to generations of both readers and company employees. The paper has flourished over the years: its circulation steadily rising to a current level of 18,000 copies a week in an area where the total population (excluding sheep and grouse!) is around 65,000. It has no serious competition: the only other paper in the area being a monthly 'freesheet.' This has attracted *some* advertising revenue, but *NEN* remains a financially sound and profitable publication.

Timothy was a shrewd enough businessman to realise that publishing a weekly newspaper would not occupy the time of all his production staff for the whole week. So, in common, with many other, similarly sized newspaper companies he established a printing business which would utilise equipment and employee time when newspaper production was completed for the week. However, printing work has been generally regarded as the 'poor relation' at the company; a view that was certainly reflected in the Willis family attitudes. The new managing director appears, though, to be taking a different approach and is looking at ways to improve the effectiveness and efficiency of this part of the business.

The company employs thirty-one staff organised into four departments each with a manager who reports to the managing director. The editorial department is headed by Ian McCullem and has six journalists and a photographer while the production department, the responsibility of Harold Plumb, employs fourteen staff. The administrative support to the company's operations is in the hands of the office manager and her team of four employees. In addition there is a small team of three advertising staff, including the sales manager.

Many of the staff are long-serving employees, some of who have been with the company for all their working lives. Labour turnover is very low. The only leavers tend to be women in the office roles who choose to start a family and younger journalists who move to further their careers. A trade union is recognised for production workers and a different one for journalists, but both rarely get involved in company matters. The style of the company, perhaps not surprisingly given its family ownership, is paternalistic, although with the last two managing directors being women, 'maternalistic' has been suggested as a better metaphor.

Ian McCullem and the editorial department

Born and bred locally, Ian McCullem is in his mid-thirties and has been a journalist all his working life having joined the *NEN* after finishing his college course in journalism some fifteen years ago. He progressed rapidly through the grades of reporter and took over as editor of the paper four years ago when the then incumbent decided to vacate the position. Ian's predecessor is still employed by the company as a journalist but there has been no sign of this causing any difficulties in working relationships. Ian is highly regarded by his fellow journalists and in the community as a whole.

Under his stewardship the paper has maintained its strong readership loyalty despite making a number of changes of which the Willis family were initially unsure. However, all have proved to be a success and as a result Ian suffers from very little proprietorial interference in the way he manages the editorial side of the business. Very early on in his post as editor, he abandoned the paper's tradition of having classified advertisements on the front page, replacing them with news stories. He also introduced changes which affected the work of a number of the journalists. Three of the reporters were given responsibility for particular parts of the news carried by the *NEN*: motoring, sport and farming, the latter being a chief topic of interest amongst the readership. Each of these reporters now compiles the material for these sections, often writing much of the copy themselves but where necessary seeking assistance from colleagues. Ian's policy is to confirm with each of these reporters at the start of the week the number of pages they intend to provide and to leave them to get on with the work, only checking the final material a few hours before the paper is to be printed. He has, however, made it clear to these journalists that he is always available for advice and guidance should they need it. Although quite regular in the beginning, such requests have declined over time.

Although effectively working autonomously on their respective pages, these journalists are still expected to contribute to the rest of the paper. In particular, Ian holds a regular meeting with the whole editorial team at the beginning of the week to identify likely newsworthy stories. These are discussed and responsibility for their coverage determined. Usually this is through personal choice but Ian reserves the right to allocate reporters to particular stories if necessary. This rarely happens since the involvement in the decision-making process usually leads to staff volunteering for jobs even if their preference is for another story.

Most of the editorial staff are in their twenties and the *NEN* is often their first job after leaving college. The company has been able usually to recruit locally: only one of the last four appointments coming from outside the area. However, working for the paper is rarely seen as a lifetime occupation for journalists who, as indicated earlier, move to other organizations as part of their career development. For example, one left three years ago to join an evening paper in the south of Scotland, while the most recent leaver resigned a few months ago to join a local independent radio station as a news journalist. Recognising the reality of this situation, Ian sees part of his responsibility to be development of journalistic careers and the paper is becoming recognised as a place to go to obtain a good 'on-job' training.

Harold Plumb and the production department

Harold is also a local man, in his late forties, who joined Timothy Willis Ltd over twenty years ago as a typesetter – an employee who types material provided by reporters or advertising staff ready for it to be transferred for printing. He took up the position of production manager almost fifteen years ago following the enforced retirement, on ill-health grounds, of the then general manager and a reallocation of duties amongst the management team. Moving straight from the shopfloor into a management role was something of a shock for him, particularly as he was offered no training and very limited guidance from the company on what was expected of him.

Harold has three sections in the production department for which he is respons-ible: typesetting, where the seven operators sit at computer stations inputting advertising and editorial copy for the newspaper; the print floor, which has three machines each with its own operator producing work for the 'jobbing print' side of the business; and finishing, where completed print jobs are trimmed, if necessary, glued, and wrapped ready for despatch to customers. The typesetting department also sets material for the printing machines but this work has to be fitted in around the demands of the paper, which is given priority.

About the time of Harold's promotion, the company was going through what amounted to one of the most significant changes in its history. Until the end of the 1970s the paper had been produced by what is known as the 'hot metal' method. This method was considered to be slow, inefficient and produced poorer quality newspapers than that available from newer, computer-based technology. A substantial investment was therefore made by the company in updating its production operations. However, Willis was unable to afford a new printing machine capable of producing the *NEN* and since this time, printing of the paper has been subcontracted to a printer about thirty miles away.

The changes in technology meant that some typesetters, particularly the older ones, were unable to adapt to the new work and, in line with the company's paternalistic approach, were given jobs in the finishing department rather than being required to take redundancy. However, some of the remaining typesetters are quite slow at the work and the department is not as efficient as it could be.

The 'jobbing' print work is also a cause for concern. New print machines were also purchased at the same time but no formal training was given to the operators. The majority of the work is 'short run' jobs from the local area including parish magazines, advertising posters, personal and business stationery and business documents. This means that the printers spend much of their time cleaning the machines after one job and getting ready for the next with a comparatively short time actually printing.

Harold is not a printer by trade and is unable to give much help even if he were asked. This is unlikely as the printers seem to have little respect for him. Morale throughout the production department is low but nowhere lower than on the print floor. The operators hardly speak to, and refuse to help, each other. All are concerned with 'protecting their own back'. Each of them at one time or another has been threatened by Harold with the sack if they 'don't pull their socks up'; this despite the fact that only the managing director has the authority in the company to dismiss an employee. When faced with problems, Harold's preferred style is to shout and 'ball out' the employee and even, on more than one occasion, to threaten physical violence.

However, there have been no voluntary leavers amongst production employees, partly due, it is supposed, to the limited job opportunities locally, certainly ones that pay as well as Timothy Willis.

The managing director has become increasingly concerned at the poor utilisation of employee and machine time and the financial losses that the print side are incurring. When she has broached this to Harold his response has been to blame this on the laziness of the staff. The MD is less than convinced since there appears to very little planning of work and jobs are allocated to machines apparently at the last minute.

The company has also received a number of complaints from print customers about late delivery of work and missed deadlines despite their having received an assurance from Harold that their work would be completed on time. One or two have also remarked on Harold's rudeness to them both on the telephone and face to face. There are now a number of other print companies becoming established in the area, who appear to be cheaper and more reliable than Timothy Willis and a loss of customers could damage the company's profitability and lead to job losses.

Activity brief

1 Utilising the exposition in Mullins (Chapter 13) of Theory X and Theory Y, and the Leadership Grid, how would you characterise the differences in approach Harold and Ian take to people and management? How effective does each appear to be as a manager?

2 What are the variables, both personal and organisational, that may have influenced the pattern of management displayed by Ian and Harold? (You may find Likert's analysis of management in Chapter 13 of Mullins a useful starting point for answering this question.)

*Case study provided by Derek Adam-Smith, University of Portsmouth.

Great expectations and hard times: A tale of two managers

The following case study is based on research carried out by Dr Colin Hales and Michael Nightingale for the Hotel and Catering Institutional Management Association and the then Hotel and Catering Industry Training Board. The research used depth interviews with the managers' role sets and the managers themselves, together with structured observation of the managers' work.

Alex

Alex is the manager of a busy unit of a family restaurant chain owned by a large food, drink and leisure company which has shown steady growth over the past twenty years. The restaurant, situated beside a main road, is open daily and offers a standard low-price fixed menu of popular dishes and waitress service for up to 150 people. The site also offers washroom facilities, a small shop and a children's play area. All areas of work in the restaurant – cooking, service, cleaning/maintenance, billing and record keeping – are standardised and codified in detailed operating manuals. Alex, who has worked for the company for the past five years, is thirty-four, married, educated to HND level, and has switched careers from retail to catering management. He works shifts with two (variable) days off in seven. He has a deputy manager, restaurant manager and chef reporting to him directly and he, in turn, reports to an area manager.

A number of people, therefore, have expectations about what Alex *ought* to be doing in his job: his immediate boss, senior line and head office managers, his deputy manager, other staff in the unit, the restaurant's customers and, of course, Alex himself. Despite some differences, there is considerable agreement among these expectations and, indeed, many of them are explicitly communicated in such things as company regulations, operating manuals, standard forms and controls.

Broadly speaking, Alex is expected to deal with eight key areas:

1 *Staffing* Ensuring adequate staffing levels, recruiting/selecting staff (waitresses and cooks), conducting training, allocating duties, organising rotas and holidays, dealing with grievances and keeping staff records.

2 *Premises/Equipment* Making sure that they are kept clean and well maintained.

3 *Materials* Controlling stock, ordering goods and checking deliveries.

4 *Money* Controlling costs, controlling cash and completing financial returns.

5 *Customers* Liaising with customers, monitoring customer satisfaction with the service and dealing with customer requests and complaints.

6 *Operations* Organising, monitoring and checking work.

7 *Quality* Ensuring that company product and service standards are maintained.

8 *Business performance* Meeting sales/profit targets, developing promotions and new business ideas, and making the business grow.

Predictably, Alex's managers emphasise the 'money', 'customers', 'quality' and 'business performance' aspects of the job, whilst his staff place more emphasis on 'staffing', 'materials' and day-to-day 'operations' matters. Alex himself acknowledges that these are what his job is about, with two notable exceptions: first, he does not believe that it is his job to train his staff; and second, he does not see it as his responsibility to develop new business for the restaurant.

In terms of how he spends his time, Alex concentrates on maintaining the provision of a standard service by ensuring that the restaurant has an adequate supply of staff, materials and equipment and by monitoring the operational performance of the restaurant, using standard control procedures. The key *tasks* which occupy most of his time are:

● Ordering/controlling materials.

● Controlling money (cash receipts and expenditure).

● Monitoring operational performance.

● Maintaining company quality standards.

● Planning and maintaining staff levels.

This means that, in terms of *activities*, Alex concentrates on the following matters (in descending order of time spent):

1 Cashing up (emptying the till, counting the takings) and putting them in bags to take to the bank).

2 Stocktaking (day-to-day checks plus a full stocktake lasting five hours on a Sunday evening).

3 Ordering goods (completing order forms and telephoning for goods which run out unexpectedly, and checking deliveries).

4 Talking to customers at the till and dealing with customers' requests or complaints.

5 Helping out in areas of operational work (cooking, moving stock, working the till, cleaning, making minor repairs to equipment and, occasionally, serving in the restaurant).
6 Drawing up staff rotas, allocating duties and recording time sheets.
7 Checking the quality of food and service by observing staff at work.

There are two activities which, in view of other people's expectations of him, are conspicuously absent from Alex's work: first, training (except for the occasional cursory instruction to an employee on how to do something, usually in response to an employee request); and secondly, any kind of 'entrepreneurial' activity such as local advertising, offering special promotions or generating new business ideas.

This absence of entrepreneurial activity is not surprising, however, given the number of rules and procedures within which Alex has to work. Such things as menus and prices, methods of food preparation and presentation, restaurant decor/furniture and nominated suppliers of materials are all determined by head office. The only area of choice available to Alex is where to purchase fresh vegetables.

Yet much of what Alex does is chosen, rather than imposed. For example, he chooses to carry out stocktaking and cashing-up himself rather than delegating them and he is quite happy – indeed, rather enjoys – working the till, replacing light bulbs and broken toilet seats, and cooking at the griddle. On the other hand, he is content to exercise indirect 'paper' control over the restaurant, leaving the more direct management of staff to his deputies.

This is reflected in the manner in which Alex does his job. He spends most of his time at his desk in a small, windowless office, away from the restaurant. For the remainder of the time, he is operating the till in the restaurant, working in the stock room, or is out, paying in takings to the local bank. About a third of his time is spent on various forms of paperwork: completing weekly trading reports, records of takings, ledgerbook, staff time sheets, stock records and checking delivery notes, price lists, invoices, and so on. About a sixth of his time is spent helping out on operational tasks. The remaining time is spent in some form of interaction with others. A small proportion of these contacts are scheduled meetings – usually in the form of regular meetings with the area manager to discuss day-to-day issues or, less frequently, with the regional manager. The remaining contacts are either telephone conversations, usually with suppliers about orders and deliveries, or unscheduled meetings, which are many, varied, generally short-lived and are usually initiated by someone else (either a member of staff or a customer). These unscheduled meetings are mainly either brief exchanges with customers as they pay their bill or they are interruptions from staff – requests for information or assistance – during paperwork. It is not unusual, for example, for Alex to be interrupted during completion of the weekly trading report by a cook asking for help in opening a can of fruit cocktail.

Alex, therefore, tends to be much more attuned to expectations which are either immediate – that is, they come from face-to-face contact with his staff or his immediate boss – or specific – that is, they are explicitly stated in regulations and manuals. He is much less aware of the more general expectations of senior managers in the company or of customers. Therefore, he tends to do the things he *must* do, rather than exploring what he *could* do. As a result, his job is predominantly one of routine paperwork and 'helping out'.

Rose

Rose is the manager of a domestic services unit responsible for the cleaning and housekeeping of a large National Health hospital in the Midlands. In common with other hospitals, it is undergoing considerable changes in funding and structure. Most relevant here is the move towards 'contracting out' ancillary services such as cleaning, laundry and catering through a process of competitive tendering in which existing in-house services, such as domestic services, are invited to participate. The provision of domestic services, however, continues to be subject to stringent regulations, imposed by the health authority, relating to hygiene standards. The domestic services unit is strongly unionised and staff are fearful of, and opposed to, the impending changes.

Rose, who has worked in hospital domestic services for seven years, is twenty-nine, single and educated to HND level. She reports directly to the hospital administrator and has six supervisors reporting to her, each in charge of cleaning in a particular area of the hospital (a group of wards, for example).

A very diverse set of people have expectations about what Rose *ought* to be doing in her job: her immediate boss (the hospital administrator), other senior managers (such as personnel), her immediate subordinates (the supervisors), the domestic staff of the hospital, trade union representatives, the nursing and medical staff, and the patients. Therefore, she is subject to different and conflicting pressures, not only from 'above' and 'below', but also from three different areas within the hospital – administration, domestic services and health care – each with its own distinct culture. Because it is a time of change and uncertainty, there are many new and ambiguous expectations emerging in addition to those currently expressed more explicitly in hospital regulations.

In broad terms, Rose is *expected* to work on seven key areas:

1 *Staffing* On a day-to-day basis, this means ensuring adequate staffing levels, recruiting and selecting domestic staff, conducting training, allocating duties, organising shifts and holidays, dealing with grievances, and keeping staff records. In the longer term, however, it means managing, or reconciling, the administrators' requirements – that the domestic services unit become more efficient and competitive through changes in work practices and possible redundancies – with the staff and union expectations that their jobs remain secure. These long-term expectations also colour, and make more difficult, short-term issues such as allocating duties, recruiting new staff and dealing with grievances. They also give rise to ongoing industrial relations work, meeting and negotiating with trade union representatives.

2 *Premises/equipment* Making sure that all surface areas of the hospital and linen are kept scrupulously clean.

3 *Information* Explaining existing and new regulations and policy, and offering technical advice when required.

4 *Operations* Organising, directing and monitoring the work of domestic staff.

5 *'Client' liaison* Liaising with nursing and medical staff.

6 *Quality* Negotiating and reconciling the competing and often ambiguous standards of service quality defined by nursing, medical, domestic and administrative staff and ensuring that these negotiated standards are met.

7 *Self* Being knowledgeable, acting as a source of information and advice and being involved in the process of change within the hospital.

Therefore, although there is general agreement about the *areas* of work which make up Rose's job, there is considerable disagreement over *what* she should be trying to achieve in these areas. Rose not only recognises these areas as central to her job but also that the job is 'political' in that she must manage these conflicts. Because of this she perceives her job as having clear priorities and, consequently, sees certain tasks, such as staff induction, training and development and acting as a technical adviser, as less important, at least for the present.

Rose, therefore, spends her time trying to bring about an increasingly efficient and effective cleaning service to the satisfaction of both administrative and nursing/medical staff. This means that she has a preoccupation with day-to-day staffing matters and long-term staffing issues. The key *tasks* which occupy most of her time are:

● Planning and ensuring adequate levels of staffing in the short term.

● Maintaining good industrial relations.

● Ensuring and maintaining standards of cleanliness.

● Controlling the cost of the domestic services function.

● Bringing about a lower level of staffing in the long term through the restructuring of work.

She is, therefore, mainly engaged on the following activities (in descending order of time spent):

1 Organising staff duties, rotas and holidays.

2 Dealing with staff grievances.

3 Checking work quality and hygiene standards.

4 Negotiating with union representatives and handling disputes.

5 Identifying the need for equipment repairs and new materials.

6 Discussing organisational policy changes for staff.

Contrary to others' expectations, but consistent with Rose's own priorities, three activities are absent: first, staff training; second, acting as a general technical adviser; and third, general liaison with nursing and medical staff. In the prevailing atmosphere of crisis and uncertainty, in which staffing and industrial relations issues are to the fore, Rose sees these other activities as unaffordable luxuries.

Indeed, the climate of change has made Rose's job less clearly defined than before. Under these circumstances, although the restructuring issue is *what* must preoccupy her, Rose has considerable choice about *how* she handles it. She chooses to make the job people-oriented and 'political', trying to reconcile competing interests, ameliorating the impact of change on domestic staff, and fighting for the integrity and continued existence of the domestic services unit within the hospital. This means that her approach is proactive and highly involved in hospital matters.

This is reflected in the manner in which Rose does her job. She spends a significant amount of her time out of the office, either at meetings or touring the hospital, speaking to domestics, nurses or administrative staff and checking the progress and quality of work. Indeed, interactions of one kind or another take up most of Rose's time. Many of these are scheduled and time-consuming committee meetings, policy meetings or negotiations, involving a wide variety of people (administrators, the personnel department, trade union representatives and medical staff). In addition, Rose also spends much of her time on more fleeting unscheduled meetings or conversations – with domestic, nursing and administrative staff. Many of these are instigated by Rose herself, seeking out people to obtain or give information, to deal with problems and to request or give assistance. Paperwork takes up relatively little of her time and is largely concerned with staff/personnel matters. Telephone calls are mainly internal, again predominantly about staff-related matters.

Rose's mobile, proactive involvement in the hospital reflects her general awareness of the politics of the organisation. She defines her job not only in terms of the more formal demands of her superiors and the medical staff but also in terms of the more ambiguous expectations of her supervisors and staff. Out of this uncertainty she has created the kind of job which she feels she *ought* to do: the proactive, personalised management of a key political issue.

 ## Activity brief

1 Compare and contrast the two jobs in terms of:
   (a) Mintzberg's 'managerial roles';
   (b) Stewart's 'job types' and 'contact patterns'; and
   (c) Stewart's 'demands, constraints and choices' model.
   How useful are these frameworks for pointing up the similarities and differences between the two jobs?

2 How far and in what ways are the two managers influenced by:
   (a) the internal environment of the organisation; and
   (b) the external environment?

3 How far can the similarities and differences between the two jobs be explained by the fact that they are both in the service sector but one is in the private sector whilst the other is in the public sector?

4 Which of the two managers is the more effective? Give your reasons, indicating in particular how you define 'effective'. What other evidence, if any, would you require in order to judge the managers' effectiveness?

Case provided by Dr. Colkin Hales, University of Surrey.

The successful executive

This is the story of Lynette Thompson, who runs a very successful business. She started out as a self-employed European Community legislation consultant. For the first three years, Lynette balanced the tasks of designing and running consultancy programmes for a select group of clients.

As time progressed, Lynette's workload became increasingly difficult to cope with. She travelled extensively in the UK and Europe providing consultancy programmes for her client companies. At the same time, she was her own book-keeper, administrative assistant and researcher.

Gradually, Lynette's workload increased to such an extent that she found herself working seven days a week. She felt she could cope as her office was in her home. However, Lynette's constant fear was that she would become ill, and not be able to work. She also had a home, a husband, a teenager and two dogs to think about and make time for.

Lynette did not feel her earnings justified the hire of a secretarial assistant or a researcher, so she continued to work an increasing number of hours; she also increased her travelling. She felt compelled to take on more challenging consultancy programmes in order to make a name for herself, and to grow and develop professionally.

Lynette believed in networking as a way to increase business. She joined two successful international business organisations. Soon, she found herself on a subcommittee, with more responsibilities. She agreed to run a monthly advisory programme without a fee. This was a good networking strategy, but it increased the pressures on her already overloaded life.

Adding further pressure, in the third year of running her own business Lynette began to publish a monthly newsletter for her clients. This provided a useful complement to her consultancy activities, and kept her clients abreast of new developments in the labyrinth of European legislation.

In year four, Lynette began to feel the physical repercussions of her activities. More fatigued than usual, one day she found herself almost unable to get out of bed. This frightened her, particularly as she prided herself on eating well, staying healthy and keeping fit.

She adhered to a daily routine of fitness. Even so, Lynette often rose at 4.30 a.m. to fly to a European destination, and worked with her clients until late each evening. She did try to make an hour for herself every evening prior to dinner, and kept up a regular routine of personal and professional reading.

What had gone wrong? Lynette began a round of visits to her doctor and to the local hospital for tests. The tests showed that she was extremely fit – great blood pressure, no cholesterol problems, good heart, and so forth. Yet she was beginning to feel more and more ill. She began to have regular headaches, lose her naturally clear complexion, suffer weight loss, and find her energy level severely depleted.

Despite these signals, Lynette felt she had no choice but to persevere with her strenuous programme. One day, she found she could not go on. Her system collapsed.

Out of sheer desperation, Lynette went to an acupuncturist and a naturopathic doctor. This doctor discovered the problem. He diagnosed an infection of the liver and the malfunction of her adrenal glands – the accelerator pedal of the body. This came as a great shock to Lynette, who couldn't understand how this could have happened to her. She had no choice but to cancel most of her consultancy engagements for the next two-month period, and began a strict dietary regime, taking recommended minerals, vitamins and medicines to eliminate the liver and adrenal problems.

Gradually, over a period of six months, Lynette began to recover her mental and physical wellbeing. However, her illness caused her to look seriously at her working life. She realised that some radical changes were necessary. But where to begin?

 # Activity brief

1 What could Lynette have done differently to deal with her pressures, and cope with the immense stress she was under?

2 What would you recommend she do, once she reached the point of having to submit to her illness and cancel some of her work?

3 What role do you think gender played in the case of Lynette? Could that have been one of the issues which drove her on?

4 What can you do, as an individual, to plan a strategy for 'managing' stress in order to avoid a situation similar to that of Lynette?

5 What needs to be done at an organisational level (i.e. by management within an organisation) to help all of its employees to recognise the symptoms and causes of stress – and ultimately to cope?

Further reading

Brewer, K. C. (1991), *The Stress Management Handbook*, National Press Publications.

Froggatt, H. and Stamp, P. (1991), *Managing Pressure at Work*, BBC Books.

Hamilton, R. (1993), *Mentoring*, The Industrial Society.

Motivation cassettes: based on the book by P. Makin and P. Lindley, *Positive Stress Management*, Kogan Page, 1994.

Mullins, L. J. (1993), *Management and Organisational Behaviour*, Pitman, 190–2, 486–7, 532–53.

Scott, D. (1993), *Stress That Motivates*, Kogan Page.

Shea, G. F. (1992), *Mentoring*, Kogan Page.

Case contributed by Sunny Stout, Sun Training.

 # What is management?

See Mullins, pp. 391–7.

Chemical company

See Mullins, p. 427.

 Activity one: The jigsaw test

Logistics

The group should be divided into three smaller groups: Organisation A, Organisation B and Observer group. The composition of each organisation is as follows:

A customer   A chairman
A distributor   A production manager
A development manager   Production workers
Development staff

Whilst each organisation is identical in terms of work roles, Organisation A has a supportive climate with management and subordinates working together to sustain the business, and Organisation B has an authoritarian climate, with management and subordinates working apart.

Materials required

- 5m of fishing line (40–50 lbs breaking strain).
- A supply of medium-sized paper clips.
- A supply of A4 laser copier paper (80–100 grams weight).

Task

Each organisation must select their own roles from their respective team members. Your task is divided into phases 1–3 below.

Phase 1 Innovation (10 minutes)

Rules

- *Organisation A* The subordinates must *respect* management directives, leadership and decision-making. Management must *support* both each other and their workforce.

- *Organisation B* The subordinates *must not* advise management. Management must *control* the workforce using their authority and power.

Task

You are to produce a product to your customer which is a simple paper dart. Each paper dart must be delivered to the customer over a distance of four metres, unassisted, using only the materials supplied. Your objectives for this phase, therefore, are:

1 To design the paper dart.

2 To construct the transport system for product delivery.

You will *not* be allowed to proceed to the next phase until you have achieved these objectives – the organiser's decision is final!

You should collect from the organiser a 5m length of fishing line, a supply of A4 paper clips, and some A4 paper.

Phase 2 Manufacturing (20 minutes)

Rules

- *Organisation A* Subordinates are *empowered* to control the manufacturing process and improve efficiency. Management are to analyse workforce behaviour, *advise and support* the workforce. (NB: Management will be entitled to a 50 per cent share out of the total profits made during the manufacturing phase.)

- *Organisation B* Subordinates are *not empowered* to control the manufacturing process or to improve efficiency but only to *respond* to management directives. Management must *control* the manufacturing process; decisions made by the chairman are final. (NB: Subordinates will be entitled to a 50 per cent share out of the total profits made during the manufacturing phase.)

Task

The key objective during this phase is to deliver as many paper darts as possible to the customer within the time allowed. Each paper dart successfully received by the customer wins the organisation a profit of £100,000. Management in both teams must record the number of successfully received paper darts.

Each team member is to take their place according to the layout shown in Figure 12.1. The constructed transport system must separate management from the workforce. The following are the tasks for each section of the organisation:

- *Development* To create a model paper dart and pass it to Production together with an additional sheet of A4 paper. The department then continues to resource production.

- *Production* To receive the model dart from Development and replicate it. The finished product is passed to Distribution. The department then repeats the manufacturing process.

- *Distribution* To receive the dart from Production and attach the paper dart to the transport system for despatch. Each paper dart is detached by the customer.

Phase 3 Share out (10 minutes)

The management of both teams calculate the total profit gained during their manufacturing phase. Each chairman will then allocate 50 per cent of the profits to those entitled to receive them.

Fig. 12.1 Team layout for Organisations A and B

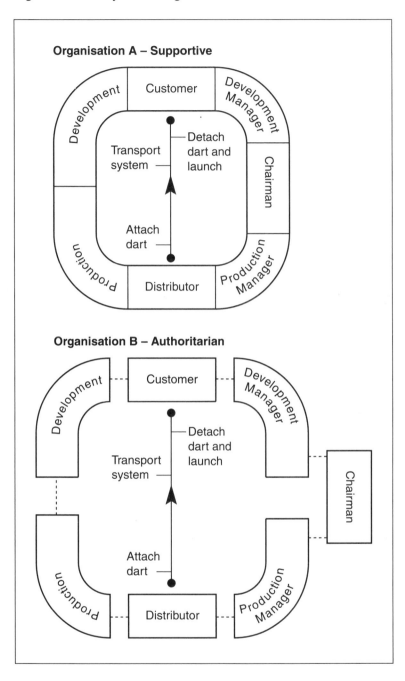

Phase 4 Plenary session

This should be led by the Observer group using the questions below. They should also present their perceptions as to the *nature* and *performance* of both organisations.

Organisation A

1 What behaviours emerged when innovation became a joint effort between management and subordinates (motivation vs roles)?

2 Did management experience a greater accessibility to the attitudes of their empowered workforce (attitude vs influence)?

3 Did management experience any dilution of leadership identity, power or influence as a result of working with an empowered workforce (self-perception vs power-redistribution)?

Organisation B

1 What perceptions were experienced by the subordinates when their management controlled innovation (perception vs leadership)?

2 Did the subordinate workforce react to the unequal distribution of management authority (conflict vs authority)?

3 Did management favour a subordinate, challenge an equal or desire the role of chairman (power vs politics)?

Activity provided by Nick Cox, Executive MBA Programme, University of Portsmouth.

 Activity two

This activity is a time management exercise. Read the text below and then, in small groups, answer the questions at the end.

Suzanne Potts has been an area sales manager for Page Fashions in the South-West for the last six months and is an energetic manager who, prior to her promotion, had been with the company for five years as a store manager. Page Fashions have both stand-alone high street shops and also shop-in-shops in many of the large department stores.

She believes that she manages her time effectively but recognises that sometimes distractions prevent her from accomplishing what she considers to be the most important aspects of her job. Suzanne generally likes to do some informal planning of what she thinks must be achieved each day.

On Monday evening Suzanne was relaxing at home, thinking about some of the things she knew needed to be done the next day. In her mind she prepared her schedule for the following day.

Planned schedule

AM   Check progress of new manager at shop-in-shop, Badgers, Bournemouth.

10.00	Appointment with David Douglas, store director, Badgers, Bournemouth.
PM	Follow-up customer care training, Page stand-alone shop, Bournemouth and complete an area managers' sales and branch administration checklist.
	Ring regional sales director to discuss arrangements for appraisal next week.
	Ring Jane Pearson, recruitment officer, about vacancies in the area.

Actual schedule

8.30	Arrives at Page shop, Bournemouth, has a cup of coffee and discusses the recently received new range with the manager.
9.00	Leaves to walk to Badgers across the precinct.
9.05	Arrives at Badgers to talk to Sarah Brooks, the new manager. However, Sarah has an appointment with personnel at 9.15 to discuss the customer service training sessions organised by Badgers and had expected to see Susan after her appointment with Mr Douglas.
9.15	Suzanne notices the department is looking untidy and starts to remerchandise it. The part-timer assists and gets extra stock from the stockroom to fill up the department. Suzanne is pleased to be able to serve two customers who each buy a complete outfit.
9.45	The manager returns, joins in the remerchandising and helps the part-timer to put the stock on the correct hangers.
9.50	The Page shop, Exeter, rings Suzanne with an urgent query concerning the banking. They appear to be missing £10 from the cash register and the manager suspects a member of staff, although she does not have any evidence.
10.00	Suzanne makes a note to ring the personnel department for information concerning the member of staff and some guidance concerning the correct procedures. She leaves the floor after checking that she has made a note of all the problems associated with the query.
10.05	Suzanne arrives late for her appointment with Mr Douglas. His secretary has just put through a telephone call and asks Suzanne to sit and wait.
10.15	Mr Douglas greets Suzanne and apologises for keeping her waiting. They discuss the plans for resiting the department and the schedule previously discussed. As an additional point, he is concerned about the size of the deliveries and the amount of stockroom space that seems to be needed. Suzanne agrees to look into the problem.
11.00	Suzanne has a quick coffee in the customer restaurant and uses the time to make some notes concerning her meeting with Mr Douglas.
11.20	She returns to the department. Sarah and her part-timer have completed the remerchandising. There are one or two changes which Suzanne feels that she needs to make and which she briefly discusses with Sarah.
11.45	Sarah asks if she can talk to Suzanne about a personal problem. She needs to take some holiday to try to sort out an argument she has had with her landlord which may involve her moving out of her present accommodation. They discuss the issue at length on the shop floor and Suzanne agrees that Sarah can take two days holiday the following week.

12.20	Suzanne leaves to go back to the stand-alone shop. On the way to the shop she buys some sandwiches and a drink from Marks & Spencer.
12.45	When she arrives at the shop, the manager is at lunch. Suzanne eats her sandwiches and then sits in the office and makes her phone calls to head office.
1.00	Jane Pearson, recruitment officer, is interviewing, so Suzanne leaves a message for her to ring back. The merchandise department checks the deliveries and allocation for Badgers and it appears that they are only marginally larger than in the previous year, but they agree to check the details and ring back.
1.15	Anne, the manager, returns from lunch and Suzanne starts to talk to her about the customer care programme. Debbie, the deputy, comes into the office to say that there is a problem with the cash register and they all go out on to the shop floor. Suzanne realises that it is a problem with the audit roll and spends five minutes fixing it. While they are out on the floor a customer complaint appears to be getting heated and Suzanne steps in to sort it out.
1.45	Suzanne returns to the office to ring her sales director concerning her appraisal next week. They discuss the format and Suzanne agrees to prepare some notes beforehand. She does this straight away while it is fresh in her mind.
2.00	The training manager rings to discuss Suzanne's nominations for the next New Manager Induction Course. They also discuss Suzanne's recommendations for an area trainer for the south-west region.
2.10	Suzanne continues her discussion with Anne about the customer care training. She then spends fifteen minutes talking to the sales assistants about their comments on the package.
2.25	The merchandise department ring Suzanne back to confirm the information regarding Badgers.
2.30	Suzanne starts to complete an area manager's report on the stand-alone branch. The report is designed to cover all aspects of the sales and general administration of the branch.
2.35	Jane Pearson returns Suzanne's call and Suzanne asks if she can ring her back because the information she requires is up in the office. She continues with her check of the branch.
3.30	Suzanne moves some fixtures because they appear to be out of line. She asks Anne to tidy the accessories fixture which looks untidy.
3.45	Suzanne and Anne have a cup of tea and discuss Anne's forthcoming wedding.
4.05	Suzanne phones Jane Pearson to discuss staff vacancies.
4.20	She decides to do a full administration check with Anne. There are a number of queries outstanding which Suzanne tries to sort out.
5.25	Anne goes down to the shop floor to ensure that the cashing up is done properly and to tidy the shop before closing.
5.40	Suzanne agrees with Anne to continue with the administration check on her next visit. She has completed the area manager's report on the shop

floor and stockroom, and hands it to Anne. There are a number of critical points which Suzanne asks Anne to put right.

5.45   Suzanne leaves to go home.

6.00   On her way home, Suzanne makes a mental note to write to Mr Douglas about the stock problem and the reply from the merchandise department.

Questions

1 How effective has Suzanne's day been?

2 What has she achieved?

3 What impression has she created with each of the people she has visited?

4 Has any time been wasted? If so, how much and on what?

5 What work is outstanding?

6 What advice would you give to Suzanne?

Activity contributed by Jackie Rainford, Common Sense Training Ltd.

 Debate one

'The modern organisational form means that managers are an unnecessary luxury. They have been replaced by 'upside-down' organisation charts and empowered employees.'

Starting points

For

● At the end of the day all managers do is to coordinate. Empowered employees don't need the degree of coordination applied by traditional managers.

● If managers are needed for some specialist task in the future, they can be 'bought in' or 'leased' as necessary.

Against

● There will always be a need for someone to integrate the activities of the business, even if that person isn't necessarily called 'a manager'.

● Mullins says, '"management" is not homogenous. It takes place in different ways and at different levels of the organisation.' The statement for debate implies that it is only present at senior levels: this is simply not true.

Further reading

Mintzberg, H. (1990), 'The Managers Job: Folklore and Fact', *Harvard Business Review Classic*, March–April, 163–76.

Semler, R. (1989), 'Managing Without Managers', *Harvard Business Review*, Sept.–Oct., 76–84.

Stewart, R. (1976), *Managers and Their Jobs*, Macmillan.

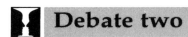

Debate two

'There is no real difference between "management" in the private and public sectors.'

Starting points

For

- All organisations are concerned with planning and forecasting – there is no difference between public and private sector.

- Whatever the organisation, problems will be faced, alternative solutions discussed, selected and implemented – in other words, one of the main aspects of the managers job.

Against

- The aims and goals of public sector organisations are different, particularly in terms of profit. This is bound to have an affect on the way managers manage.

- There is generally a demand for public sector organisations to account publically for their performance. This is bound to have an impact on what managers do and how they manage people far more than in a private sector organisation.

Further reading

Bourn, J. (1979), *Management in Central and Local Government*, Pitman.

Mullins, L.J. (1993), *Management and Organisational Behaviour*, 377–8, Pitman.

 # Look, it really works!

One of the authors was involved in a customer care initiative in a company who had (rightly) decided that the ethos of customer care should pervade the whole organisation. The board of directors were to receive the first tranche of training and it would then cascade throughout the company.

The trainer decided to use the same activity throughout all the courses, which involved participants in constructing a parachute-type contraption that, when filled with a fresh egg, would enable the egg to be dropped from a given height and land unbroken. Participants were given forty minutes to complete their task. The following happened.

1 At the end of the allotted time, the board of directors were still arguing about who was going to do what. The production director (who was an engineering graduate) poured cold water on any idea that was suggested quoting laws of physics, stress and aerodynamics; the managing director had taken the role of chairman but no one was following his lead; the personnel director was trying, in vain, to act as a gatekeeper; the finance director had switched off completely

and was reading a newspaper; and the marketing director was more concerned with the look of the finished article than whether it could do the job.

2 A second group was made up of canteen assistants, cleaners and general maintenance workers. Halfway through the exercise the trainer went up to the group to see how they were doing, expecting them to ask for further time. Not only had they completed the task but they had even tried out a prototype. When asked how they did it so quickly, one member of the group replied: 'Well we all decided who was going to do what and then we got on with it.' Looking a bit guilty, she added, 'And it helped that Freda had done something similar before, so she was a sort of adviser.'

The moral of this story? Things go much more smoothly when you can agree on what's got to be done and who's going to do it. In this case it also helped that a previous situation and solution could be transferred to a new situation – but don't forget that what has worked in the past may not *always* work in the future.

 ## Assignment one

Context

This assignment is based upon the material presented in the first case study in this chapter, 'Effective behaviour: hard news or soft sell?'.

You have been asked by the managing director of Timothy Willis Ltd to apply your understanding of organisational behaviour theory to the problems she is facing in the production department of the company.

Task

Prepare a report for the managing director which:

1 Identifies the factors which you believe are important in explaining Harold Plumb's approach to the management of his staff.

2 Provides reasoned recommendations on the action she might take to improve the productivity and morale in the production department.

The report is expected to be between 1,500 and 2,000 words in length.

Alternatively

Make a short, individual or group, seminar presentation on the matters requested in the task making the assumption that the tutor and rest of the seminar group are the managing director and key members of the Willis family.

Assignment provided by Derek Adam-Smith, University of Portsmouth.

Assignment two

Mullins (pp. 377–8) discusses the differences and similarities between public and private sector organisations.

Imagine that you are a management consultant who has been brought in by a public sector organisation to advise on either:

- the change to privatisation; or
- a management buy-out.

Task

Write a paper for the senior management team outlining the changes which will be needed in, for example, management style, culture and organisation structure, and give suggestions as to how these might be achieved.

 # Assignment three

See Mullins, p. 390.

! Pause for thought

1 Mary is a well-qualified, widely experienced, highly professional nurse in her early fifties. She has worked within the National Health Service for the whole of her career, holding the post of 'Sister' for many years.

Sweeping and fundamental changes have been, and still are, taking place within the service. Imposed from the very top, these are cultural as well as organisational and financial. Control by 'market forces', the formulation and implementation of a Patients' Charter, together with stated objectives and measurable targets are all part of these changes. Management responsibilities which once concerned only the topmost levels are now devolved down through the organisation to unit level and include responsibility for budgeting, purchasing, staff appraisal, cost control, feasibility studies and the compilation of various statistical and management reports.

Until recently, Mary's role, one of 'team leader' for a specific aspect of health care, was very much a 'hands on' appointment, working with a close-knit team of professionals. Over a very short period of time her role and job title were changed to 'manager' although no training or development were given to enable Mary to cope with this change, other than a dramatic increase in the requirement to attend meetings.

Although she seems to cope as well as anyone in the new situation, Mary believes and insists that she is a professional nurse and *not a manager!* She regrets the move away from her traditional role towards increasing managerial responsibilities and activities. She is particularly competent at team-building, able easily to develop and maintain interpersonal relationships. Her senior manager considers that she is carrying out her new duties and responsibilities well.

There are many implications for both present and future managerial and organisational effectiveness in this situation: the questions raised are many and varied:

- Can such changes be imposed autocratically from the top, as in this situation, with a high guarantee of success?

- What skills (if any) are transferable between the technical and managerial role needs, and what are the implications for future individual and team motivation and relationships?

- How should training and development be viewed in this type of situation?

- What are the moral and ethical implications of arbitrarily changing a job which the job holder finds satisfying and rewarding into one which is considerably less so?

'Pause for thought' provided by David Callas, Development Consultants.

2 In his book *The Age of Unreason* (1989), Charles Handy describes managers of the future as 'portfolio people' who will simultaneously have a variety of paid and unpaid jobs rather than the generally accepted career/job pattern of today.

Even post-recession this may sound a little implausible for some people but the market for 'executive temps' or 'interim managers' is a growing one (*Management Today*, May 1994). Originating in The Netherlands as their answer to restrictive employment legislation, the concept spread first to the USA and has now reached British shores.

The reasons for using these near-board-level people are many and varied: when an organisation needs specific skills to start up, turnround or close a department, division or subsidiary; when specialist skills are needed for a short time only or for a fill-in post between a senior person leaving and a new person being appointed. The agencies who specialise in this growing breed of 'leased manager' appear to be somewhat élitist in their approach. They stress the difference between *their* temps and the growing band of freelance consultants as one of commitment to both providing solutions *and* implementing them.

Is this the way forward for both organisations and surplus-to-requirements full-time executives in the future? What is the difference (if any) between this élite band and Handy's concept of the 'shamrock' organisation?

❓ Still not convinced?

1 David was a managing director who believed firmly in the art of delegation – so much so that by 11.30 every morning his desk was free of post except for one or two letters to dictate to his secretary. Now in case you've misunderstood, David didn't see *all* the company's post and pass it out accordingly, this was his *own* post. Thus everyone else also had their own little piles – plus, by 11.45 each morning, most of David's as well. If, during the day, calls came in to him or problems arose, they also would be delegated. If he was able to find the appropriate person at their desk, the delegated duty would probably be passed over by phone. If a manager rashly left their desk they would return to find a Post-It note stuck to it. One person came back from a week's holiday to find not only the entire desk covered in Post-It notes but also half the wall . . .

David never followed up to see if the job had been done, he made the assumption that you would get on with it – he didn't even necessarily require you to report back when it was completed.

Was this too good to be true: the manager who delegated according to all the rules in the textbooks and who then, secure in the knowledge that the work would be done, takes the afternoon off? Or was there more here than meets the eye? What about perception, personality, motivation and control? You see, you cannot just look at one aspect of 'managing' in isolation without considering all the other variables as well.

2 The Oast House Theatre has been recently restored. The original Kentish oast house has been converted to a studio theatre and artists' workshops, while a new extension has been added on to house the main theatre, cafeteria and bars.

The money to convert the theatre came mostly from government and EU grants, donations and fund-raising events. Its organisation structure is not particularly unusual: there is a board of management made up of local dignitaries, patrons of the Arts and some well-known names from the world of theatre and entertainment. Their job is to oversee the strategy of the Oast House and to use their network of contacts to raise both money and public awareness. Reporting to the board of management is the Oast House director and reporting to him are a cook and a part-time administration assistant. These last three are the only people at the Oast House who are currently paid for their labours, although it should be said that they all frequently work over and above their paid hours.

All other 'employees' from cafeteria assistants to bar staff and box office are volunteers who give their services free. They do so for a variety of reasons: some because they genuinely want to see the Oast House as a working theatre; some younger ones because they are doing drama or stage management courses; some because it provides an opportunity to socialise and get out of the house; and some for all of these reasons.

Can you see how 'managing' these people is very different from managing paid employees? Anything resembling an autocratic style, they'll be off like a shot and there's nothing anyone can do about it. On the other hand, it's very necessary to present the Oast House as a professional organisation and high standards have to be maintained. The theatre director has to walk a very narrow tightrope between these requirements and ensuring that everybody's individual motivations and aspirations are met, at least in part.

❗ A final pause for thought*

Mark was the personnel manager for an engineering company. One day, faced with a particularly difficult industrial relations problem he gave up trying to find a solution, left it all on his desk and walked over to the window to look out.

Lost in thought, he didn't hear his boss come in until he walked over and tapped him on the shoulder. Startled, Mark turned round and somewhat guiltily said, 'Sorry, I know I've got this union problem to sort out – I was just thinking about it.' His boss replied, 'Thinking is as much a part of management as doing things,' and walked out.

Mark said many years later that he had never forgotten his boss's comment – too often we associate management only with activity. Perhaps Mark's boss had read Mullins?

*With thanks to Brian Sutcliffe for the original idea.

Appendix 1
Guidelines for Chapter 4

 ## General assessment of your handwriting

Below you will find the general meanings of the movements of handwriting that you looked at in Chapter 4, 'Activity two'. If you feel that any interpretation is totally wrong it is probably because there is a modifying factor in your writing which needs deeper analysis than this brief test allows.

1 Size

(a) Large middle zone
You are aware of your own worth and have good confidence levels. Because you enjoy meeting and being with people you find work with an aspect of social activity particularly rewarding – personnel, conference office, public relations, and so on. Sometimes you find concentrating a bit difficult if there is a lot going on around you.

(b) Small middle zone
You are able to concentrate well no matter what is going on around you. You like to immerse yourself in the work in hand. You are not pushy by nature. You enjoy working in an academic environment and are excellent with fiddly, detailed work such as figure work, data entry and working with your hands on intricate work.

(c) Mixed
You are a highly strung person and as a result can work fast without tiring easily. You get a lot done in a short space of time. Variety is the key to maintaining your interest and keeping you mentally stimulated. You enjoy activity in your work rather than pure administration or deskwork.

2 Letter connections

(a) All joined up
You have a very logical train of thought. You don't like being interrupted from what you are doing and are keen to achieve what you set out to do. You are good at work where you need to use deductive thinking.

(b) All disconnected

You are an intuitive person. You can sense an atmosphere when you walk into a room. You will know instinctively if you like a working environment or not, without knowing why. You are excellent at coming up with ideas and relate well to other people's creative ideas. Although you get along well with others you keep emotional distance. You find you are sometimes distracted from what you set out to do.

(c) A mixture

You have a combination of good ideas and a logical mind enabling you to put those ideas into action. You are able to come up with practical solutions to problems and find alternative ways to reach your goals. You are a good troubleshooter.

3 Loops

(a) Loopy

You have imagination and a visual mind and will get more job satisfaction in a creative or artistic environment – graphic design, art studios, interior design companies, fabric manufacturers, photographic companies, and so on.

(b) Loopless

You are a practical and down-to-earth person with good technical skills. You have a natural aptitude for working with electronic equipment and an innate feel for technical matters.

4 Overall shape

(a) Rounded

Affectionate and warm-hearted, you are a good pacifier and look to others to give you work to do. You relate well to people, especially children, and teaching or administrative posts, amongst others, are well within your scope.

(b) Angular

You are prepared to work extremely hard for your employer and are therefore an asset to any company. You are thorough in whatever you undertake and don't give up easily. You are a natural researcher and are good at finding essential information quickly. You can find a needle in a haystack if required!

(c) Stretched

You are interested in anything new and exciting and variety is the keyword for you. You find it difficult sometimes to make decisions and work more happily in an environment where decisions are made elsewhere. You love challenges and are prepared to have a go at anything.

(d) Mixed

Adaptability is one of your strongest assets. You are able to turn your hand to a variety of jobs and are also able to handle chopping and changing tasks when necessary.

5 M's and N's

(a) Humped
You are a patient person and can deal in a kindly way with others and won't push them to do anything they don't want to. You learn best by hands-on experience.

(b) Angular
Determined and thorough, you complete what you set out to do. You love research work and have an analytical mind that can be put to good use in business. You like to get your teeth into a problem and can be relied upon not to give up until it is sorted out.

(c) Pointed
You are very curious and inquisitive and always want to know a little bit more about things. You pick up new information quickly and are therefore easy to train. You respond well to state-of-the-art environments and innovative atmospheres.

(d) Mixed
Versatile and adaptable, you are able to handle differing situations in differing ways and can find alternative solutions to problems.

6 Margins

(a) About equal
You are a visually minded person with an eye for the aesthetic. You appreciate well-designed and harmonious surroundings and will work best in an environment that pleases the eye.

(b) Wider on the left
You are a person who is a little bit on the shy and formal side. You are happier if you are introduced to a newcomer than having to go up and meet them. You also feel ready to meet change head on.

(c) Wider on the right
You are a little apprehensive of what the future holds for you and will need to feel that a job is absolutely right for you before you will commit yourself.

Note: *Very narrow margins all round* are the sign of a natural communicator who is never at a loss for something to say and therefore is excellent at putting others at their ease.

7 Capital 'I'

(a) As large as the other capitals
You have a good sense of your own self-worth and a realistic level of confidence.

(b) Larger than the other capitals
You have a good level of self-confidence but need to be careful not to take on more than you can really handle as you take disappointments and failures very much to heart.

(c) Smaller than the other capitals
You are modest by nature and prepared to work in an undemanding way. It takes you more effort to blow your own trumpet. Your confidence levels could be improved with an insight into assertiveness training.

8 Signature

(a) Larger than your writing
You are good at putting forward a lively and confident image even when you don't feel brilliant underneath. You have an excellent interview technique and the ability to make others feel at their ease and think well of you.

(b) Smaller than your writing
You like to be private and dislike intrusions into your personal affairs. You need to be recognised for your professional merits more than for your personality.

(c) Same size as your writing
You are a person who can be taken at face value and you expect the same of others. You are natural and spontaneous and neither oversell nor undersell your capabilities.

Note: *Underlined signature*. Underlining is a sign of self-assertion and a desire for recognition. It helps confidence levels an indicates that you are satisfied with your talents and ready to put them to good use.

9 Spaces

(a) Fairly close together
You are an excellent team member and work best as part of a group or team. You need to have others around to maintain a feeling of enthusiasm and spirit.

(b) Fairly wide apart
You are happy working on your own and relish being given responsibility to get things done without interference and supervision.

(c) A mixture
Very flexible in your working methods, you are happy working on your own or with a team or a combination of both. You are adaptable and enjoy variety in the work you do.

10 Slant

(a) Vertical
You are a person who likes to know all the facts before making a decision. You mange to stay cool-headed in stressful situations.

(b) Right slant
You are an emotional person who relates in a friendly way to others. You need to have people around you with whom you can establish a rapport.

(c) Left slant

You tend to be a very cautious person and are wary of new situations and acquaintances. You are excellent at telephone communications. Job satisfaction is a very important priority for you.

(d) Mixed

You are adaptable and impressionable. You prefer to have decisions made for you, and variety and changes in routine in your work are essential for you as you thrive on a varied programme.

11 Legibility

(a) Clear and easy to read

You are a natural communicator. You are good at explaining complicated facts in an easy to understand way. You are thorough and conscientious in what you undertake.

(b) Some letters skimmed over

You get things done quickly and can be considered a fast worker. You don't particularly enjoy fiddly work but always keep sight of the end result in whatever you undertake.

12 Lines

(a) Going up

You are enthusiastic and optimistic and have good energy levels.

(b) Going down

You need to make sure you are getting enough rest and relaxation so that your energy levels are replenished and you can put your best foot forward.

(c) In an arc

If the arc goes *up* in the middle you tend to take on more than you can handle and need to learn to pace yourself better so that you can complete the jobs you undertake. If the arc goes *down* in the middle you are a bit unsure that you can undertake the jobs you are given but you always manage to fulfil your commitments.

(d) Horizontal

If you say you will do something then you stand by your word. You are reliable and prepared to take on responsibility. A steady worker and employee.

*Assessment provided by Corinne Bible, Chairman, British Institute of Graphologists Examinations Board.

Appendix 2
Guidelines for Chapter 5

Guidance notes

1 The difference between HIV and AIDS

HIV and AIDS are not the same thing. HIV is the virus that attacks the body's defences and eventually makes that person prone to a variety of other diseases that eventually result in death. These fatal diseases are usually what is referred to as 'AIDS' (Acquired Immune Deficiency Syndrome).

However, *it may be many years, often more than ten, before a person infected with HIV starts to become unwell.* As medical treatment develops, the incapacitating nature of AIDs can, in some cases, be limited for increasingly longer periods.

2 How HIV – the virus that causes AIDS – is spread

The virus is spread only in the following ways:

- Sexually, through unprotected intercourse with an infected partner, male or female, 'gay' or 'straight'. Using a condom reduces the risk.

- From exposure to infected blood (e.g. through sharing drug injecting equipment). All blood for transfusion in the UK has been screened for HIV since 1986, and blood products are treated to destroy the virus. There is no risk in giving blood.

- From an infected mother to her unborn child.

3 How you can't get HIV

HIV is not spread through normal social contact. It is not spread by touch, or through water or air, or by coughing or sneezing.

You cannot be infected by working alongside someone with HIV or AIDS, or by sharing ordinary, everyday utensils and appliances (e.g. cutlery, cups, glasses, telephones, toilets, washing facilities). There has been no case where a family member sharing a house with someone infected with HIV or AIDS has been infected by sharing food utensils or household appliances.

4 Workplace issues

Unless an organisation currently finds it necessary to screen all recruits for the presence of other potentially debilitating conditions (e.g. heart problems, cancers), *there is no need to introduce special measures to try to detect people with HIV.* The chances of employing someone who is going to be unable to work as a result of an AIDS-related illness is probably less than employing someone with a heart condition or other common medial complaint such as a bad back. If illness is a concern, then a general medical to determine *immediate fitness to work* of *all* recruits is probably the best solution.

There is no need for any special precautions to be taken. In the area of first aid, basic hygiene procedures taught on recognised courses are sufficient. As a universal rule all employees (whether trained first-aiders or not) should have access to gloves, so that if they need to help in any emergency direct contact with blood can be avoided. *This applies to all cases of injury, not just if someone is thought or known to have HIV.*

There is no need to feel threatened or afraid. People with AIDS or who are HIV-positive (in other words who have the HIV virus in their blood) need understanding and support: you should not feel frightened or give way to prejudice. Instead, give the same sympathy and support you would expect from your workmates if you were seriously ill.

An employer may find it useful to develop a policy specifically relating to HIV and AIDS, or to incorporate it in an existing policy such as Health and Safety or Equal Opportunities. The following guidelines are provided by the National AIDS Trust:

- The policy must address both HIV and AIDS separately, and the company's response to each should acknowledge that they are separate conditions. HIV and AIDS can be integrated into existing policies, such as those concerning equal opportunities, sickness leave, and so forth.

- In an integrated policy, mention must be made of HIV and AIDS, to ensure that staff can obtain the information they need on company practice without having to ask specific questions.

- Any policy must clearly state that discrimination, in any aspect of company activity, against anyone who is HIV positive or who has AIDS will not be tolerated.

- The policy should state clearly that AIDS will be treated in the same manner as any other progressive or debilitating illness.

- The policy must contain a clear statement on confidentiality, explaining the way in which confidential information will be treated.

- The policy must make clear, by outlining or referring to discipline and grievance procedures, what action will be taken if staff breach the terms laid down.

- The best model policy will cover areas such as opportunities for redeployment, retraining, flexible working, compassionate leave, and so on. Where possible these should apply not only to those infected with HIV but also to carers.

Further information

Information relating to HIV/AIDS and workplace issues can be obtained from the following sources.

1 National AIDS Trust Employers' Initiative: contact Vanessa Hardy, 6th Floor, Eileen House, 80 Newington Causeway, London, SE1 6EF. Tel.: (071) 383 4246.

2 Terrence Higgins Trust Positive Management Initiative, 52–54 Grays Inn Rd, London WC1X 8JU. Tel.: (071) 831 0330.

3 Centre for AIDS and Employment Research: contact Dr David Goss, Portsmouth Business School, Locksway Rd, Portsmouth, Hants. Tel.: (0705) 844172/844223.

Further reading

Adam-Smith, D., Goss, D., Sinclair, A., Rees, G., Meudell, K. (1992), 'AIDS and Employment: Diagnosis and Prognosis', *Employee Relations*, **18** (3), 29–40.

Goss, D. and Adam-Smith, D. (1994), 'Empowerment or Disempowerment? The Limits and Possibilities of Workplace AIDS Policy', in P. Aggleton (ed.), AIDS: Foundations for the Future, Falmer.

Goss, D. and Adam-Smith, D. (1994), 'Preconditions for Policy: The Role of AIDS Education in the Workplace', in V. Hardy (ed.), *Socio-economic Impact of AIDS in Europe*, Cassell.

IDS (1987), *AIDS and Employment*, IDS Study No. 393, Incomes Data Services.

IDS (1993), *AIDS Returns to the Agenda*, IDS Study No. 528, Incomes Data Services.

Keay, D. and Leach, M. (1993), 'Positive Thinking about HIV', *Human Resources*, spring, 36–40.

LAGER (1990) *HIV and AIDS: Policy Guidelines*, Lesbian and Gay Employment Rights.

National AIDS Trust (1992), *Companies Act! The Business Charter on HIV/AIDS*, NAT.

Sim, J. (1992), 'AIDS, Nursing and Occupational Risk', *Journal of Advanced Nursing*, **17**, 569–75.

Smithurst, M. (1990), 'AIDS: Risks and Discrimination', in B. Almond (ed.), *AIDS: A Moral Issue*, Macmillan.

Wilson, P. (1993), *HIV and AIDS in the Workplace*, National AIDS Trust.

References

Banas, G. E. (1992), 'Nothing Prepared me to Manage AIDS', *Harvard Business Review*, July–August, 26–33.

Belbin, R. M. (1993), *Team Roles at Work*, Butterworth-Heinemann.

Bengtsson, A. (1993), 'Stardust, Fantasy and Performance Excellence', *Training and Development*, September.

Berger, P. (1963), *Invitation to Sociology*, Penguin.

Canals, J. (1994), *Competitive Strategies in European Banking*, Clarendon Press.

Drucker, P. F. (1961; first pub. 1955) *The Practice of Management*, Heinemann.

Feldman, D. C. (1981), 'The Multiple Socialisation of Organization Members', *Academy of Management Review*, April, 310.

Ferner, A. and Hyman, R. (1994), *Industrial Relations in the New Europe*, Blackwell.

Festinger, L. (1957), *A Theory of Cognitive Dissonance*, Stanford University Press.

Handy, C. (1989), *The Age of Unreason*, Business Books.

Handy, C. (1993), *Understanding Organisations*, 4th edn, Penguin.

Hellriegel, D. and Slocum, J. W. Jr (1974), 'Measures, Research, and Contingencies', *Academy of Management Journal*, June, 225–80.

Hoffmann, S. (1967), 'Heroic Leadership', in L. J. Edinger (ed.), *Political Leadership in Industrial Societies*, Wiley.

Kanter, R. (1983), *The Change Masters*, Simon & Schuster.

Kimmage, P. (1990), *A Rough Ride*, Stanley Paul.

Lambert, R. (1968–9), 'Processus d'influence et performance de groupe', *Bulletin de Psychologie*, **22**, 800–10.

Lawrence, P. R. (1958), 'The Changing Patterns of Organizational Behavior', *Harvard Business Review*.

Lee, R. and Lawrence, P. (1985), *Organizational Behaviour: Politics at Work*, Hutchinson.

Legge, I. (1989), 'Human Resource Management: A Critical Analysis', in J. Storey (ed.), *New Perspectives on Human Resource Management*, Routledge.

Legge, K. (1978), *Power, Innovation and Problem Solving in Personnel Management*, McGraw-Hill.

Lenk, H. (1969), *Sport, Culture and Society*, Macmillan, 393–7.

Lewis, R. (1989), *Stage People*, Weidenfield & Nicolson.

Lord, R. G., DeVader, C. L. and Alliger, G. M. (1986), 'A Meta-analysis of the Relation between Personality Traits and Leadership Perceptions: An Application of Validity Generalization Procedures', *Journal of Applied Psychology*, August, 402–10.

Maccoby, M. (1988), *Why Work: Motivating and Leading the New Generation*, Simon & Schuster.

Metcalf, D. (1994), *What has human resource management achieved in the workplace?* Vol. 8, No. 3, May, Employment Policy Institute.

Meudell, K. A. and Gadd, K. (1994), 'Culture and Climate in Short Life Organisations', *International Journal of Contemporary Hospitality Management*, **6** (5).

Mole, J. (1990), *Mind Your Manners*, Industrial Society Press.

Morgan, G. (1993), *Imaginization*, Sage Publications.

Mullins, L. J. (1992), *Hospitality Management: A Human Resources Approach*, Pitman.

Mullins, L. J., Meudell, K. A. and Scott, H. (1993), 'Developing Culture in Short-life Organisations', *International Journal of Contemporary Hospitality Management*, **5** (4).

Peters, T. J. and Waterman, R. H. (1982), *In Search of Excellence*, Harper & Row.

Roddick, A. (1991), *Body and Soul*, Ebury Press.

Sashkin, M. (1991), *Pillars of Excellence: Organizational Beliefs Questionnaire*, Organization Design and Development Inc.

Semler, R. (1993), *Maverick!*, Century.

Sheldon, W. H., Stevens, S. S. and Tucker, W. B. (1940), *The Variety of Human Physique*, Harper.

Shubert, A. (1990), *A Social History of Modern Spain*, Unwin Hyman.

Society of Occupational Medicine, *What Employers Should Know about HIV and AIDS*.

Staw, B. M. and Ross, J. (1980), 'Commitment in an Experimenting Society: A Study of the Attribution of Leadership from Administrative Scenarios', *Journal of Applied Psychology*, June, 249–60.

Taguiri, R. and Litwin, G. H. (eds) (1968), *Organizational Climate*, Graduate School of Business Administration, Harvard University.

Tolman, E. C. and Holzick, C. H. (1930), 'Introduction and Removal of Reward and Maze Performance in Rats', *University of California Publications in Psychology*, **4**, 257–75.

Torrington, D. (1994), *International Human Resource Management*, Prentice Hall.

Torrington, D. and Hall, L. (1991), *Personnel Management: A New Approach*, 2nd edn, Prentice Hall.

Whyte, W. (1956), *The Organization Man*, Doubleday Anchor Books.

MANAGEMENT AND ORGANISATIONAL BEHAVIOUR

Laurie J Mullins

This best-selling book presents a managerial approach to the study of organisational behaviour with an emphasis on improving work performance through a better understanding of human resources. It is concerned with interactions within the structure and operation of organisations, the process of management and the behaviour of people at work. The central theme is the need for organisational effectiveness and the importance of the role of management as an integrating activity.

The book is written with the minimum of technical terminology and the format is clearly structured. The concepts and ideas presented provide a basis on which to formulate a critical appraisal of different perspectives on the structure, operation and management of organisations, and interaction among the people who work in them.

Management and Organisational Behaviour
● contains exercises and case studies for practical assignments and group work
● open text design and clear writing style make the book accessible to students
● is printed in attractive 2-colour text throughout.

Laurie J Mullins is Principal Lecturer, Department of Human Resource Management, The Business School, University of Portsmouth

ISBN 0 273 60039 7

ORGANISATIONAL CULTURE

Andrew Brown

This exciting new text gives an overview of a subject which is becoming increasingly popular with both academics and practitioners. It examines the linkages between culture and the concepts of organisational change, human resource management and strategic issues.

The reader is given an introduction to the origins of the current interest in organisational culture with examples drawn from real-life companies. Building on these fundamental concepts key issues in the study of culture, such as problems of definition, the development of cultures, sub-cultures and national cultures, are examined in detail.

All concepts and theoretical points addressed are illustrated with specific case examples and the final section draws together these concepts and speculates on future trends in organisational culture.

Organisational Culture includes case material from well-known companies including: Renault and Volvo, Shell, Royal Mail and Bassett Foods Plc.

The case study 'The Management of Change in the NHS' was awarded a prize in the 1994 European Case Clearing House Awards.

Andrew Brown is Lecturer in Organisational Behaviour, School of Management and Finance, University of Nottingham.

ISBN 0 273 60454 6

WORK PSYCHOLOGY

John Arnold, Cary L Cooper and Ivan T Robertsom

Work Psychology examines the contribution of psychological theory to our understanding of human behaviour at work. Its accessible and user-friendly style makes it suitable for readers unfamiliar with the theory of work psychology as well as those with a basic grounding in the subject. The text covers both personnel issues such as selection and training and organisational issues such as decision making, thus making it a comprehensive study of human behaviour in the workplace.

The new edition contains completely up-to-date material throughout with additional coverage of organisational culture and design. There is also new material on change and development and the issue of power at individual, group and organisational levels.

Throughout the text, real-life examples and illustrations are used to support the theory and to show how the concepts dealt with actually apply to work settings.

Work Psychology features:

- greater emphasis on organisational issues than in other work psychology texts
- contains case studies and illustrations throughout
- logically structured with clear chapter headings making it extremely easy to use

John Arnold is Lecturer in Organisational Psychology, **Cary L Cooper** is Professor of Organisational Psychology and **Ivan T Robertson** is Professor of Occupational Psychology, all at Manchester Schools of Management, UMIST.

ISBN 0 273 60324 8